The Federal Administrative Agencies

The Need for Better Definition of Standards

The Oliver Wendell Holmes Lectures

DELIVERED AT THE HARVARD LAW SCHOOL
IN FEBRUARY 1962 UNDER A FUND ESTABLISHED
OUT OF A LEGACY TO THE LAW SCHOOL
FROM THE LATE JUSTICE HOLMES

The Federal Administrative Agencies
The Need for Better Definition of Standards

HENRY J. FRIENDLY

HARVARD UNIVERSITY PRESS
CAMBRIDGE, MASSACHUSETTS · 1962

© Copyright 1962 by the President and Fellows of Harvard College

All rights reserved

Distributed in Great Britain by Oxford University Press, London

---

Library of Congress Catalog Card Number 62-20247

Printed in the United States of America

TO

F F

WITH AFFECTION AND GRATITUDE
FOR NEARLY TWOSCORE YEARS
OF FRIENDSHIP AND TUTELAGE

Preface

A half dozen years ago I was recounting to Mr. Justice Frankfurter some professional experiences which seemed to me to show that the regulatory agencies did not combine the celerity of Mercury, the wisdom of Minerva, and the purity of Diana to quite the extent we had been taught to expect, or at least to hope, in the 1920's when the spirit of Commissioner Eastman was abroad throughout the land. The Justice's suggestion that I put some of these thoughts in writing did not appear feasible to me as a practitioner at the time; but the idea he implanted stayed with me after I was appointed to the United States Court of Appeals for the Second Circuit in 1959.

A first effort, inflicted on the editors of the *Columbia Law Review* at their Sixtieth Anniversary dinner in April 1960, was later published in that distinguished journal. To draw a bill of particulars against the regulatory agencies was easy enough. On what I conceded to be the much "harder subject of what we should do about it," I offered, as a negative, that the problem would not be solved by dividing the agencies into three parts, as was then being quite seriously proposed, in what seemed to me a vain hope that somehow the parts would function better than the whole, and, as an affirmative, that the road to agency salvation lay in the appointment of good men, with some suggestions how that goal might be achieved. Amiable critics, who agreed with most of the bill of particulars, and also with my negative, found my affirmative too facile. I came to think they were right; but judicial labors prevented me from thinking more about the problem until the winter of 1961 when the gracious invitation of the faculty of my own law school to deliver the Oliver Wendell Holmes Lectures a year later forced me to do that.

The result is the theme of what follows — that the basic deficiency, which underlies and accounts for the most serious troubles of the agencies, is the failure to "make law" within the broad confines of the agencies' charters; that once this basic deficiency is remedied, other ills will largely cure themselves; and that shadows and miseries will long be with the agencies if it is not. Quite plainly, recognition of all this does not lessen the need for good men — if anything, it heightens the importance of obtaining commissioners who, in Mr. Eastman's phrase, possess "ability to grasp and comprehend facts quickly and to consider them in their relation to the law logically and with an open mind." Yet it should also aid in attracting such men. Formulating definite and potentially somewhat enduring policy for an agency affords a challenge altogether absent from the Rabelaisian "judiciary, tribonian and praetorial throw of dice" engaged in by some of Mr. Justice Bridlegoose's recent administrative counterparts.

I am not so naive as to suppose that attaining the more definite standards for the agencies urged in these lectures will be altogether easy. The competing interests are strong; the agencies operate in areas where there is relatively little consensus on values; and often, perhaps even usually, there is much to be said on both sides. Sometimes, when administrative drift has lasted too long, the agency may indeed have rendered itself helpless, and Congress must come to the rescue if rescue there is to be. Yet the task need not be by any means so intractable as is sometimes claimed. The decisional problems, though difficult, are not unsolvable; the very circumstance that a standard in these areas cannot be assuredly right affords the comforting corollary that, by the same token, it cannot be assuredly wrong — not to speak of the axiom that almost any standard is better than none, because Congress then will at least know what the agency is doing and can alter the standard if it sufficiently disagrees. Agency members must acquire enough sophistication to realize how far the bark of the pressure-threateners exceeds their bite. A commissioner of known character and ability will have little to fear if — and the "if" is all-important —

the President and the Senate revive the tradition of almost automatic reappointment of conscientious commissioners that was followed for so many years. We need a recrudescence of the spirit that led the railroads to urge Mr. Eastman's reappointment regardless of his holding views with which they strongly disagreed, and of corresponding wisdom and firmness in the White House and on Capitol Hill. This should not be too much to expect once its importance is clearly seen. Moreover, as these chapters emphasize, the very definition of standards will lessen the opportunity for pressures on the agencies and the consequent temptation to exert them.

I have thought it best that the lectures should be printed substantially as delivered. The reader is asked to bear this in mind when he encounters statements that might have been tempered or qualified if I had not had obligations to an audience that patiently listened on three successive winter nights. The book departs from the lectures in only a few respects. Obvious ones are the addition of footnotes and the insertion of chapter divisions. Another is that my material, condense it as I tried, outran what I could reasonably expect in endurance even from so willing an audience; the book thus contains some examples and detailed discussion of decisions that were omitted in the oral presentation. Although the field is developing so rapidly that it is impossible to keep fully up to date, I have included references to some important events, such as President Kennedy's significant message of April 6, 1962, since the lectures were given. Finally, I have had the benefit of some helpful criticism, notably from two of the great masters, Professor Louis L. Jaffe of the Harvard Law School and Professor Kenneth Culp Davis of the Law School of the University of Chicago.

Where I have strayed into expressions on the merits of issues that may come before me on the bench, full rights of recantation are reserved.

The more general sections of the manuscript were read by Joseph L. Weiner, LL.B., Columbia, 1926, who made many thoughtful suggestions stemming from his long experience with administrative agencies. Much help has been rendered by Peter B. Edelman, LL.B., Harvard, 1961, and Leonard Poryles, of New York Law School. Other heavy obligations are acknowledged in the footnotes — in addition to Davis and Jaffe, such names as Dickinson, Sharfman, Cushman, Landis, Redford, Bernstein, and Schwartz constantly recur. My wife, already experienced as a daughter in the strange ways of judges, has cheerfully acquiesced in my application of many evenings and weekends to what seems this rather small result. I am grateful, finally, to Dean Griswold and to the committee of the faculty of the Harvard Law School chaired by Professor Freund, who did me the high honor of inviting me to deliver the Holmes Lectures and thus afforded me an opportunity for reexamining this significant field of law.

Henry J. Friendly

New York City
July 1962

Contents

I. Why More Definite Standards of Administrative Adjudication Are Needed ... 1

II. An Early Success: Section 4 of the Interstate Commerce Act ... 27

III. Definition of Standards by Agency and Legislature in National Labor Relations ... 36

IV. The Licensing of Radio and Television Broadcasting ... 53

V. Competitive Domestic Air Route Certification ... 74

VI. The Minimum-Rate Power of the Interstate Commerce Commission ... 106

VII. The Road to Improvement ... 141

Index ... 177

WORKS CITED FREQUENTLY

DAVIS — DAVIS, ADMINISTRATIVE LAW TREATISE (1958).

DOYLE REPORT — Senate Committee on Commerce, Special Study Group on Transportation Policies in the United States, *Report Pursuant to S. Res. 29, 151 and 244 of the 86th Cong.*, S. REP. No. 445, 87th Cong., 1st Sess. (1961).

I. & R. BOARD REPORT — Board of Investigation and Research, *Report on Practices and Procedures of Governmental Controls*, H.R. DOC. No. 678, 78th Cong., 2d Sess. (1944).

LANDIS REPORT — LANDIS, REPORT ON REGULATORY AGENCIES TO THE PRESIDENT-ELECT, printed for the use of the Senate Committee on the Judiciary, 86th Cong., 2d Sess. (1960).

SHARFMAN — SHARFMAN, THE INTERSTATE COMMERCE COMMISSION (1931–1937).

STAFF REPORT — STAFF OF THE SUBCOMMITTEE ON LEGISLATIVE OVERSIGHT OF THE HOUSE COMMITTEE ON INTERSTATE AND FOREIGN COMMERCE, 86TH CONG., 2D SESS., REPORT PURSUANT TO § 136 OF THE LEGISLATIVE REORGANIZATION ACT AND H. RES. 56 (Comm. Print 1960).

I

Why More Definite Standards of Administrative Adjudication Are Needed

WHEN Dean Griswold extended his faculty's invitation to deliver the Holmes Lectures, my initial impulse was that I should decline — with deep gratitude that the bid had been extended and a hope that it might be renewed when a longer period away from the stir of the marketplace might have permitted reflections more nearly worthy of expression here. However, I thought of the uncertainty of human affairs, and also of the advice given by Mr. Justice Brandeis when Felix Frankfurter received a far more important call, to teach at the Harvard Law School — "I would let those who have the responsibilities for selecting you decide your qualifications and not have you decide that." [1] Recalling some of the earlier lectures on Justice Holmes's foundation, and, most poignantly, those given four years ago by that flashing and unique personality who gladdened our spirits and enriched our minds to the end of his happily long life,[2] I cannot but think my initial impulse was right; but it is too late to change.

For my topic I have turned to a field in which I took my first steps some thirty-five years ago under the guidance of those same two great men, Professor Frankfurter, as he then was, and Mr. Justice Brandeis — that part of administrative law relating to the regulation of business by agencies of the federal government.[3]

[1] FELIX FRANKFURTER REMINISCES 78 (Phillips ed. 1960).
[2] L. HAND, THE BILL OF RIGHTS (1958).
[3] The federal regulatory agencies within the scope of these lectures — the ICC, the FTC, the FCC, the SEC, the NLRB, the CAB, the FPC, and the constantly name-changing Shipping Board — have perhaps occupied rather more space in legal writings than, relatively, they deserve. Too little attention has been given to state regulation of utilities supplying such vital services as the telephone, electrical energy, and water, and to other aspects of state administrative law; after a score

Fate willed that many of my years at the bar should be spent in that widening pasture — some would liken it rather to "that Serbonian bog . . . where armies whole have sunk" — and I have continued to be concerned with it on the bench, although the Second Circuit's poor score in reversing administrative findings [4] appears to have caused practitioners with a choice of forum to steer their petitions for review toward more hospitable harbors.

Twenty years ago, the Attorney General's Committee on Administrative Procedure reported that "taken together, the various Federal administrative agencies have the responsibility for making good to the people of the country a major part of the gains of a hundred and fifty years of democratic government." [5] A decade later, Mr. Justice Jackson proclaimed that "the rise of administrative bodies probably has been the most significant legal trend of the last century and perhaps more values today are affected by their decisions than by those of all the courts, review of administrative decisions apart." [6]

In that same opinion, however, he spoke of "malaise in the administrative scheme." [7] The feeling of malaise, which had been

---

of years the Benjamin report, *Administrative Adjudication in the State of New York*, remains without a worthy successor. For a lively account of one such agency, see Catterall, *The State Corporation Commission of Virginia*, 48 VA. L. REV. 137 (1962); apparently the Virginia commission's informal contacts with the regulated avoid many problems encountered just across the Potomac!

Likewise, too little has been written on significant areas of federal administrative law outside the major regulatory agencies; for an indication of the importance of some of these other areas see GELLHORN & BYSE, ADMINISTRATIVE LAW: CASES AND COMMENTS 639–75 (4th ed. 1960), and Kerner v. Flemming, 283 F.2d 916, 922 (2d Cir. 1960). Much also would be learned from comparative study of the work of the commissions and of the regulatory activities of other departments and agencies. See, *e.g.*, Bernstein, *The Regulatory Process: A Framework for Analysis*, 26 LAW AND CONTEMP. PROB. 329, 342 (1961).

[4] Cooper, *Administrative Law: The "Substantial Evidence" Rule*, 44 A.B.A.J. 945, 948 (1958).

[5] ATTORNEY GENERAL'S COMMITTEE ON ADMINISTRATIVE PROCEDURE, FINAL REPORT 20 (1941).

[6] FTC v. Ruberoid Co., 343 U.S. 470, 487 (1952) (dissenting opinion). See also BERNSTEIN, REGULATING BUSINESS BY INDEPENDENT COMMISSION 296 (1955).

[7] 343 U.S. at 482.

temporarily eased by the Administrative Procedure Act in 1946,[8] but was by no means cured, again became acute with the exposures by the Subcommittee on Legislative Oversight of the House Committee on Interstate and Foreign Commerce in 1958.[9] A spate of intense criticism followed. Radical remedies were demanded — the disinterestedness of the agencies was to be assured, in somewhat Byzantine fashion, by shearing them of many of their vital functions [10] and building a blank wall between the regulators and the regulated.[11] Fortunately in this instance, the legislative paralysis, of which I shall later have more to say, prevented hasty action; and Mr. Landis' *Report on Regulatory Agencies to the President-Elect* seems to me quite as valuable for what it does not recommend as for most of what it does.[12] I do not mean by this either that no functions can usefully be removed

[8] 60 Stat. 237 (1946), 5 U.S.C. §§ 1001–11 (1958). For contrasting views *compare* Mr. Justice Jackson in Wong Yang Sung v. McGrath, 339 U.S. 33, 40 (1950), *with* Parker, *The Administrative Procedure Act: A Study in Overestimation*, 60 YALE L.J. 581 (1951).

[9] See H.R. REP. No. 2711, 85th Cong., 2d Sess. (1959); STAFF OF THE SUBCOMMITTEE ON LEGISLATIVE OVERSIGHT OF THE HOUSE COMMITTEE ON INTERSTATE AND FOREIGN COMMERCE, 86TH CONG., 2D SESS., REPORT PURSUANT TO § 136 OF THE LEGISLATIVE REORGANIZATION ACT AND H. RES. 56 (Comm. Print 1960) [hereinafter cited as STAFF REPORT].

[10] The plan that has properly received the most attention is contained in the *Memorandum to the President* accompanying Mr. Louis Hector's resignation from the Civil Aeronautics Board. See Hector, *Problems of the CAB and the Independent Regulatory Commissions*, 69 YALE L.J. 931 (1960). Many of these proposals find their source in the Hoover Commission's suggestion for an administrative court. See U.S. COMMISSION ON ORGANIZATION OF THE EXECUTIVE BRANCH OF THE GOVERNMENT, LEGAL SERVICES AND PROCEDURE 84–88 (1955). The still earlier history, going back to 1934, is reviewed in Heady & Linenthal, *Congress and Administrative Regulation*, 26 LAW AND CONTEMP. PROB. 238, 240–45 (1961). For a perceptive comment on such proposals see SCHWARTZ, FRENCH ADMINISTRATIVE LAW AND THE COMMON LAW WORLD 317–20 (1954).

[11] See, *e.g.*, H.R. REP. No. 2711, 85th Cong., 2d Sess. (1959); H.R. 4800, H.R. 6774, 85th Cong., 2d Sess. (1959).

[12] LANDIS, REPORT ON REGULATORY AGENCIES TO THE PRESIDENT-ELECT (printed for the use of the Senate Committee on the Judiciary, 86th Cong., 2d Sess. (1960)) [hereinafter cited as LANDIS REPORT]. For an appreciative comment see McFarland, *Landis' Report: The Voice of One Crying in the Wilderness*, 47 VA. L. REV. 373 (1961).

from the agencies or that no code of ethics can properly be enacted for them. I do mean that three-quarters of a century of distinctive American development ought not be abruptly reversed when the proffered alternative is so unattractive and ill defined; and that unless codes of ethics for the agencies are most carefully tailored to their special problems, which differ from those of the courts, the codes will do great harm, or will be flagrantly violated, or both.[13]

Progress in the new administration there surely has been. Congress revived the President's authority, under the Reorganization Act of 1949, to submit plans for altering the internal organization of the agencies.[14] The President's plans for such reorganization of the CAB and FTC have become effective; [15] that for the FCC, which the House rejected as a plan,[16] has largely been enacted as a law; [17] and although the plan for the SEC also met defeat,[18] a bill to that end remains pending. The Administrative Conference of the United States has been constituted, under the strong leadership of Judge Prettyman.[19] Some agencies have taken significant steps on their own account — the ICC and the CAB to place opinion-writing on a more responsible basis,[20] the FPC in a too

---

[13] See Friendly, *A Look at the Federal Administrative Agencies*, 60 COLUM. L. REV. 429, 439-44 (1960).

Neither do the more general criticisms of the commissions, such as those by Professor Bernstein in his stimulating book, give me any ground for belief that this form of regulation can or ought to be abandoned. Many of his criticisms seem predicated upon an overestimate of the extent to which regulation today is a war of tooth and claw between government and the regulated, and an underestimate of the extent to which it is a means of deciding among the regulated. Also I should want to know a good deal more about the supposedly superior "new forms, techniques, and ideas," *id.* at 297, before abandoning the old ones.

[14] Act of April 7, 1961, 75 Stat. 41.

[15] See 26 Fed. Reg. 5989, 6191 (1961).

[16] See 107 CONG. REC. 9705-19 (daily ed. June 15, 1961).

[17] Act of Aug. 31, 1961, 75 Stat. 420.

[18] By the Senate. See 107 CONG. REC. 10220 (daily ed. June 21, 1961).

[19] Exec. Order No. 10934, 26 Fed. Reg. 3233 (1961).

[20] See AMERICAN BAR ASS'N SECTION OF PUBLIC UTILITY LAW, REPORT 34 (1961); N.Y. Times, April 8, 1961, p. 42, col. 3. It is understood that one member of the FTC has announced his intention not to avail himself of its "Division of Special Legal Assistants" for opinion-writing.

delayed endeavor to break the logjam created by the Supreme
Court's decision in the *Phillips* case.[21] Beyond all this and some
excellent appointments, one gets a general sense that the agencies
have raised their hearts. While that spirit prevails may be a good
time to consider whether the current malaise does not derive in
large part from a cause which, although recognized,[22] has in my
view been insufficiently so, and which must be remedied if the
malaise is not to become something worse.

The Task of Administrative Adjudication

The thesis presented is this: A prime source of justified dissatisfaction with the type of federal administrative action which
I will shortly specify is the failure to develop standards sufficiently
definite to permit decisions to be fairly predictable and the reasons

[21] Phillips Petroleum Co. v. Wisconsin, 347 U.S. 672 (1954); see *In re* Phillips
Petroleum Co., 24 F.P.C. 537 (1960), *aff'd*, Wisconsin v. FPC, UTIL. REG. REP.
¶ 10224 (D.C. Cir. Nov. 30, 1961), *cert. granted*, 369 U.S. 870 (1962); Statement
of General Policy No. 61-1, 24 F.P.C. 818 (1961).

[22] See, *e.g.*, HENDERSON, FEDERAL TRADE COMMISSION 334 (1927); 3-B SHARF-
MAN, THE INTERSTATE COMMERCE COMMISSION 764-65 (1936) [hereinafter cited
as SHARFMAN]; Schwartz, *Comparative Television and the Chancellor's Foot*, 47
GEO. L.J. 655, 657-58, 694-95 (1959); REDFORD, NATIONAL REGULATORY COMMIS-
SIONS: NEED FOR A NEW LOOK 14-15 (1959); *Hearings Pursuant to S. Res. 234
Before a Subcommittee on Administrative Practice and Procedure of the Senate
Judiciary Committee*, 86th Cong., 2d Sess. 218 (1960) (testimony of Mr. Hector):
"the greatest single source of uncertainty and, consequently, injustice to those who
are regulated by the Federal Government" is "that agencies do not make policy
because policy is hard to make and because it is far easier to take up each case as it
comes along and figure out what to do on a flexible ad hoc basis"; Cooper, *The
Executive Department of Government and the Rule of Law*, 59 MICH. L. REV. 515,
527 (1961); S. REP. NO. 168, 87th Cong., 1st Sess. (1961); Individual Views of
Senator Dirksen, *id.* at 18: "Policies should be openly and clearly announced."
Need for better articulation of standards was also the theme of Mr. Justice Jackson's dissent in FTC v. Ruberoid Co., 343 U.S. 470, 487 (1952), although one may
question whether that was altogether the appropriate case for it; the case dealt
with a different aspect of the need for definiteness, namely in the drawing of agency
orders, an issue recently debated in Quaker Oats Co., FTC Docket 8119, decided
April 25, 1962.

For an effective expression of the need for definite standards, made by an
agency chairman since these lectures were delivered, see Law Day Statement of
FPC Chairman Swidler, April 30, 1962.

for them to be understood;[23] this failure can and must be remedied.

Quite deliberately I have said simply "the" failure without further elaboration at this juncture; I will show later that responsibility has been multiple. There have been failures, perhaps excusable, by Congress at the time of initial enactment, failures by the agencies to sharpen the vague contours of the original statute, failures by the legislature to supply more definite standards as growing experience has permitted or even demanded, and failures by the executive to spur the legislature into activity.[24] All these failures have been interdependent: failure by the agency to make clear what it is doing impedes both executive challenge and legislative response.[25] I do not assert that failure has been universal; we shall see victories as well as defeats. The victories help to show the defeats need not have been suffered.

My first task must be to define the type of administrative action I mean to discuss.

To begin with some negatives, I shall not be discussing areas where Congress has confided to an administrative agency the enforcement of a rule stated in such clear language as to leave nothing to discretion and little to interpretation — the kind of task more usually given to the executive departments. For examples you may take the duty of the Interstate Commerce Commission to enforce the Safety Appliance Act,[26] or of the SEC to require the filing of notifications of registration by investment companies.[27] Neither shall I be dealing with areas where the

[23] Compare LLEWELLYN, THE COMMON LAW TRADITION: DECIDING APPEALS 17-18, *passim* (1960); and 1 DAVIS, ADMINISTRATIVE LAW TREATISE, *Preface* at iii-x (1958) [hereinafter cited as DAVIS], making a similar criticism with respect to administrative law decisions of appellate courts.

[24] See BERNSTEIN, *op. cit. supra* note 6, at 291-93.

[25] See Jaffe, *An Essay on Delegation of Legislative Power*, 47 COLUM. L. REV. 359, 364 (1947).

[26] 27 Stat. 531 (1893), 45 U.S.C. §§ 1, 2, 4 (1958); 35 Stat. 476 (1908), 45 U.S.C. § 17 (1958).

[27] Investment Company Act of 1940, 54 Stat. 803, 15 U.S.C. § 80a-8 (1958).

agency is an actor rather than a decider, such as the conduct of a vote on a railroad reorganization by the ICC [28] or the holding of an election (as distinguished from the decision whether and for what unit to hold one) by the NLRB.[29]

My frame of reference likewise does not include cases where the agency is empowered to promulgate detailed rules and regulations of its own, with no legal consequences to anyone unless and until it does. Examples are the authority of the Federal Reserve Board to regulate margin requirements [30] and of the SEC to lay down rules governing short sales.[31] Here it is plain that the legislature did "not bring to a close the making of the law," [32] and that the agency is doing the kind of thing the legislature might well have done on its own account were it not for the need of frequent and rapid change. In such cases the very lack of any effective action by the legislature usually compels the agency rather speedily to frame rules and regulations which supply the needed definition. Although true "delegated legislation" of this kind falls outside my subject, I cannot forbear the comment that the relative lack of criticism in such areas, where a fair degree of precision has been achieved through rules and regulations, supports my thesis of the need for attaining similar specification in others. In such instances the regulators have stated in fairly definite terms what the regulated may do and what they may not; if the regulated do not like the prescription, they may endeavor to have it changed either by the agency or, failing that, by the Congress; meanwhile they know where they stand and that they all stand alike.[33]

---

[28] Bankruptcy Act § 77(e), 49 Stat. 918 (1935), 11 U.S.C. § 205(e) (1958).
[29] 49 Stat. 453 (1935), as amended, 29 U.S.C. § 159 (1958).
[30] Securities Exchange Act, 48 Stat. 886 (1934), as amended, 15 U.S.C. § 78g (1958).
[31] Securities Exchange Act, 48 Stat. 891 (1934), 15 U.S.C. § 78j (1958).
[32] FTC v. Ruberoid Co., 343 U.S. 470, 486 (1952) (dissenting opinion by Mr. Justice Jackson).
[33] Other reasons for the relative success in this area may be that the process does not demand detailed factfinding and that, partially on that account, it is more

The area of federal administrative action with which I shall be dealing can best be described as those instances where Congress has adopted a general standard which a commission or board is to apply. There are numerous examples: just and reasonable rates, undue preference or prejudice, public convenience and necessity, discrimination discouraging membership in a labor organization, bargaining in good faith, unfair methods of competition, are a sufficient sampling.

Although I call the process of applying such standards, whether for the past or for the future, "administrative adjudication," I have no intention of indulging in the sport, once so popular, of attempting to determine how far such action is judicial or legislative or executive, even "softened with a *quasi*." [34] However it may be with others, my own litmus paper is not sensitive enough for me to do the job. I am told, for example, that the decision whether there shall be a new air route between *A* and *B* is quasi-legislative, as is also the decision whether the route shall go through *C* and *D* or through *E* and *F*, but that determination whether *G* or *H* airline should run it is quasi-judicial; [35] frankly I do not see why — as Professor Manley Hudson used to say, to our discomfiture, "I

---

comprehensible to, and receives more personal attention from, the members of the agency.

[34] Springer v. Philippine Islands, 277 U.S. 189, 210 (1928) (dissenting opinion by Mr. Justice Holmes). See also FTC v. Ruberoid Co., 343 U.S. 470, 487–88 (1952) (dissenting opinion). Some of the developments of this theme would do credit to Humpty Dumpty. A fine specimen is Representative Mann's explanation, in the debates on the Hepburn amendments, why the ICC's power to fix future rates would not be "legislative":

> We do not give to the Interstate Commerce Commission the power to fix rates. We say by legislative act what the rate shall be. . . . The rate shall be just, reasonable, and fairly remunerative . . . and then we leave to the Commission the administrative power to determine what in each particular case is the just, reasonable, and fairly remunerative rate. . . . [T]he Legislature finds what the rates shall be and puts these rates into force; and all the Commission is given power to do is the administrative act of making the computation." 40 CONG. REC. 2245 (1906).

[35] This seemed implicit in Hector, *supra* note 10, at 960–62; at least it was so understood by the CAB. See Comments of the CAB on the Hector Memorandum to the President 17–18, March 29, 1960; CAB Staff Analysis and Evaluation of the Hector Memorandum to the President 20–21.

get it all — but the 'therefore'." [36] Again we have been informed, by the very highest authority, that "awarding reparation for the past and fixing rates for the future involve the determination of matters essentially different," the former being "quasi-judicial" because it looks to the redress of private wrongs and to the past, whereas the latter is "quasi-legislative" because it deals with the public and the future.[37] Yet legislatures have prescribed remedies for past private wrongs,[38] and some injunctions, particularly, where, as under section 208 of the Taft-Hartley Act, no past wrong has been done, seem to fit rather precisely the Supreme Court's description of action in a "quasi-legislative capacity, to prevent further injury to the public." Increasingly we are coming to recognize that to a not inconsiderable extent, as a French jurist has said, "the two powers are of the same nature." [39] Furthermore, I cannot see that generally anything of consequence would follow from the classification if there were satisfactory means for making one. It is rather notable that after going to such pains to draw a sharp distinction between past and future ratemaking, the Supreme Court sensibly added that "testimony showing the un-

[36] Under the Administrative Procedure Act, § 2(d), all licensing is "adjudication." 60 Stat. 237 (1946), 5 U.S.C. § 1001(d) (1958).

[37] Baer Bros. v. Denver & R.G.R.R., 233 U.S. 479, 486 (1914). The Interstate Commerce Commission insisted on this distinction in its *Annual Report* for 1938, explaining that "the great bulk" of its duties "are quasi-legislative, i.e., they consist of the application of a general rule laid down by the Congress to specific cases" — something that many people would consider a pretty good description of judicial activity — although "confusion of thought has arisen because of the fact that in the performance of its quasi-legislative duties the Commission employs a procedure which resembles that employed by courts." ICC ANN. REP. 26 (1938). One wonders just who was confused. See also *id.* at 24. For an admirably clear treatment of the whole problem, see Board of Investigation and Research, *Report on Practices and Procedures of Governmental Controls*, H.R. Doc. No. 678, 78th Cong., 2d Sess. 52–59 (1944) [hereinafter cited as I. & R. BOARD REPORT].

[38] Private divorce acts, a practice whose validity was sustained against separation of powers attack in Maynard v. Hill, 125 U.S. 190 (1888), are a sufficient example.

[39] RIPERT, LES FORCES CRÉATRICES DU DROIT 119 (1955), citing the famous Article I of the Swiss Civil Code of 1912; see HOLMES, THE COMMON LAW 35 (1881); I. & R. BOARD REPORT 9.

reasonableness of a past rate may also furnish information on which to fix a reasonable future rate and both subjects can be, and often are, disposed of by the same order." [40]

On the other hand, I find valid and important the distinction, previously noted, between what anyone would recognize as a clear delegation of legislative power, with no quasi about it — I have cited the SEC's rulemaking power for short sales as an instance — and the application to a myriad of instances of a general standard which the legislature itself has made legally effective. Literally, both come within Professor Jaffe's "single generalization" that "power should be delegated where there is agreement that a task must be performed and it cannot be effectively performed by the legislature without the assistance of a delegate or without an expenditure of time so great as to lead to the neglect of equally important business"; [41] practically, as he recognizes,[42] they are very different. The SEC's rules in regard to short sales [43] are the sort of things which Congress could have put out on its own; they are no more detailed than many provisions of the income tax. The reasons for delegation in that instance are simply that Congress doesn't have the time, or the will,[44] to do all these things and that, even if Congress initially promulgated a set of rules on short sales every bit as good as the SEC's, it would be too hard for Congress to effect change, in an area where speedy change may be needed.[45] In contrast, the very nature of Congress, with one

[40] Baer Bros. v. Denver & R.G.R.R., 233 U.S. 479, 486 (1914). The distinction may be important on the issue of the constitutional right to a trial-type hearing.

[41] Jaffe, *supra* note 25, at 361.

[42] *Id.* at 363.

[43] 17 C.F.R. §§ 240.10a–1, –2 (1949).

[44] Probably it is this matter of the will that accounts for Congress' retention of the details in income and estate taxation.

[45] This was one reason why the interests that were to be regulated by the Securities Exchange Act preferred a broad delegation of truly legislative power to the Commission. See the statement by the then President of the New York Stock Exchange: "Instead of having a fixed rule of law, which can only be changed by an act of Congress and cannnot be changed if Congress is not in session — instead of having a fixed rule of law, we advocate the power being put in a commission to make those rules and regulations, which, if they are wrong, they can immediately

house having 100 members and the other 435, makes it wholly unfit to determine the rail and truck rates on new automobiles or who should run the television station in Kankakee; the difficulty is not just lack of time but an institutional lack of aptitude. Unlike the short sale rules, such decisions involve not a prescription for the whole or even a segment of an industry but the application of a standard to a concrete case, requiring not only the determination of the standard but also the accurate ascertainment and proper weighing of scores of subsidiary facts to which the standard must then be applied, and, in the first example, the consideration of a vast complex of relationships. From a practical standpoint, therefore, it may be slightly misleading to characterize true administrative adjudication as "delegation" by the legislature; a body cannot "delegate" in any meaningful sense the performance of action it would be incapable of taking on its own even if it had the time and the desire. Yet even this distinction should not be pressed too far; only a thin line separates rulemaking of the sort required to trigger a regulatory statute into operation from rulemaking to which an agency may resort, in the course of its "adjudicative" function, in sharpening an already effective command.[46] We shall thus do well to recognize that administrative adjudication is sui generis, and that it must work out its problems in its own way.

The Feasibility of Adjudicative Standards

With the area of our study thus delimited, let us return to the thesis.

In the instances of administrative adjudication which I gave

---

change." *Hearings on H.R. 7832 and 8720 Before the House Committee on Interstate and Foreign Commerce*, 73d Cong., 2d Sess. 726 (1934). For the development of the Securities Exchange Act, see CUSHMAN, THE INDEPENDENT REGULATORY COMMISSIONS 331-39 (1941). Note also the approval by the Investment Counsel Association of America of the grant of rulemaking power to the SEC by the 1960 amendment of the Investment Advisers Act, "as preferable to specific and inflexible statutory standards." S. REP. NO. 1760, U.S. CODE CONG. & AD. NEWS, 86th Cong., 2d Sess., 3502, 3510 (1960).

[46] See pp. 146-147 *infra*.

some time back, the legislative direction was very general.[47] As has recently been said, "The statutes from which they [the agencies] derive their authority are so often couched in broad general terms" as to endow them "with a discretion so wide that they can offer a more or less plausible explanation for any conclusion they choose to reach with respect to many, perhaps the great majority, of the matters coming before them." [48] In an oftquoted passage Professor Davis puts it thus: "Because of history or context, vague phrases of this sort may sometimes have considerable meaning. But sometimes they do not have. Sometimes telling the agency to do what is in the public interest is the practical equivalent of instructing it: 'Here is the problem. Deal with it.' " [49] Some years ago the Board of Investigation and Research explained in what manner this comes about — how an original draft of a statute "which may convey a fairly definite impression despite generality in its terms" is so watered down in the course of enactment that "the final product is not unlikely . . . to amount to little more than a direction to the agency to govern a certain situation justly, reasonably, and in the public interest." [50] One could make a case that the great divide between the giving of

---

[47] Much earlier examples could have been given; nearly two hundred years ago the Assembly of Vermont, confessing that it "cannot so well distinguish" between the state's various rivers and ponds, authorized the various towns to "appoint proper persons and places for ferries; and further regulate the price thereof according to the profits of such ferries, and price of labor; to be varied from time to time as occasion shall require." ATTORNEY GENERAL'S COMMITTEE ON ADMINISTRATIVE PROCEDURE, FINAL REPORT 15 (1941), citing VERMONT LAWS REVISED 77–78 (Haswell ed. 1787). A similar early Maryland statute is quoted in GELLHORN & BYSE, ADMINISTRATIVE LAW: CASES AND COMMENTS 1–2 (4th ed. 1960).

[48] STAFF REPORT 6. See to the same effect, with respect to the Interstate Commerce Commission's rate decisions under conflicting statutory mandates, Murphy, *Problems in Transportation Ratemaking*, 26 ICC PRAC. J. 1138, 1143–44 (1959); Senate Comm. on Commerce, Special Study Group on Transportation Policies in the United States, *Report Pursuant to S. Res. 29, 151, and 244 of the 86th Cong.*, S. REP. NO. 445, 87th Cong., 1st Sess. 120–24 (1961) [hereinafter cited as DOYLE REPORT].

[49] 1 DAVIS § 2.03, at 82.

[50] I. & R. BOARD REPORT 12. See also Cooper, *The Executive Department of Government and the Rule of Law*, 59 MICH. L. REV. 515, 526–27 (1961).

instructions by Congress in language which, despite its generality, history had freighted with meaning,[51] and simply telling the agency to do what it thought best, was the Transportation Act of 1920, where, in placing the railroads under the "fostering guardianship"[52] of the Interstate Commerce Commission, Congress vested the Commission with a gamut of new powers — over construction and abandonment, security issues, minimum rates, divisions, and so forth — with all too scant directions as to how to exercise them.[53] We have had a legion of such enactments since then.[54]

Certainly it would be better if Congress could be somewhat more specific at the outset. Where the conflicting forces are too great, it is asking overmuch of an agency to make policy when Congress could make none. The lesson taught in Mr. Landis' explanation of the impossible task the SEC would have had if the "death sentence" of the Holding Company Act had been passed in its original breadth[55] is still a good one for legislators to ponder. Professor Schwartz is quite right in thinking the ideal for

[51] See American Power & Light Co. v. SEC, 329 U.S. 90, 104 (1946).

[52] Dayton-Goose Creek Ry. v. United States, 263 U.S. 456, 478 (1924).

[53] See 3-A SHARFMAN 366, 504; 3-B SHARFMAN 626; LANDIS, THE ADMINISTRATIVE PROCESS 13 (1938).

[54] It is hard to remember today that the only other federal regulatory commissions dealt with in these lectures which existed prior to 1920 were the Federal Trade Commission, created in 1914, and the Shipping Board, created in 1916. Before 1920 the primary regulatory duties of the Interstate Commerce Commission were to administer the commands as to just and reasonable maximum rates and discrimination, concepts with a long history at common law. See the famous quotations from Lord Hale's *De Jure Maris* and *De Portibus Maris* and the references to the dicta in Bolt v. Stennett, 8 T.R. 606, 101 Eng. Rep. 1572 (1800), and Aldnutt v. Inglis, 12 East 527, 104 Eng. Rep. 206 (1810), in Munn v. Illinois, 94 U.S. 113, 126–28 (1877). The same was true as to the Shipping Board, which, in addition to the general provisions of §§ 17 and 18, had been given a specific list of prohibited discriminatory acts in § 16. 39 Stat. 734–35 (1916), as amended, 46 U.S.C. §§ 815–17 (1958). The general grant of power in § 5 of the Federal Trade Commission Act, 38 Stat. 719 (1914), also employed a term with well-known common law connotations. How different, and how much vaguer, some of the new concepts introduced in 1920 actually were, seems not to have been fully appreciated at the time, see, as to the minimum rate power, pp. 108–110 *infra*.

[55] LANDIS, THE ADMINISTRATIVE PROCESS 55–56 (1938).

such a statute is to "steer a middle course between the Scylla of attempting to include every possible detail and the Charybdis of embodying no standard at all." [56] Indeed, President Kennedy himself has adjured that statutes should not "couch their objectives in such indecisive terms as to leave vast areas open for the free play of agency discretion." [57] However, for reasons we will later examine, it would be chimerical to suppose these good counsels will be greatly heeded; fairly broad standards in initial legislative grants to administrative agencies are likely to remain with us, as to some extent, when the statute deals with a novel field, they should.

My thesis is that where the initial standard is thus general, it is imperative that steps be taken over the years to define and clarify it — to canalize the broad stream into a number of narrower ones. I do not suggest this process can be so carried out that all cases can be determined by computers; I do suggest it ought to be carried to the point of affording a fair degree of predictability of decision in the great majority of cases and of intelligibility in all.

It will scarcely have escaped attention that the application of standards of greater or less generality to concrete cases is not a function peculiar to administrative agencies; it has long been practiced by other institutions not unknown to law students. Indeed, at one end of the administrative spectrum, it is hard to dis-

[56] SCHWARTZ, INTRODUCTION TO AMERICAN ADMINISTRATIVE LAW 45 (1958). Professor Bernstein expresses a similar thought: Congress "abdicates its legislative responsibility if it provides a regulatory agency merely with slogans rather than working criteria for defining the public interest." *Op. cit. supra* note 6, at 263. See also DOYLE REPORT 120. Compare the statement by an English author, ROBSON, JUSTICE AND ADMINISTRATIVE LAW 607–08 (3d ed. 1951): "[T]he wrong method of control is to give jurisdiction to administrative tribunals in vague terms containing undefined or undefinable standards, and to expect that economic conflict will thereby be resolved." Cf. Borchardt, *Congress and Administrative Law*, 30 GEO. WASH. L. REV. 429, 465 (1962).

For a recent instance of overly detailed legislative specification of standards, doubtless reflecting a close balance of the opposing forces, see § 14b, added to the Shipping Act by 75 Stat. 762 (1961), 46 U.S.C. § 813a (Supp. III 1962), dealing with the "dual-rate" system.

[57] H.R. Doc. No. 135, 87th Cong., 1st Sess. 2 (1961).

cern much difference between either the problems or the decisional processes of the agencies and those of the courts. A grievance on the score of unfair competition can come before a court at the suit of a plaintiff seeking an injunction or damages, or before the Federal Trade Commission on a complaint issued by the Commission but often having its real origin in a private source; and, after all these years, it is still uncertain just how far the statutory test on such a complaint, "unfair methods of competition, and unfair or deceptive acts or practices in commerce," [58] differs from that of the common law — an uncertainty going back to the congressional debates [59] and the initial Supreme Court decision,[60] much criticized but never overruled.[61] The same provision of the Clayton Act, section 7, may be invoked either in a proceeding beginning in the Federal Trade Commission under section 11 with enforcement by a court of appeals, or in a suit by the United States in the district court under section 15 without prior administrative action.[62] Again, when the NLRB has to determine whether an employee was discharged for union activity [63] or for inefficiency, it seems to be doing much the same kind of thing to which courts are accustomed. I am not undertaking to say that administrative adjudication is exactly the same as judicial adjudication even in such cases; [64] certainly it is very different in those at the

[58] 38 Stat. 719 (1914), as amended, 15 U.S.C. § 45(a)(1) (1958).
[59] See 51 CONG. REC. 11112, 11113, 11178–80, 12874–75 (1914); CUSHMAN, *op. cit. supra* note 45, at 205; HENDERSON, THE FEDERAL TRADE COMMISSION 35–36 (1924).
[60] FTC v. Gratz, 253 U.S. 421 (1920).
[61] Later cases tell us, not very helpfully, that the statutory phrase "has a broader meaning but how much broader has not been determined." FTC v. Raladam Co., 283 U.S. 643, 648 (1931); FTC v. R. F. Keppel & Bro., 291 U.S. 304, 310–12 (1934); A. L. A. Schechter Poultry Corp. v. United States, 295 U.S. 495, 552–53 (1935) (concurring opinion).
[62] 38 Stat. 734, 736 (1914), as amended, 15 U.S.C. §§ 18, 21, 25 (1958).
[63] 49 Stat. 452 (1935), as amended, 29 U.S.C. § 158(a)(3) (1958).
[64] The view that it is lies behind the American Bar Association's proposals to transfer such cases to a Trade Court, and a Labor Court, S. 1273, S. 1275, 86th Cong., 1st Sess. (1959); see Benjamin, *A Lawyer's View of Administrative Procedure — The American Bar Association Program*, 26 LAW & CONTEMP. PROB. 203, 220–22 (1961).

opposite end of the administrative spectrum, such as the *Class Rate Investigation of 1939*,[65] dealing with the classification and level of railroad class rates throughout the nation, a type of proceeding as to which I strongly endorse current criticisms of overjudicialization of hearing procedures and evidence-taking.[66]

Be all that as it may, there is still enough resemblance between administrative and judicial adjudication to suggest that the former can draw some useful lessons from the latter. "[T]he tendency of the law," Holmes told us eighty years ago, "must always be to narrow the field of uncertainty."[67] Of course, neither Holmes nor others who have sought to follow him ever supposed that complete certainty would be attainable; some critics have thus been beating not merely a dead but a phantom horse. The issue is one of goal: is it worth while for judges and administrators to attempt to state a principle and abide by it until circumstances dictate a new one, or should such an effort be downgraded in favor of subjective creation, largely undefined and uncontrolled?

John Dickinson has described how a legal standard, even one originally given to the jury to administer, "may become hardened in the course of time into a definite rule . . . ." He cites "the crystallization of the vague early rule that notice of the dishonor of a negotiable instrument must be given within a reasonable time into the definite rule that where the parties live at different places, the notice must be sent off on the following day, while if they live in the same town it must be given in time to be received on the following day (Williams *v.* Smith, 2 B. & Ald., 496, 500)"; and the hardening of the standard of due care in some states into the "stop, look, and listen" rule.[68] Mr. Justice Buller's famous

[65] 262 I.C.C. 447 (1945), *aff'd sub nom.* New York v. United States, 331 U.S. 284 (1947).

[66] LANDIS REPORT 17; REDFORD, NATIONAL REGULATORY COMMISSIONS: NEED FOR A NEW LOOK 14–15 (1959); I. & R. BOARD REPORT 66–67. I have made a similar criticism, *supra* note 13, at 435. See p. 144 *infra*.

[67] THE COMMON LAW 127 (1881). See also COHEN, *Jurisprudence as a Philosophical Discipline*, REASON AND LAW 142 (1950).

[68] DICKINSON, ADMINISTRATIVE JUSTICE AND THE SUPREMACY OF LAW IN THE UNITED STATES 143 (1927). For other instances, see *id.* at 205.

opinion in *Lickbarrow v. Mason* [69] tells how in earlier days mercantile cases "were left to a jury, and they produced no general principle. From that time we all know, the great study has been to find some certain general principles which shall be known to all mankind, not only to rule the particular case then under consideration, but to serve for the future." An analogy closer to the field here under review relates to the "rule of reason" applied under Section 1 of the Sherman Act. From the outset certain types of contracts, the so-called per se violations, have been recognized to create "a conclusive presumption which brought them within the statute" [70] as so construed, whether in fact they were reasonable or not. And even outside this area the courts have been concerned to make their applications of the rule of reason intelligible — to show that generally similar facts will bring about similar treatment. Neither is this process unique to the Sherman Act; "all great statutes force the judge at some point or other, be he ever so reluctant, to devise a 'common-law' of the statute." [71]

It would seem that if courts have been able thus to crystallize general standards, administrative agencies should be able to do something of the sort, even though they can hardly take as many generations to get the job done.[72] The Sherman Act example is enough to validate Dickinson's statement that "to make the presence or absence of an issue of contested social policy the test of

[69] 2 T.R. 63, 100 Eng. Rep. 35 (K.B. 1787).

[70] Standard Oil Co. v. United States, 221 U.S. 1, 65 (1911); United States v. Trenton Potteries Co., 273 U.S. 392 (1927); United States v. Socony-Vacuum Oil Co., 310 U.S. 150 (1940); Klor's, Inc. v. Broadway-Hale Stores, Inc., 359 U.S. 207 (1959); see Rahl, *Per Se Rules and Boycotts Under the Sherman Act: Some Reflections on the Klor's Case*, 45 VA. L. REV. 1165 (1959). For an illuminating discussion of the importance of clear principles in the antitrust area, see Bok, *The Tampa Electric Case*, 1961 SUPREME COURT REVIEW 267, 315–319.

[71] Jaffe, *An Essay on Delegation of Legislative Power*, 47 COLUM. L. REV. 359, 360–61 (1947).

[72] The *I. & R. Board Report* points out that "Law made by the courts is made slowly and indirectly, and ordinarily it emerges only after a succession of decisions have followed one upon another, clarifying and confirming until a new principle is molded," whereas regulation "must move quickly and directly if it is to be at all effective." I. & R. BOARD REPORT 55.

whether or not a field of human relations admits of the development of a body of law is . . . to set up a mistaken criterion."[73] He suggests that the test is rather "the possibility of isolating facts pertinent to all the cases which may form the basis for a rule" and that "the real reason for the special difficulty of developing legal rules in the fields of economic regulation which happen also to raise issues of debatable policy is that the situations which form the subject-matter of such regulation are generally so complex and unique that the factors which are determining in one case seldom repeat themselves in others."[74] I do not contend that economic regulation of business is susceptible of the same degree of definiteness as commercial law; I do suggest that, during three-quarters of a century of regulatory experience in the railroad field and several decades in others, many patterns have recurred frequently enough so that by now it should be possible to articulate bases of administrative determination more specific than we have generally had, even though these cannot be expected to be as immutable as the law of the Medes and Persians.[75]

[73] DICKINSON, *op. cit. supra* note 68, at 215.
[74] *Id.* at 215-16. Dickinson thought that such advances as can be made must come from the courts, rather than from the agencies themselves. *Ibid.* The reasons given, *id.* at 234-35, are: (1) that "The technical equipment which the commissions are supposed to possess, and the limited and specialized nature of their work, in a measure operate to unfit them for the task of developing general rules of law"; (2) that "among the rules of law to be developed and applied are those delimiting the scope and nature of the administrative body's activities. These, of course, cannot be left for that body to determine for itself"; and (3) that "the function of an administrative body is to get something done, not to adjudicate controversies nor to mark out and delimit rights." The second reason is surely unsound; a proposal that the agencies themselves do more to define the standards which they apply does not mean that the courts will lose power to keep the agencies from straying beyond their fences. The other two reasons are not convincing to me, although quite understandable in a pioneering work written thirty-five years ago; and the suggestion that administrative "determinations, if the supremacy of law is to be maintained, must be subject ultimately to the check of an adjudicating body primarily interested in general rules of delimitation between opposing rights," *id.* at 235, either would vest the courts with powers of review altogether too broad or would be ineffective for Dickinson's stated purpose if it did not.
[75] Professor Bernstein has thus put the desideratum: "When policies are broad

The Need for Better Definition

The need for achieving better definition of standards in administrative adjudication appears to me so compelling that I should hardly have thought the case had to be argued. But since there is highly respectable opinion which, at least seemingly, is to the contrary,[76] let me state the principal reasons:

The first is the basic human claim that the law should provide like treatment under like circumstances. Cardozo's statement, "It will not do to decide the same question one way between one set of litigants and the opposite way between another," [77] applies also to the administrative agencies, at least if we insert the caveat, "so long as the economic circumstances remain basically the same." We are not looking for oak trees to shelter twentieth century counterparts of St. Louis in the halls of the commissions any more than in the courthouses.[78] Still less can we tolerate the cozening of agency members and staffs which too wide discretion breeds. Rather, as Mr. Justice Douglas has said: "Law has

---

and vague, they generally prove to be unsatisfactory guides to decision in adjudicated cases. And when policies are too tight and specific, they may be applicable only to relatively few cases. What is needed is an appropriate balance between the two extremes . . . ." Bernstein, *The Regulatory Process: A Framework for Analysis*, 26 LAW & CONTEMP. PROB. 329, 332 (1961).

[76] See, e.g., 2 SHARFMAN 367-71. Professor Sharfman even looked at least with equanimity on a practice whereby "when the findings are changed, they are not only made operative for the future, but produce retroactive effects — the carriers are made liable to reparation even on shipments moved under the rates originally prescribed by the Commission," citing Traffic Bureau v. Atchison, T. & S.F. Ry., 140 I.C.C. 171 (1928). *Id.* at 369. The Supreme Court later took a different view. See Arizona Grocery Co. v. Atchison, T. & S.F. Ry., 284 U.S. 370 (1932). For a contrasting and much sounder tack, see 3-B SHARFMAN 763. Professor Davis also becomes quite enthusiastic over wide administrative discretion. See 1 DAVIS §§ 2.04, 2.05, 2.06, 2.11. Although his discussion seems directed to the constitutional validity of the delegation rather than to the manner of its exercise, the general tendency of this portion of his analysis is to downgrade the rule of law in administrative adjudication. For an opposite view, see PRETTYMAN, TRIAL BY AGENCY 10 (1959).

[77] THE NATURE OF THE JUDICIAL PROCESS 33 (1921). See HART, THE CONCEPT OF LAW 155-59 (1961).

[78] See POUND, INTRODUCTION TO THE PHILOSOPHY OF LAW 63 (rev. ed. 1954).

reached its finest moments when it has freed man from the unlimited discretion of some ruler, some civil or military official, some bureaucrat. Where discretion is absolute, man has always suffered." [79]

A second reason for definite standards of administrative adjudication is the social value in encouraging the security of transactions.[80] An airline considering an investment of $100,000,000 in additional jet transports, which it thinks necessary to give adequate service on its routes over a decade, ought to have some notion whether it will be allowed to serve the existing and anticipated traffic, along with other airlines then certificated, or whether its very success in traffic development will become the basis for additional authorizations. So ought the lenders who will be providing most of the money. A trucker contemplating the purchase of a new fleet should know the degree to which he will or will not be protected from ratecutting by other truckers or by competing modes of transportation. Although no such assurances are afforded in unregulated sections of the economy, a greater degree of predictability is a proper offset for some of the hampering effects of regulation. Perhaps the agency will say it can give no assurances; that, too, is an answer, and even such a statement is better than constant ambiguity and shift. Moreover, as these examples show, the need is not merely for definiteness at any given time but also for some degree of stability. Recognition of that need should not preclude an overruling of a policy which changed conditions or further reflections demand; [81] it will ensure

---

[79] Dissenting in United States v. Wunderlich, 342 U.S. 98, 101 (1951). See also his dissent in New York v. United States, 342 U.S. 882, 884 (1951), and Parker, *Why Do Administrative Agencies Exist? A Reappraisal*, 45 GEO. L.J. 331, 351 (1957). Compare Max Weber's description of "cabinet justice" in a patrimonial society, LAW IN ECONOMY AND SOCIETY 264, 266 (1954).

[80] RIPERT, LES FORCES CRÉATRICES DU DROIT I (1955): "De la permanence des règles dépend l'utilité de l'action, car aucune prévision ne peut être faite que sur la considération de ce qui existe."

[81] In view of the Commission's responsibility to adapt to fundamentally changing circumstances, there can be no quarrel with the Interstate Commerce Commission's early statement that it does not have "the same reason for applying the

that such a reversal will be deliberate and public, rather than inadequately considered, and too adequately concealed — in many instances from the members of the agency themselves.

Third, a clear statement of the standards the agency is applying is necessary if administrative adjudication is to be consistent with the democratic process.[82] Professor Bernstein's assertion that "the commission has significant antidemocratic implications" [83] is not to be dismissed so readily as has been done.[84] We still live under a Constitution which provides that "all legislative Powers herein granted shall be vested in a Congress of the United States, which shall consist of a Senate and House of Representatives"; [85] even if a statute telling an agency "Here is the problem:

---

maxim *stare decisis* which exists in courts of law." Board of R.R. Comm'rs v. Atchison, T. & S.F. Ry., 8 I.C.C. 304, 308 (1899). For example, the Commission would surely be justified in taking a different view today as to the degree to which a reduction in rail competition should preclude approval of a merger from the view it would have taken when railways had a near monopoly. However, the Commission has soundly recognized limitations on the disregard of previous decisions. In the cited case itself the Commission adhered to its earlier decision, believing that money may have been "invested and industries built up upon the strength" of it, and that hence it must control "in the absence of some showing that new conditions have intervened, or that the effects of the original holding have been other than were anticipated . . . ." *Id.* at 309. Later the Commission said "[W]hen, upon a given state of facts, we reach a conclusion regarding certain rates we will adhere to that conclusion in subsequent proceedings regarding the same or similar rates unless new facts are brought to our attention, conditions are shown to have undergone a material change, or we proceeded on a misconception or misapprehension." American Glue Co. v. Boston & M.R.R., 191 I.C.C. 37, 39 (1932). See also the Commission's recent statement in *Ex parte* No. MC-55, sheets 36–37 (1961).

[82] BERNSTEIN, REGULATING BUSINESS BY INDEPENDENT COMMISSION 293 (1941).
[83] *Ibid.*
[84] 1 DAVIS § 2.16, at 155. The author says that "by various means, formal and informal, prominent and concealed, direct and devious, the people's representatives influence the exercise of delegated power"; such concealed and devious methods seem to me the antithesis of the democratic process. There is much more in Professor Davis' point that "appropriate legislative supervision or reexamination" may be a safeguard; but, as we shall see, this can scarcely be effective unless the administrators say what they are doing, and adhere to what they have said unless and until a change is clearly indicated.
[85] U.S. CONST. art. I, § 1.

deal with it" be deemed to comply with the letter of that command, it hardly does with the spirit. It is quite true that the "law" made by Congress itself reaches the citizen only through application by the executive or the judiciary,[86] that the executive can give a particular law either a strong or a weak enforcement, and that "courts continue to mold the common law, as well as to engage in creative interpretation of statutes and of constitutions."[87] However, the executive is accountable to the electorate; and the courts, themselves a basic part of the constitutional scheme, legislate "only interstitially,"[88] spell out what they are doing, apply uniformly any new rule they have forged, and usually stick to it for a considerable period. The legislature thus knows what the courts have done and is free to change this if it desires. The people would not otherwise tolerate even the modest degree of lawmaking in which the courts necessarily indulge. They should be no more tolerant of unbridled discretion on the part of administrative agencies; in the long run, they will not be.

A fourth reason for a crystallization of standards is that this is necessary to the maintenance of the independence which the agencies so highly prize. The revulsion against the revelations of pressure on the commissions from businessmen, legislators, and the executive branch has been too much concerned with the symptoms and too little with the cause. One reason, not the only reason but nevertheless a reason, why there are no similar pressures on judges is the relative definiteness of the rules the judges apply; even in the courts, pressure is more likely to be attempted on the committing magistrate, with his wide range of undefined discretion, than on the appellate judge. Lack of definite standards creates a void into which attempts to influence are bound to rush; legal vacuums are quite like physical ones in that respect.[89] Al-

---

[86] Compare RIPERT, op. cit. supra note 80, at 364: "Il faut donc prêter attention à la vie de la loi après sa naissance."

[87] 1 DAVIS § 2.05, at 98.

[88] Mr. Justice Holmes dissenting in Southern Pac. Co. v. Jensen, 244 U.S. 205, 221 (1917).

[89] McMAHON, Regulation of Broadcasting: Study for the Committee on Inter-

though pressure produces diffuse decisions, it is likewise true that diffuse decisions produce pressure; and pressure from one party to a case, or even a reasonable fear of it, arising from experience, will produce pressure from others.[90] It is hardly coincidence that the two commissions believed to have been most subjected to pressure, the FCC and the CAB, are agencies which have conspicuously failed to define the standards governing their decisions. Indeed, it may not be unduly cynical to ask whether, if there really were no intelligible criteria in the award of a television license, so that the record, made at so much pain, was quite irrelevant to the decision, it would not be somewhat hypocritical to become so exercised over methods of persuasion that could permissibly be used in other instances where choice is under no legal control. On the other hand, as the administrators sharpen their standards for decision, they will not only end the cruder forms of influence from interested individuals, but also will reduce pressures from the executive and from Congress, in such forms as threats to deny or the actual denial of reappointment or pronunciamentos by individual legislators or committees. This does not mean that there would or should be an end to efforts to persuade agencies to alter rules that have become outmoded, or are contended to be; but such efforts, whether by parties to the cause or by members of the legislature or the executive, would then be in the open, and related to the rule rather than the case. Congress could affect agency decision mainly by performing its assigned task of legislating, and the President by performing his of recommending legislation.

Finally, the clear definition of standards affords a miscellany of intra-agency advantages. Perhaps the most important is educating the agency members — much will be learned from the discussions among the members and with the staff that are essential

---

state and Foreign Commerce, House of Representatives, 85th Cong., 2d Sess. on H. Res. 99 (85th Cong., 1st Sess.) 155–56 (1958).

[90] See Note, *Ex Parte Contacts With the Federal Communications Commission*, 73 HARV. L. REV. 1178 (1960).

to the framing of a policy, whether in a decision or in a statement or rule. It should reduce the volume of cases; absence of standards encourages the filing of applications which their presence would render hopeless. It will help protect against the "aimless drifting" periods when a heretofore able commission is rendered temporarily helpless by incompetence or diverseness.[91] Beyond that I will borrow Professor Redford's list [92] — better defined standards inform examiners and "thus increase their opportunities to make decisions which will not be appealed or will stand upon appeal"; [93] "they inform the staff, facilitate delegation, and lay the basis for responsible evaluation of policies"; [94] and they save the time of administrators and reduce expense and delay by avoiding the need for treating each case as *res nova*. Indeed, I would emphasize the point as to delegation even further. In these large agencies a considerable amount of delegation to subordinates is inevitable; definition of standards is required if the agency members are to be the masters of the staff rather than the slaves of anonymous Neros, each fiddling his own tune.

[91] I. & R. Board Report 29.

[92] National Regulatory Commissions: Need for a New Look 12–13 (1959). See also Borchardt, *supra* note 56, at 466.

[93] I would hazard the guess that examiners of the NLRB have suffered reversals in unfair labor practice cases much less frequently than have those of the FCC and CAB in comparative hearings on television licenses and new route cases; and that the NLRB's clearer definition of standards, discussed below, is the main reason for this.

Another advantage of definition of standards, in the case of the NLRB, is the aid this gives the Board's regional directors in determining whether there is "reasonable cause to believe" the validity of a charge of unfair labor practice, warranting an application for an injunction under 61 Stat. 149 (1947), as amended, 29 U.S.C. § 160(*l*) (Supp. I 1959) — often the only truly effective method of enforcement.

[94] The first two considerations are of peculiar importance because of the fact, noted many years ago in Henderson, The Federal Trade Commission 328 (1924), "that most government affairs are run by men of average capabilities, and that it is necessary to supply such men with a routine and a readymade technique . . . ." See also, supporting many of the foregoing observations, former Commissioner Arpaia's address to the 1953 Annual Meeting of ICC Practitioners, quoted in Gellhorn & Byse, Administrative Law: Cases and Comments 1077–78 (4th ed. 1960).

Of course, as in most matters, there is another side. Perhaps the point was best put by a great judge, too painfully conscious of the limitations of his own calling. Judge Learned Hand once criticized what he thought was the tendency of commissions to "fall into grooves, just as the judges are so apt to do," characteristically adding, "and when they get into grooves, then God save you to get them out of the grooves." [95] I doubt we need bother the deity; we hold our own keys to salvation. I would say, in respectful answer, that the danger Judge Hand feared can be overcome if the agencies keep looking out of the grooves with a view to deflecting their course if that should appear desirable, and if the President and Congress keep looking into them with the same objective, and that the consequences of having no grooves at all are very much worse, as we are going to see.

If I have convinced you that the goal of more definite standards in administrative adjudication is well worth attaining, I have as yet advanced nothing, save the example of the courts, to show this can be done. Neither have I indicated whose is the responsibility for attaining the goal and in what manner that is to be accomplished. For these and other reasons the time has come to forsake the heady mountain air of generalities and descend to the pastures where the daily work of the agencies is done. Such a descent to the particular is the more necessary, toilsome though it be, because laborers in this vineyard have so generally declined to make it. Perhaps somewhat illogically in my role as a critic, I shall begin with two areas that show what can be accomplished when the agency and the legislature do their part; evidence of

[95] *Hearings To Study Senate Concurrent Resolution 21 Before a Subcommittee of the Senate Committee on Labor and Public Welfare*, 82d Cong., 1st Sess. 224 (1951) (reprinted in GELLHORN & BYSE, *op. cit. supra* note 94, at 40-41, and in HAND, THE SPIRIT OF LIBERTY 241-42 (3d ed. 1960)). One commentator has read Judge Hand as criticizing, not what I am here advocating, but rather a refusal by agencies "to cope with problems which, though superficially the same as older ones, are really different and thus require specialized handling." Rothman, *The National Labor Relations Board and Administrative Law*, 29 GEO. WASH. L. REV. 301, 317 (1960). If Judge Hand meant only that — and the reading is surely supportable — I would happily agree.

failure will come later and in ample measure. Only when we have acquainted ourselves in some degree with the detailed workings of administrative adjudication in a variety of fields will we have earned the privilege of generalizing again.

II

An Early Success:
Section 4 of the Interstate Commerce Act

MY first example has a long history; a review of this neatly illustrates the interplay of timely administrative specification of standards and suitable legislative response. In my days as a student, when so much of federal administrative law concerned a single statute, Professor Frankfurter spoke of it familiarly as "the fourth section"; today, with the burgeoning of federal regulatory legislation and the reduced role of the railroads in the transportation scheme, I had better present it more formally as the long-and-short-haul clause embodied in Section 4 of the Interstate Commerce Act. Here is how it appeared in the Act of February 4, 1887:

> SEC. 4. That it shall be unlawful for any common carrier subject to the provisions of this act to charge or receive any greater compensation in the aggregate for the transportation of passengers or of like kind of property, under substantially similar circumstances and conditions, for a shorter than for a longer distance over the same line, in the same direction, the shorter being included within the longer distance; but this shall not be construed as authorizing any common carrier within the terms of this act to charge and receive as great compensation for a shorter as for a longer distance: *Provided, however,* That upon application to the Commission appointed under the provisions of this act, such common carrier may, in special cases, after investigation by the Commission, be authorized to charge less for longer than for shorter distances for the transportation of passengers or property; and the Commission may from time to time prescribe the extent to which such designated

common carrier may be relieved from the operation of this section of this act.[1]

The first point to note is that the fourth section was itself a specification of a more general standard. Section 3 made it unlawful "for any common carrier subject to the provisions of this act to make or give any undue or unreasonable preference or advantage to any particular person, company, firm, corporation, or locality, or any particular description of traffic, in any respect whatsoever, or to subject any particular person, company, firm, corporation, or locality, or any particular description of traffic, to any undue or unreasonable prejudice or disadvantage in any respect whatsoever." The Commission would thus have had power, under section 3, to ban what Congress specifically made unlawful by section 4. Congress was not willing to leave things at that — it selected a particular type of discrimination and made that per se illegal, as it later did, in Section 16 of the Shipping Act, with respect to certain types of discrimination on the sea that had proved especially offensive.[2] Moreover, the fourth section served a protective as well as a prohibitive purpose; a lower rate for the longer than the shorter haul sanctioned by the fourth section could not violate the third.[3] This type of specification at the very outset is, I suggest, highly desirable; it is unfortunate that Congress no longer seems so willing — or able — to look a problem squarely in the face.

However, section 4 raised its own problems. The Commission dealt with them in *In re Southern Ry. & S.S. Ass'n*,[4] springing from a petition of the Louisville & Nashville Railroad Company filed on April 5, 1887, the very day the act took effect.[5] The decision, written by Judge Cooley, the Chairman, was rendered on

[1] Ch. 104, 24 Stat. 380. My discussion of the fourth section through 1920 has drawn heavily on Professor Sharfman.
[2] 39 Stat. 734 (1916), amended by 49 Stat. 1518 (1936), 46 U.S.C. § 815 (1958).
[3] Intermountain Rate Cases, 234 U.S. 476, 482–483 (1914).
[4] 1 I.C.R. 278 (1887). The opinion was also printed in the Commission's *First Annual Report* at 64 (1887).
[5] See 1 I.C.R. 15 (1887). Similar petitions were filed by other companies.

June 15 — a speed itself worthy of emulation. The quality was even more so; if Cooley had deliberately set out to write an opinion that would forever be a model for administrators, he could scarcely have done better.[6]

The first question to which the Commission addressed itself was this: Did section 4 prohibit generally the charging of more for the shorter than the longer distance save when the Commission had granted relief, or did it prohibit this only when the circumstances and conditions were substantially similar, with applications to the Commission under the proviso required only when they were, or when the carriers were so uncertain about the dissimilarity as to desire protection? Reviewing the language, the practicalities of administration, and the legislative history, the Commission adopted the latter construction. Although, on that view, the L & N's application need not have been filed, the Commission thought "it may be proper to consider the application on its merits, especially as the question, What is a case of dissimilar circumstances and conditions within the meaning of the law? must in general be a mixed question of law and fact, upon which differences of opinion would be expected to arise," and the railroads were "entitled to the benefit of such conclusions as we have already reached upon the general merits of their applications, that they may be guided thereby in the preparation of their tariffs respectively." [7]

Although long quotations are boring, still I must give some indication of what Judge Cooley said for the carriers' guidance; it is such an admirable illustration of what all commissions should do early in their careers, and then do again later on. The essence

---

[6] Perhaps there are lessons in the circumstance that Cooley did not want the Interstate Commerce Commission post. He wrote his wife when rumors of his appointment were heard: "I really begin to think that I am in danger of being named on the Railroad Commission. . . . I don't think there is anything in it for me to feel elated." III DORFMAN, THE ECONOMIC MIND IN AMERICAN CIVILIZATION, *Bibliographic Notes* at xx n.13 (1949).

[7] 1 I.C.R. at 281–82.

of the opinion is condensed into two propositions, one affirmative, the other negative. Here is the affirmative:

> *FIFTH.* That the existence of actual competition which is of controlling force, in respect to traffic important in amount, may make out the dissimilar circumstances and conditions entitling the carrier to charge less for the longer than for the shorter haul over the same line in the same direction, the shorter being included in the longer, in the following cases: 1, when the competition is with carriers by water which are not subject to the provisions of the statute; 2, when the competition is with foreign or other railroads which are not subject to the provisions of the statute; 3, in rare and peculiar cases of competition between railroads which are subject to the statute, when a strict application of the general rule of the statute would be destructive of legitimate competition.[8]

Now comes the negative:

> *SIXTH.* The Commission further decides that when a greater charge in the aggregate is made for the transportation of passengers or the like kind of property for a shorter than for a longer distance over the same line in the same direction, the shorter being included in the longer distance, it is not sufficient justification therefor that the traffic which is subjected to such greater charge is way or local traffic, and that which is given the more favorable rates is not.
>
> Nor is it sufficient justification for such greater charge that the short haul traffic is more expensive to the carrier, unless when the circumstances are such as to make it exceptionally expensive, or the long haul traffic exceptionally inexpensive, the difference being extraordinary and susceptible of definite proof.
>
> Nor that the lesser charge or the longer haul has for its motive the encouragement of manufacturers or some other branch of industry.
>
> Nor that it is designed to build up business or trade centers; nor

---

[8] 1 I.C.R. at 291. One instance was when a circuitous route had been set up to serve out-of-the-way localities; there "the greater charge for the shorter haul preserves the proper advantage of situation, and has in itself no element of injustice to localities," whereas a contrary rule would "be fatal to competition." 1 I.C.R. at 289.

that the lesser charge on the longer haul is merely a continuation of the favorable rates under which trade centers or industrial establishments have been built up.

The fact that the long haul traffic will only bear certain rates is no reason for carrying it for less than cost at the expense of other traffic.[9]

To get the full flavor of Judge Cooley's opinion, it ought to be read, in full, as against the vacuous and weasel-worded utterances characteristic of our day. The railroad lawyer who studied it in June of 1887 must have come away feeling he had learned quite a lot; he had eaten meat, not gelatin. The opinion did not settle every fourth-section case for him, something that would have been manifestly impossible, but it told him pretty well how the land lay.[10] Moreover, the Commission had provided the most effective possible answer to the fears, expressed in Congress, that the proviso had endowed it "with a greater power than that which is wielded by any sovereign in Europe where anything like constitutional government prevails. Indeed, the Czar of Russia could not have a more arbitrary power," since "the commission in its discretion has the power to suspend the law in case of one railroad company and to refuse to suspend it in case of another railroad company located by the side of the one relieved if it chooses to do so." [11]

Five years later the Commission took another important step by eliminating Judge Cooley's "rare and peculiar cases" of competition between interstate railroads at the more distant point as a dissimilar circumstance or condition, an exception which the carriers had so expanded as to make it the rule, and directed that henceforth any interstate rail competition should be only a basis

---

[9] 1 I.C.R. at 291.
[10] Twenty-seven years later Chief Justice White was to say: "These comprehensive views announced at the inception as a matter of administrative construction were subsequently sustained by many decisions of this court . . . ." Intermountain Rate Cases, 234 U.S. 476, 483 (1914).
[11] 18 CONG. REC. 571 (1887) (remarks of Senator Brown).

for applying for fourth-section relief.[12] However, the latter definition of the general standard received a rude jolt when the Supreme Court held, in 1897, that the Commission had been wrong in so requiring fourth-section applications in all cases where competition between interstate railroads was the ground relied on; this was not demanded, the Court held, if the circumstances were in fact dissimilar, and a carrier could decide this for itself and take a chance on a court's holding it right, as the Supreme Court there did.[13] Congressional reaction to the decision was slow in coming but rather violent when it came, in the Mann-Elkins Act of 1910.[14] The "under similar circumstances and conditions" language was wholly eliminated — thereby enacting the stricter construction which the Commission, altogether properly as a matter of interpretation, had rejected twenty-three years before; henceforth dissimilarity of circumstances and conditions was simply a basis for seeking fourth-section relief.[15]

Another provision of the Mann-Elkins amendment of section 4 is relevant to our study. The amended section contained a completely new prohibition, rather unrelated to its original purpose; this made it unlawful for a carrier "to charge any greater compensation as a through route than the aggregate of the intermedi-

[12] Trammell v. Clyde S.S. Co., 4 I.C.R. 120 (1892).

[13] ICC v. Alabama Midland Ry., 168 U.S. 144, 173 (1897). This was the occasion for the famous remark of Mr. Justice Harlan, alone dissenting, "Taken in connection with other decisions defining the powers of the Interstate Commerce Commission, the present decision, it seems to me, goes far to make that Commission a useless body for all practical purposes, and to defeat many of the important objects designed to be accomplished by the various enactments of Congress relating to interstate commerce." *Id.* at 176.

[14] Ch. 309, § 8, 36 Stat. 547 (1910). The constitutionality of this provision of the act was sustained in Intermountain Rate Cases, 234 U.S. 476 (1914).

[15] The act further provided that "whenever a carrier by railroad shall in competition with a water route or routes reduce the rates on the carriage of any species of freight to or from competitive points, it shall not be permitted to increase such rates unless after hearing by the Interstate Commerce Commission it shall be found that such proposed increase rests upon changed conditions other than the elimination of water competition." 36 Stat. 548. This was held not to apply to rates reduced with the authority of the Commission. Skinner & Eddy Corp. v. United States, 249 U.S. 557 (1919).

ate rates subject to the provisions of this Act."[16] The interest of this is that the amendment gave statutory force to what had been a policy announcement of the Commission. In its *Tariff Circular No. 6–A*,[17] issued shortly after passage of the Hepburn Act of 1906,[18] the Commission announced that "it would be its policy to consider the through rate, which is higher than the sum of the locals between the same points, as prima facie unreasonable, and that the burden of proof would be upon the carrier to defend such higher through rate." The Mann-Elkins Act took this announcement, made it more specific, and placed it beyond administrative recall — the practice now was not just "prima facie unreasonable," it was unlawful, save that the Commission might grant relief from it as from other fourth-section prohibitions.[19] It is scarcely likely that, without the Commission's pronouncement, Congress would have taken the occasion to legislate; here it did legislate and the legislation has stood, apparently without complaint, although perhaps without much effect, for over fifty years. What Professor Jaffe has called "a permanent creative partnership between legislation and administration"[20] will not work unless the administrative agency, by this kind of definition, continuously presents to the legislature possible solutions which the latter may affirm, modify, or reject. Neither will it work unless the legislature keeps itself abreast of what the agency is doing and employs its ability to legislate.

Further workings of this interplay are illustrated by the amendments to the fourth section in Transportation Act, 1920.[21] The Commission's authority to grant relief under the section was restricted in three respects. The Commission was not to permit "the establishment of any charge to or from the more distant

[16] 36 Stat. 547.
[17] 20 ICC Ann. Rep. 170 (1906).
[18] Ch. 3591, 34 Stat. 584 (1906).
[19] 25 ICC Ann. Rep. 19–20 (1911).
[20] *An Essay on Delegation of Legislative Power*, 47 Colum. L. Rev. 359, 364 (1947).
[21] Ch. 91, § 406, 41 Stat. 480.

point that is not reasonably compensatory for the service performed"; [22] in permitting a circuitous route to lower the rates to or from competitive points while maintaining higher charges to or from intermediate points, "the authority shall not include intermediate points as to which the haul of the petitioning line or route is not longer than that of the direct line or route between the competitive points," and the Commission was not to grant relief "on account of merely potential water competition not actually in existence." In each instance Congress here affirmed positions the Commission had already announced: [23] in the light of experience, Congress chose to take the Commission's specifications of the general standard, which would otherwise have remained subject to reargument and reconsideration, and to vest them with the force of law.

While such enactment of criteria developed by the agency has the advantages of added certainty and of avoidance of constant reargument, it may prove premature; the legislature must be ready to act if further experience demonstrates the adoption to have been unwise. Such, in some degree, has been the further history of section 4. The Transportation Act of 1940 [24] eliminated the 1920 proviso with respect to intermediate points on circuitous routes; evidently this was too mechanical a limitation. And in 1957 Congress in effect went back to pre-Mann-Elkins days in one respect by providing that no relief application was required when a carrier operating over a circuitous route wished to meet

---

[22] As will later be seen in our study of the minimum rate power, pp. 112-118 and 129-130 *infra*, determination of this is not nearly so simple as it sounds. The Commission held the provision to forbid rates "lower than necessary to meet existing competition." Transcontinental Cases of 1922, 74 I.C.C. 48, 71 (1922).

[23] Fourth Section Violations in the Southeast, 30 I.C.C. 153, 177 (1914); New Orleans Cotton Exchange v. Louisville & N.R.R., 46 I.C.C. 712, 748-49 (1917); Memphis-Southwestern Investigation, 55 I.C.C. 515, 562-66 (1919); *cf.* Meridian Traffic Bureau v. Director General, 57 I.C.C. 107, 110 (1920) (granting relief because of strong potential water competition). See also 34 ICC ANN. REP. 47-48 (1920).

[24] Ch. 722, § 6, 54 Stat. 904.

the charges of a carrier operating over a more direct route,[25] the Commission having advised that almost all such applications were granted in any event.[26]

So endeth the long but to me rather beautiful story of section 4. It shows how agency and legislature can work fruitfully together — the agency by announcing specifications of the statutory standard which it will regularly apply, the legislature by legislating, here four times in forty-seven years, when it deems those specifications sufficiently proven, and then modifying its own enactments if subsequent experience so suggests. Whether the story has been as beautiful in its economic results as in its exemplification of the gradual working out of standards by agency and Congress, I do not pretend to judge.[27]

[25] 71 Stat. 292 (1957), 49 U.S.C. § 4 (1958).

[26] H.R. REP. No. 577, 85th Cong., 1st Sess. 3 (1957).

The *Doyle Report* severely criticizes the 1957 change as having "the effect of perpetuating avoidable economic waste in the transportation system in order to artificially equalize competition between direct and indirect routes"; it is "strongly recommended that section 4 of the act be retained as written prior to 1957 and that the sense of the Congress be expressed that equalization of intramodal circuity through relief from provisions of section 4 be limited to that circuity which, in the judgment of the regulatory agency, results only in negligible increased cost to the national economy . . . ." DOYLE REPORT 344–45.

[27] The 1955 *Report of the Presidential Advisory Committee on Transport Policy and Organization* recommended, p. 13, that Congress remove any requirement of prior approval where rail or water carriers wished to meet actual competition and the charge was not less than a minimum reasonable rate. Secretary Weeks explained that the change was intended to be "procedural" only and that such rates "would have to meet the full present requirements of section 4" if challenged by suspension or complaint. *Hearings Before a Subcommittee on Transport Policy and Organization of the House Committee on Interstate and Foreign Commerce*, 84th Cong., 1st Sess. 25 (1955). The provision forbidding a through rate higher than the aggregate of the locals was to be deleted. See *ibid*.

Administration of the fourth section has, of course, raised a host of problems other than those treated in the text. Here as elsewhere I have made no attempt at anything like complete analysis.

III

Definition of Standards by Agency and Legislature in National Labor Relations

AN agency that has done much to translate the general words of its charter into more specific guides for behavior by the regulated and decision by the regulators is the National Labor Relations Board. Time and again the Board has announced that certain conduct would, or presumptively would, violate one of the broad prohibitions of the National Labor Relations Act, whereas other conduct would not, or presumptively would not. Indeed, the Board has sometimes been held by the courts to have gone too far in doing this. The history is instructive on both counts. Perhaps the Labor Board's field lends itself to crystallization more readily than those of the transportation and communications agencies. Probably also the pressures on the NLRB in a particular case are generally less strong than those with respect to the award of supposedly valuable franchises, although, as I have suggested, failure to define standards is a cause of pressures as well as a result. Still, when the Board has done so much in the way of specification, it is somewhat hard to believe that other agencies could not have done more. In this area also Congress has effectively intervened, in the Taft-Hartley Act of 1947 and again in the Landrum-Griffin amendments of 1959. Although I shall place a number of examples before you, I shall make no attempt at completeness either in breadth or in depth; to do so would be to write a not inconsiderable portion of the treatise on labor law we so badly need.

A good instance with which to begin is the problem of union solicitation on company property. Literally, any employer prohibition of such solicitation might have been considered a violation of section 8(1), making it an unfair labor practice for an employer to interfere with or restrain employees in the rights of self-organization guaranteed in section 7.[1] Actually no such absolute would have been tolerated. The problem, as the Supreme Court later put it, required "working out an adjustment between the undisputed right of self-organization assured to employees under the Wagner Act and the equally undisputed right of employers to maintain discipline in their establishments."[2]

The Board might have left the problem for *ad hoc* determination in each case, taking account of factors in favor of allowing such solicitation — confinement of the workers, isolation of the place of employment, antiunion activities of the employer, and so forth — and of others working against it. Such a course would have multiplied litigation; moreover, the very lack of a settled rule might have promoted employer interference save in the clearest cases. The Board took a different tack. In *Peyton Packing Co.*,[3] it made an announcement typifying what an administrative agency ought to do:

> The Act, of course, does not prevent an employer from making and enforcing reasonable rules covering the conduct of employees on company time. Working time is for work. It is therefore within the province of an employer to promulgate and enforce a rule prohibiting union solicitation during working hours. Such a rule must be presumed to be valid in the absence of evidence that it was adopted for a discriminatory purpose. It is no less true that time outside working hours, whether before or after work, or during luncheon or rest periods, is an employee's time to use as he wishes without unreasonable restraint, although the employee is on company property. It is therefore not within the province of an employer to promulgate and enforce a rule prohibiting union solicitation by an employee outside of working hours, although on company property. Such a rule must be presumed to be an unreasonable impediment to self-organization and therefore discriminatory in the

---

[1] 49 Stat. 452 (1935), as amended, 29 U.S.C. §§ 157, 158(a)(1) (1958).
[2] Republic Aviation Corp. v. NLRB, 324 U.S. 793, 797–98 (1945).
[3] 49 N.L.R.B. 828, 843–44 (1943).

absence of evidence that special circumstances make the rule necessary in order to maintain production or discipline.

When the issue came before the Supreme Court in the *Republic Aviation* case, that body could "perceive no error in the Board's adoption of this presumption," which "was the product of the Board's appraisal of normal conditions about industrial establishments." [4] Neither, apparently, could Congress when it made its thoroughgoing revision of the Labor Act in 1947.[5]

A subsidiary development — the so-called *Bonwit Teller* rule — was less successful. In 1944 the Board had laid down an exception to *Peyton Packing Co.* for retail department stores.[6] "Because of the unique manner in which the latter type of enterprise conducts its operations," the Board permitted "prohibiting union solicitation at all times on the selling floor." The Bonwit Teller store in New York had availed itself of this permission. With an election due on September 15, 1949, its president addressed the employees on the selling floor after an early closing on September 9. Three days later the union sought an opportunity to address the employees under similar conditions; its request was not acknowledged. In a 1951 decision the Board held "that an employer who chooses to use his premises to assemble his employees and speak against a union may not deny that union's reasonable request for the same opportunity to present its case, where the circumstances are such that only by granting such request will the employees have a reasonable opportunity to hear both sides. What the particular circumstances are which give rise to the obligation to grant such request is a matter the Board must face on a case-to-case basis." [7] The Board was satisfied that such circumstances existed in *Bonwit Teller*; one was the company's permissible use of a "broad no-solicitation rule" on the selling floor.

---

[4] 324 U.S. at 804; *cf.* NLRB v. Babcock & Wilcox Co., 351 U.S. 105 (1956).
[5] Ch. 120, 61 Stat. 136 (1947).
[6] May Dep't Stores Co., 59 N.L.R.B. 976, 981 (1944).
[7] Bonwit Teller, Inc., 96 N.L.R.B. 608, 612 (1951).

What the opinion left in doubt was whether the new rule was limited to a department store that had taken advantage of the exception permitting the prohibition of solicitation on the selling floor even during nonworking hours and then had used the floor for an antiunion speech, at least when no other unfair labor practice had been committed. On review the Second Circuit held the rule must be thus confined.[8] However, the Board proceeded to apply the doctrine even in an industrial establishment with no rule against solicitation,[9] saying, in a 1953 decision, that refusal by the employer to accord a union equal opportunity to express its case by speechmaking on company time and premises violated section 8(a)(1) "despite any dicta or views to the contrary which may be found in the decision of the court of appeals in the *Bonwit Teller* case." [10]

This bold assertion was to stand only for some nine months. Before the year was out, the Board, whose composition had been altered in the meanwhile, proceeded to bring the *Bonwit Teller* doctrine back where the Second Circuit had placed it. Henceforth, "in the absence of either an unlawful broad no-solicitation rule (prohibiting union access to company premises on other than working time) or a privileged no-solicitation rule (broad but not unlawful because of the character of the business), an employer does not commit an unfair labor practice if he makes a preelection speech on company time and premises to his employees and denies

---

[8] Bonwit Teller, Inc. v. NLRB, 197 F.2d 640 (2d Cir. 1952), *company's petition for cert. denied*, 345 U.S. 905 (1953).
[9] Biltmore Mfg. Co., 97 N.L.R.B. 905 (1951).
[10] Metropolitan Auto Parts, Inc., 102 N.L.R.B. 1634, 1635 (1953). Chairman Herzog disagreed, believing that "the spirit and legislative history of Section 8(c) do not seem to me to encourage this Board to find that an employer's insistence on monopolizing his own property as a platform constitutes a violation of the amended Act, absent that discrimination which arises whenever he treats his no-solicitation policy as a one-way street." *Id.* at 1638. The *Metropolitan* case was followed in Seamprufe, Inc., 103 N.L.R.B. 298 (1953); Onondaga Pottery Co., 103 N.L.R.B. 770, 777–82 (1953); and Stow Mfg. Co., 103 N.L.R.B. 1280, 1306, 1309 (1953), despite continued judicial disapproval, NLRB v. American Tube Bending Co., 205 F.2d 45 (2d Cir. 1953).

the union's request for an opportunity to reply."[11] In addition to legal arguments, the Board found that even if the doctrine "had been well conceived in principle, it proved unworkable in the arena of practical labor-management relations," since it "visualized the [sic] first one party and then the other should address the employees, and so on *seriatim* and *ad infinitum*, thus compelling a game of wits and an endless jockeying for position, winner's prize being the treasured backfence advantage of having the last word."[12] Simultaneously the Board established a rule "which will be applied in all election cases" whereby "employers and unions alike will be prohibited from making election speeches on company time to massed assemblies of employees within 24 hours before the scheduled time for conducting an election."[13]

Critics might say that the birth, advance, and retreat of *Bonwit Teller*, all within three years, not to speak of further uncertainties thought by some to have been created by the Supreme Court's decision in the *Steelworkers'* case,[14] show that specification of standards is not such a good idea after all. I disagree. The difficulty was an imprecise articulation in an area where precision was extremely important. The Board was operating dangerously close to the mandate of section 8(c) of the act as amended in 1947[15] that "the expressing of any views, argument, or opinion, or the dissemination thereof, . . . shall not constitute or be evidence of an unfair labor practice under any of the provisions of this subchapter, if such expression contains no threat of reprisal or force or promise of benefit" — an amendment enacted for the specific purpose of overriding the Board's decision in *Clark*

---

[11] Livingston Shirt Corp., 107 N.L.R.B. 400, 409 (1953). See also May Department Stores Co., 136 N.L.R.B. No. 71 (1962).

[12] 107 N.L.R.B. at 407.

[13] Peerless Plywood Co., 107 N.L.R.B. 427, 429 (1953). Applications of this rule are discussed in Koretz, *Employer Interference With Union Organization Versus Employer Free Speech*, 29 GEO. WASH. L. REV. 399, 409–11 (1960).

[14] NLRB v. United Steelworkers of America, 357 U.S. 357 (1958), commented on in Koretz, *supra* note 13, at 406–09.

[15] 61 Stat. 142, 29 U.S.C. § 158(c) (1958).

Bros.[16] *Bonwit Teller* should have been limited to the two situations to which the Board has now confined it. Judicial approval was secured only on that narrow basis, and over the dissent of a most distinguished judge even as to that.[17] Instead of heeding the caution,[18] the Board carried the doctrine into new ground where it could be said with some justice, as the majority later did, that the doctrine had become *Clark Bros.* "in scant disguise." [19] At least one thing must be said to the Board's credit even in this rather sorry episode. In this instance as in others, when the NLRB has become convinced of error, it has overruled the offending action candidly and clearly, not left the carcass to lie around as other agencies have been prone to do.[20]

[16] 70 N.L.R.B. 802 (1946); see S. REP. No. 105, 80th Cong., 1st Sess. 23-24 (1947); H.R. REP. No. 510, 80th Cong., 1st Sess. 45 (1947).

[17] Later the Sixth Circuit, in a 2-1 decision, held that even as so limited the doctrine violated § 8(c). See NLRB v. F. W. Woolworth Co., 214 F.2d 78 (6th Cir. 1954).

[18] Member Murdock, dissenting in *Livingston Shirt*, said that it is not improper "for the Board to adhere to an important principle arrived at through full and thorough consideration — despite the existence, particularly at the first stages of exposition, of contrary decisions by one or more circuit courts of appeals — until the Supreme Court has finally ruled on the question." 107 N.L.R.B. 400, 426 (1953). But ought this be so when certiorari has not even been sought, and the Supreme Court has thus had no opportunity to review? Admittedly the certiorari problem as to *Bonwit Teller* was complicated; the Second Circuit had not disapproved the doctrine in its narrow form but remanded for the Board to remove an excrescence in the order. If the Board had been willing to accept the limitation, there would have been no occasion for seeking certiorari; instead the Board removed the excrescence in *Bonwit Teller* but applied it in other cases. In any event there seems to have been no reason for not seeking certiorari from the Sixth Circuit decision in *Woolworth* (rendered subsequent to Member Murdock's dissent); indeed, the conflict with the Second Circuit would have made a grant rather likely.

[19] Livingston Shirt Corp., 107 N.L.R.B. 400, 407 (1953).

[20] The press has recently been reporting a spate of overrulings by the reconstituted NLRB. Although the need for stability in the labor field may well be less than in the public utility regulatory agencies, see pp. 20-21 & note 81 *supra*, too frequent overrulings, particularly when synchronized with a change in the political complexion of the commission, do not enhance the prestige of the administrative process. Similar criticisms were made after the change in the composition of the Board in the Eisenhower administration; see Ratner, *Policy-Making by the New "Quasi-Judicial" NLRB*, 23 U. CHI. L. REV. 12, 35 (1955); Note, *The NLRB*

Let us turn now to a happier story, told in Mr. Justice Frankfurter's opinion in *Brooks v. NLRB*.[21] Section 9 of the Wagner Act had empowered the Board to certify a union as the exclusive representative of the employees in a bargaining unit when the Board determined by election or "any other suitable method" that the union commanded majority support; section 8(5) made it an unfair labor practice for an employer "to refuse to bargain collectively with the representatives of his employees, subject to the provisions of Section 9 (a)."[22] The act said nothing about how frequently the Board could conduct elections or how long the employer's duty to bargain with the certified union continued. Many agencies would have said a time reasonable under the circumstances; such a choice would have created boundless opportunities for litigation. The Board adopted a working rule that a reasonable period was one year after certification, absent unusual circumstances warranting earlier termination.[23] Unless these existed, the Board would not conduct a new election within that period and would hold the employer for an unfair labor practice if he refused to bargain even on a justified claim that the certified union had lost its majority without fault on his part.[24] The Taft-Hartley Act did not deal specifically with the latter

---

Under Republican Administration, Recent Trends and Their Political Implications, 55 COLUM. L. REV. 852, 906 (1955). A good example of what would seem a rather needless overruling, by a three-to-two vote, is A.P.W. Products Co., Inc., 137 N.L.R.B. No. 7 (1962), changing the doctrine, announced as early as E. R. Haffelfinger Co., Inc., 1 N.L.R.B. 760 (1936), that monetary awards would be tolled during the period between a trial examiner's dismissal of a complaint and subsequent Board reversal. Granting that a fair case for the new view can be made, would it not have been wiser to adhere to a defensible ruling of twenty-six years' standing with which Congress had not seen fit to interfere?

[21] 348 U.S. 96 (1954).
[22] Ch. 372, 49 Stat. 453 (1935).
[23] See Kimberly-Clark Corp., 61 N.L.R.B. 90, 92 (1945), and cases cited therein. Unusual circumstances were found when the certified union dissolved or became defunct, when there was a serious schism, or when the size of the bargaining unit fluctuated radically within a short time. See cases cited in Brooks v. NLRB, 348 U.S. at 98–99, nn. 3–5.
[24] *Id.* at 99 n. 7.

problem; however, what initially had been perforce a somewhat arbitrary choice of period was surrounded with an aroma of sanctity and, indeed, made more rigid (although somewhat shorter) [25] by the provision, in section 9(c),[26] that, after a valid certification or decertification election, the Board could not conduct a second election in the same bargaining unit for a year after the first election. Without benefit of explicit statutory sanction, the Board continued to hold employers for an unfair labor practice if they refused to bargain within the "certification year," even if the union had lost its majority through no unfair practice by the employer. The courts of appeals differed as to the validity of this specification of the employer's duty; the Supreme Court sustained it in *Brooks*. Whether the Court would have done so but for the Taft-Hartley prohibition of a new election for a year after the last one, we shall never know.

A closely related crystallization of a legislative standard is the Board's so-called "contract-bar" rule. In its initial form this was that the Board would generally refuse to hold an election during a reasonable period after the making of a valid collective bargaining agreement, now two years.[27] Nothing in the statute demanded this; the Board could have dealt with the problem on an *ad hoc* basis. The legislative history of the Taft-Hartley Act shows that

[25] "[E]ven 'unusual circumstances' no longer left the Board free to order an election where one had taken place within the preceding 12 months." *Id.* at 102.

[26] 61 Stat. 144 (1947), 29 U.S.C. § 159(c) (1958).

[27] The growth of the contract-bar rule is related in Local 1545, United Bhd. of Carpenters v. Vincent, 286 F.2d 127 (2d Cir. 1960), and in Leedom v. International Bhd. of Elec. Workers, 278 F.2d 237 (D.C. Cir. 1960). There is a vast literature — see Feldesman, *Contract Bar to Representation Elections*, 29 GEO. WASH. L. REV. 450 (1960), and the many articles cited by him, at 452 n.7a. See also the penetrating article, Peck, *The Atrophied Rule-Making Powers of the National Labor Relations Board*, 70 YALE L.J. 729, 738–741, 756 (1961), which, *inter alia*, criticizes the series of important 1958 decisions with respect to the contract bar doctrine, reported in 121 N.L.R.B., as involving "rule-making" without compliance with § 4 of the Administrative Procedure Act, 5 U.S.C. § 1003, and suggests that although it was sound for the Board to initiate the contract bar principle through *ad hoc* adjudication, changes after the doctrine had reached maturity ought to have been made, prospectively, by rulemaking.

Congress knew of the rule and did not intend to alter it by the new provision forbidding elections more frequently than annually.[28] Later the Board ruled it an unfair labor practice for an employer, during the period of the contract bar, to refuse to deal with the contracting union even though the union had ceased to command a majority, or to negotiate with another union even though the latter represented an uncoerced majority. The Board reasoned that "otherwise, we should have the anomalous result of an employer being permitted unilaterally to redetermine his employees' bargaining representative at a time when the Board would refuse to make such redetermination because the time is inappropriate for such action."[29] The bootstrap character of the operation will not have escaped attention — the Board's self-denying ordinance against an election during the reasonable period of a valid contract, even after expiration of the statutory year, becomes the basis for finding the employer guilty of an unfair labor practice if he negotiates with another while the Board has thus stayed its hand. However, the Board's ruling has been sustained by at least two court of appeals decisions, for one of which I cannot escape some responsibility.[30] And now, as we have seen in other instances, the contract bar has at least inferentially been recognized by Congress in the amendments of 1959.[31]

One could readily find other examples. A notable one is the holdings, under sections 8(a)(5) and (d), that evidence of certain types of conduct by employers is sufficient in itself to support a conclusion of lack of good faith in bargaining. Among these are refusal to sign a written contract, a specification created by the

[28] See S. REP. No. 105, 80th Cong., 1st Sess. 25 (1947); H.R. REP. No. 510, 80th Cong., 1st Sess. 50 (1947).

[29] Hexton Furniture Co., 111 N.L.R.B. 342, 344 (1955). See also Marcus Trucking Co., 126 N.L.R.B. 1080 (1960); cf. Shamrock Dairy, Inc., 119 N.L.R.B. 998, 1002 (1957).

[30] NLRB v. Sanson Hosiery Mills, Inc., 195 F.2d 350 (5th Cir.), cert. denied, 344 U.S. 863 (1952); NLRB v. Marcus Trucking Co., 286 F.2d 583 (2d Cir. 1961).

[31] Sections 8(b)(7)(A) and 8(f), added by §§ 704 and 705 of the Labor-Management Reporting and Disclosure Act of 1959, 73 Stat. 544, 545, 29 U.S.C. §§ 158(b)(7)(A)(f) (Supp. II 1961).

Board, sanctioned by the courts,[32] and ultimately adopted by Congress;[33] offering employees, during the course of negotiations, general wage increases higher than those offered through the union;[34] and insisting as a condition of agreement upon a subject outside the area of collective bargaining.[35] I could speak also of the importance the courts have given to specifications of standards made by the Board prior to the Taft-Hartley Act and left unchanged by that statute,[36] or, conversely, of how the Board has occasionally performed an almost equally useful service by making specifications that provoked legislative definition in the opposite sense.[37] But it is more instructive to turn to instances where the Board's efforts at definition of a general statutory standard have met judicial rebuff.

The first case is in the area, determination of intent to bargain in good faith, which I have just mentioned. This time the problem was on the employees' side: tactics that prevent fully effective conduct of the employer's business but fall short of a strike. In the so-called *Personal Products* case,[38] the Board declared that such union activities constituted a prohibited refusal to bargain; the Court of Appeals for the District of Columbia set the order aside.[39] However, the Board adhered to its position and the

[32] See H. J. Heinz Co. v. NLRB, 311 U.S. 514 (1941).
[33] 61 Stat. 140 (1947), 29 U.S.C. § 158 (d) (1958).
[34] NLRB v. Crompton-Highland Mills, Inc., 337 U.S. 217 (1949).
[35] NLRB v. Wooster Division of Borg-Warner Corp., 356 U.S. 342 (1958).
[36] See NLRB v. Gullett Gin Co., 340 U.S. 361, 366 (1951).
[37] I have already noted one instance, note 16 *supra*. Another is the redefinition of "employee" in § 2(3) so as to exclude "any individual employed as a supervisor," thereby overruling Packard Motor Car Co., 61 N.L.R.B. 4, 64 N.L.R.B. 1212 (1945), aff'd, Packard Motor Car Co. v. NLRB, 330 U.S. 485 (1947). Others are the provisions of § 10(c) directing uniform treatment to unaffiliated and affiliated organizations, overruling Brown Co., 65 N.L.R.B. 208 (1946), and Tappan Stove Co., 66 N.L.R.B. 759 (1946), and the provisos to § 9(b), framed in the light of such decisions as American Can Co., 13 N.L.R.B. 1252 (1939).
[38] Textile Workers Union, 108 N.L.R.B. 743 (1954).
[39] Textile Workers Union v. NLRB, 227 F.2d 409 (D.C. Cir. 1955). Certiorari was granted, 350 U.S. 1004 (1956), but the grant was later vacated and the petition denied, 352 U.S. 864 (1956).

issue reached the Supreme Court, again after a decision adverse to the Board by the Court of Appeals for the District,[40] in *NLRB v. Insurance Agents Int'l Union*.[41]

The Court was unanimous in holding the Board's order unsupportable, either on the ground, taken in the Board's opinion, that the Board could infer lack of good faith from the harassing activities alone, or on the basis, advanced in the Board's brief, that it "could appropriately determine that the basic statutory purpose of promoting industrial peace through the collective bargaining process would be defeated by sanctioning resort to this form of industrial warfare as a collective bargaining technique." [42] One must agree that the Board had gone too far. Nothing shows that a union's attempt thus to harass an employer is inconsistent with negotiation to reach an agreement — indeed, the very purpose of the harassment is to produce an agreement along the lines the union wants; and, with respect to the alternate ground, as Mr. Justice Brennan said, "Congress has been rather specific when it has come to outlaw particular economic weapons on the part of unions." [43]

I hold a quite different view as to another rebuff administered at the Court's next term. This concerned the Board's attempt, in *Mountain Pacific Chapter*,[44] to render more specific the application to union hiring halls of the general provisions, sections 8(a)(3) and (b)(2), making it an unfair labor practice for employers and labor organizations "by discrimination in regard to hire or tenure of employment or any term or condition of employment to encourage or discourage membership in any labor organization." The Board found that, under the not untypical contract

---

[40] Insurance Agents Int'l Union v. NLRB, 260 F.2d 736 (D.C. Cir. 1958). There was no discussion of the merits, but merely a refusal to depart from the decision in *Textile Workers Union*: "One panel of this court will not attempt to overrule a recent precedent set by another panel, even though one or more of its members may disagree with the ruling."

[41] 361 U.S. 477 (1960).

[42] 361 U.S. at 503 (separate opinion of Frankfurter, J.).

[43] 361 U.S. at 498.

[44] 119 N.L.R.B. 883 (1957).

before it, "the Union is free to pick and choose on any basis it sees fit"; that "for all the Employers know or care, the Union's purpose in selecting some and rejecting others may be encouragement toward union membership, or towards adherence to union policies"; and that "it is difficult to conceive of anything that would encourage their [workers'] subservience to union activity, whatever its form, more than this kind of hiring-hall arrangement." On the basis of that and long experience it concluded:

> that the inherent and unlawful encouragement of union membership that stems from unfettered union control over the hiring process would be negated, and we would find an agreement to be nondiscriminatory on its face, only if the agreement explicitly provided that:
> (1) Selection of applicants for referral to jobs shall be on a nondiscriminatory basis and shall not be based on, or in any way affected by, union membership, bylaws, rules, regulations, constitutional provisions, or any other aspect or obligation of union membership, policies, or requirements.
> (2) The employer retains the right to reject any job applicant referred by the union.
> (3) The parties to the agreement post in places where notices to employees and applicants for employment are customarily posted, all provisions relating to the functioning of the hiring arrangement, including the safeguards that we deem essential to the legality of an exclusive hiring agreement.[45]

When cases applying the new doctrine began to reach the courts, the Board buttressed its position with evidence that, in the absence of such protective provisions, workers would think exclusive union hiring halls would discriminate, whatever the fact as to a particular hall might be. It pointed to a great number of Board proceedings showing general abuse of union hiring halls, to many instances in which halls continued to prefer union members after Board or even court orders forbidding this, and to numerous cases

[45] *Id.* at 894, 895, 897.

revealing union "persuasion," by one means or another, to induce workers to withdraw charges of discrimination against them.

Reception of the doctrine in the courts of appeals was mixed, the Ninth and Sixth Circuits invalidating orders based on the Board's new doctrine, the First and District of Columbia Circuits sustaining them.[46] It was perhaps unfortunate that the case to reach the Supreme Court was the decision in the District of Columbia, where the majority unaccountably had not even discussed the validity of the Board's order, rather than that from the First Circuit, where Judge Aldrich had expressed its rationale more clearly than had the Board itself, saying, "The inference drawn by the Board was not that union hiring halls are presumptively operated in a discriminatory manner, but, rather, that the applicant for employment will so believe, and govern his conduct accordingly." It was surely unfortunate that the Board's brief in the Supreme Court did not contain the comprehensive documentation of its inability to deal with hiring hall discrimination on a case-by-case basis that it had presented in the courts of appeals.[47]

In *Local 357, Int'l Bhd. of Teamsters v. NLRB*, a divided Supreme Court struck down the *Mountain Pacific* rule.[48] With all

---

[46] NLRB v. Mountain Pacific Chapter, 270 F.2d 425 (9th Cir. 1959) (the final portion of the opinion, at 432, indicating the court might take a different view toward a prospective application); Morrison-Knudsen Co. v. NLRB, 276 F.2d 63 (9th Cir. 1960), *cert. denied*, 366 U.S. 910 (1961) (also involved retroactive application but the point is not mentioned); NLRB v. E. & B. Brewing Co., 276 F.2d 594 (6th Cir. 1960), *cert. denied*, 366 U.S. 908 (1961) (opinion by Judge Pope of the Ninth Circuit, who had written in the *Morrison-Knudsen* case, stresses retroactivity and procedural deficiency). *Contra*, NLRB v. Local 176, United Bhd. of Carpenters, 276 F.2d 583 (1st Cir. 1960); Local 357, Int'l Bhd. of Teamsters v. NLRB, 275 F.2d 646 (D.C. Cir. 1960). The First Circuit's opinion called attention, 276 F.2d at 586 n.4, to the statement in the Conference Report on the 1959 amendment adding § 8(f), "Nothing in such provision is intended to restrict the applicability of the hiring hall provisions enunciated in the *Mountain Pacific* case . . . ." H.R. REP. No. 1147, 86th Cong., 1st Sess. 42 (1959).

[47] My specific reference is to the brief in Morrison-Knudsen Co. v. NLRB, 275 F.2d 914 (2d Cir. 1960), *cert. denied*, 366 U.S. 909 (1961), where the court found it unnecessary to pass on the *Mountain Pacific* rule since specific acts of discrimination had been proved.

[48] 365 U.S. 667 (1961).

respect, here indulging in a luxury not normally allowed me, I find the plurality opinion of Mr. Justice Douglas considerably less than satisfying. After reciting the legislative history, it begins by saying that "there being no express ban of hiring halls in any provisions of the Act, those who add one, whether it be the Board or the courts, engage in a legislative act." But the Board did not "ban" hiring halls; it merely said it would regard them as discriminatory if they did not comply with certain easily met requirements that would lessen the tendency, which the Board found they had, to encourage union membership by leading workers to believe they would deny employment to nonmembers. To be sure, even that may be in some degree "a legislative act," but it is hard to see why it was more objectionably so than other Board rules the Court had sustained, and Mr. Justice Douglas is much too sophisticated in administrative matters to be so outraged at an agency's doing some minor legislating. The opinion continues that "nothing is inferable from the present hiring-hall provision except that employer and union alike sought to route 'casual employees' through the union hiring hall and required a union member who circumvented it to adhere to it." This strikes me as rather an *ipse dixit*, ignoring the Board's long experience with hiring halls and the repeated admonitions from Olympus that inference-drawing is the Board's business, not the courts'.[49] Finally, after noting the absence of evidence that the union had acted unlawfully, and the impossibility of simply assuming that it had, the opinion concludes, "Yet we would have to make assumptions to agree with the Board that it is reasonable to infer the union will act discriminatorily" — a position which, for the reason pointed out by Judge Aldrich and by Mr. Justice Clark in his dissent,[50] one may accept without similarly accepting the conclusion drawn from it.

Mr. Justice Harlan was evidently troubled by the plurality opinion; I wish he had been troubled enough to take himself and Mr. Justice Stewart, who joined with him, over to the other

---

[49] See, *e.g.*, Radio Officers' Union v. NLRB, 347 U.S. 17, 50 (1954).
[50] 365 U.S. 667, 691–93.

side.[51] His rather unenthusiastic concurring opinion proceeds on the ground that it was not enough that encouragement of union membership was a foreseeable result of the exclusive union hiring hall, since that alone was not prohibited. This also seems to downgrade the experience that in fact hiring halls had operated so as to discriminate unlawfully in a manner calculated to encourage union membership, and that workers would therefore believe the particular hiring hall would do so, whether in fact it would or not. Here, in contrast to the *Insurance Agents* case, the Board had accumulated a body of experience indicating that the practice branded as unfair would have the effect the statute condemned.

It is surely true that, in adopting this new policy with respect to hiring halls, the Board would have been wiser to have acted prospectively.[52] Indeed, if the decision had been so framed, union refusal to adopt the reasonable protective clauses which the Board proposed would seem the clearest possible proof of intent to discriminate in a way the act forbids. And the Board further compounded its problems in a fashion no wise counsel would have advised, when it not only applied the rule retroactively but accompanied it with the harsh *Brown-Olds* remedy, requiring employers as well as unions to reimburse dues and initiation fees paid, over many years, by hard-bitten union members who would thoroughly have approved the most discriminatory practices.[53] However, the *Brown-Olds* issue was handled separately by the Supreme Court; [54] the opinion in the *Teamsters* case does not proceed on the ground of retroactivity; and invalidation on that score would seem precluded by the second *Chenery* case. Indeed, I find the

[51] This would have led to affirmance by an equally divided Court, Mr. Justice Frankfurter not having participated, and would have postponed the issue to a case in which he did.

[52] See note 46 *supra*. See Peck, *supra* note 27, at 746–51, suggesting that this matter also ought to have been handled by rulemaking.

[53] See Morrison-Knudsen Co. v. NLRB, 275 F.2d 914 (2d Cir. 1960), *cert. denied*, 366 U.S. 909 (1961).

[54] Local 60, United Bhd. of Carpenters v. NLRB, 365 U.S. 651 (1961); see Local 357, Int'l Bhd. of Teamsters v. NLRB, 365 U.S. 667, 670–71 (1961) (following *Local 60, United Bhd. of Carpenters*).

Teamsters decision quite difficult to reconcile with *Chenery II*. The Labor Board also had "made a thorough examination of the problem, utilizing statutory standards and its own accumulated experience . . ."; its ruling, like the SEC's in *Chenery*, was "the product of administrative experience, appreciation of the complexities of the problem, realization of the statutory policies, and responsible treatment of the uncontested facts." [55] If the Board was legislating, it was doing this no more, indeed I should think considerably less, than the SEC was upheld in doing in *Chenery II*.[56]

The *Teamsters* decision raises other questions. Could the Board have averted the disaster if it had phrased its opinion in terms of rebuttable presumptions, as it did in the *Peyton Packing* case with which we began? Was it the Board's very desire to limit its decision by writing out a specific charter of permissible hiring hall activities that caused the outcry of "foul" and a charge of "legislation," rather reminiscent of Mr. Justice Sutherland, from a judge generally so understanding of the administrative process? I have felt compelled to dwell on this decision because it poses a threat to the process of definition that I advocate. I hope it will prove to be one of those authorities that rules its own facts but little else.[57] For I cannot believe the Court meant to set itself generally against the crystallization of broad standards by administrative adjudication, a process which it has so often approved for this very agency and which is so vital to the effective working of the administrative scheme.[58]

[55] SEC v. Chenery Corp., 332 U.S. 194, 207, 209 (1947).
[56] It seems more than a little surprising that neither the *Insurance Agents* case nor the *Chenery* decision was mentioned in any of the *Teamsters* opinions.
[57] *Cf.* CARDOZO, THE NATURE OF THE JUDICIAL PROCESS 178 (1921).
[58] Another instance in which Board specification would seem to have been headed for trouble but for amendment of the statute altering the problem in the future, is the test, laid down in Sailors Union of the Pacific and Moore Dry Dock Co., 92 N.L.R.B. 547, 549 (1950), and developed in Brewery & Beverage Drivers & Workers [Washington Coca Cola], 107 N.L.R.B. 299 (1953), and International Bhd. of Teamsters [Ready Mixed Concrete Co.], 116 N.L.R.B. 461, 473 (1956), for determining when picketing of the premises of a secondary employer violated

Indeed, a return to the Court's usual attitude seems already to have occurred. In *NLRB v. Katz*,[59] a refusal to bargain case, the Court unanimously upheld the power of the Board to find certain types of "unilateral action [by an employer] to be an unfair labor practice in violation of § 8(a)(5), without also finding the employer guilty of over-all subjective bad faith." The decision was explicated on the basis that such action constituted "[A] refusal to negotiate *in fact*." However, the Court also expressly reaffirmed the ruling in *NLRB v. Crompton-Highland Mills, Inc.*,[60] that an employer's institution of wage increases higher than offered a union in bargaining "conclusively manifested bad faith." *Insurance Agents* was distinguished; *Teamsters* was not mentioned. So the cloud on the validity of agency specification of standards, which that decision threatened, appears to have been rather speedily, and happily, dissipated.

---

§ 8(b)(4)(A) of the act, now extensively amended by the Act of September 14, 1959, 73 Stat. 542, 29 U.S.C. § 158 (Supp. II 1961). See the discussion in NLRB v. Local 294, Int'l Bhd. of Teamsters, 284 F.2d 887, 890–91 (2d Cir. 1960), and in Local 761, Int'l Union of Elec. Workers v. NLRB, 366 U.S. 667, 676–78 (1961). Here the Board did appear to have jumped a logical gap from its original holding in *Sailors Union* that it would *not* infer the forbidden intent when certain conditions were met, to holding that it would inevitably infer the intent when they were not — without any such substantiating experience as in regard to hiring halls.

[59] 369 U.S. 736 (1962).
[60] *Supra* note 34.

IV

The Licensing of Radio and Television Broadcasting

IT will scarcely be a surprise that my first instance of administrative failure to spell out standards of adjudication is the awarding of radio and television broadcast licenses by the Federal Communications Commission. Although Mr. Landis reserved for the Federal Power Commission the accolade of being "the outstanding example in the federal government of the breakdown of the administrative process,"[1] he kept his enthusiasm under remarkably good control when he reported of the FCC:

> The Federal Communications Commission presents a somewhat extraordinary spectacle. Despite considerable technical excellence on the part of its staff, the Commission has drifted, vacillated and stalled in almost every major area. It seems incapable of policy planning, of disposing within a reasonable period of time the business before it, of fashioning procedures that are effective to deal with its problems.[2]

Criticism of this sort follows a well-trodden path; the Commission has had a rather long turn at the whipping post. As long ago as 1949 the *Task Force Report* for the Hoover Commission summarized its conclusions with respect to the FCC as follows: "[T]he Commission has been found to have failed both to define its primary objective intelligently and to make many policy determinations required for efficient and expeditious administration."[3]

---

[1] LANDIS REPORT 54. Professor Redford awards the palm for being the worst agency to the FCC. See REDFORD, THE PRESIDENT AND THE REGULATORY COMMISSIONS 27 (1960) (Report prepared for the President's Advisory Committee on Government Organization).

[2] LANDIS REPORT 53.

[3] COMMISSION ON ORGANIZATION OF THE EXECUTIVE BRANCH OF THE GOVERNMENT, COMMITTEE ON INDEPENDENT REGULATORY COMMISSIONS, STAFF REPORT

Eight years later so restrained a scholar as Professor Jaffe accused the Commission of employing "spurious criteria, used to justify results otherwise arrived at."[4] The 1958 staff report to the House Committee on Interstate and Foreign Commerce upbraided the Commission for "chronic lack of . . . ability and imagination to make the laws work effectively,"[5] and a report to the Senate Committee spoke of the Commission's resolution of comparative proceedings "through an arbitrary set of criteria whose application . . . is shaped to suit the cases of the moment."[6] The *coup de grâce* was the exposure of a number of boudoir episodes, some having more piquancy and others less, but going, in the aggregate, beyond anything experienced, or, perhaps more accurately, discovered, in other federal regulatory agencies.

Although I do not defend the Commission's performance in awarding licenses, fairness demands that the frustrating nature of its task be acknowledged. The only guideline supplied by Congress in the Communications Act of 1934 was "public convenience, interest, or necessity."[7] The standard of public convenience and

---

on FCC 10 (1948), quoted in McMahon, Regulation of Broadcasting: Study for the Committee on Interstate and Foreign Commerce, House of Representatives, 85th Cong., 2d Sess., on H. Res. 99 (85th Cong., 1st Sess.) 113 (1958). The staff also reported: "Not a single person at the Commission who is concerned with broadcast work will even pretend to demonstrate that the Commission's decisions in its broadcast cases have followed a consistent policy, or for that matter, any policy other than the desire to dispose of cases and, if possible, to do so by making grants." McMahon, *op. cit. supra* at 155. See also *id.* at 106–15, 168.

[4] Jaffe, *The Scandal in TV Licensing*, Harper's Magazine, Sept. 1957, pp. 77, 79.

[5] McMahon, *op. cit supra* note 3, at viii.

[6] Ad Hoc Advisory Committee on Allocations to the Senate Committee on Interstate and Foreign Commerce, 85th Cong., 2d Sess., Allocation of TV Channels 9 (Comm. Print 1958) (additional comments of Edward L. Bowles), quoted in McMahon, *op. cit. supra* note 3, at 155. See also Lewis, *F.C.C. Prestige at Record Low*, N.Y. Times, Nov. 16, 1958, § 4, p. 8, col. 2; Schwartz, *Comparative Television and the Chancellor's Foot*, 47 Geo. L.J. 655, 696 (1959).

[7] Communications Act § 307(a), 48 Stat. 1083 (1934), 47 U.S.C. § 307(a) (1958). The act's general declaration of policy, Communications Act § 1, 48 Stat. 1064 (1934), as amended, 47 U.S.C. § 151 (1958), is more than usually meaningless, and seems to have been directed to the common carrier rather than the broadcasting provisions.

necessity, introduced into the federal statute book by Transportation Act, 1920,[8] conveyed a fair degree of meaning when the issue was whether new or duplicating railroad construction should be authorized or an existing line abandoned. It was to convey less when, as under the Motor Carrier Act of 1935, or the Civil Aeronautics Act of 1938, there would be the added issue of selecting the applicant to render a service found to be needed; but under those statutes there would usually be some demonstrable factors, such as, in air route cases, ability to render superior one-plane or one-carrier service because of junction of the new route with existing ones, lower costs due to other operations, or historical connection with the traffic, that ought to have enabled the agency to develop intelligible criteria for selection. The standard was almost drained of meaning under section 307 of the Communications Act,[9] where the issue was almost never the need for broadcasting service [10] but rather who should render it. The job that Congress gave the Commission was somewhat com-

[8] 41 Stat. 477 (1920), as amended, 49 U.S.C. § 1(18) (1958).

[9] This included the still vaguer term "interest." Compare the problems created by the use, in the section of the Motor Carrier Act relating to contract carriers, of the test "inconsistent with the public interest and the national transportation policy declared in the Interstate Commerce Act . . . ." 54 Stat. 919 (1940), 49 U.S.C. § 309(b) (1958), amending 49 Stat. 552 (1935). As has been well said, Congress' use of this different test "does suggest that some difference in treatment of the two types of carriers was intended, but it does not tell us what the difference was." Note, *National Transportation Policy and the Regulation of Motor Carriers,* 71 YALE L.J. 307, 310 (1961). See ICC v. J-T Transp. Co., 368 U.S. 81 (1961), dealing with the criteria added in 1957, 71 Stat. 411, 49 U.S.C. § 309(b) (1958).

[10] The Commission ultimately regarded this need as sufficiently demonstrated by a request from a qualified applicant for a technically feasible service. Southeastern Enterprises, 22 F.C.C. 605, 610–14 (1957). See Easton Publishing Co. v. FCC, 175 F.2d 344, 346 (D.C. Cir. 1949). In earlier cases the Commission had declined to consider the extent of community needs, see F. W. Meyer, 7 F.C.C. 551, 558 (1939), or community ability to support additional broadcasting facilities, see Voice of Cullman, 6 RADIO REG. 164, 169–70 (FCC 1950); but it was not until the *Southeastern* case, 22 F.C.C. at 612, 614, that it held itself to be without power to consider the economic effect of a new broadcast facility on existing services. This statement, quite unintelligible in the light of FCC v. Sanders Bros. Radio Station, 309 U.S. 470, 475–76 (1940), was disapproved in Carroll Broadcasting Co. v. FCC, 258 F.2d 440 (D.C. Cir. 1958).

parable to asking the board of the Metropolitan Opera Association to decide, after public hearing and with a reasoned opinion, whether the public convenience, interest, or necessity would be better served by having the prima donna role on the opening night sung by Tebaldi or by an up-and-coming American soprano who might prove herself the Tebaldi of tomorrow, or, more accurately, whether the optimum would be achieved by having the role sung by Tebaldi, by Sutherland, or by one of several winners of high American awards. Multiply this many hundredfold; add the seemingly capricious element that whoever was selected for the role could assign it to any of the other qualified applicants;[11] prohibit the board from getting the advice of many best able to help;[12] assume further that the decision-makers know their action is likely to please or displease persons responsible for their continuance in office, who occasionally communicate attitudes while the decision is in process — and you will have a more sympathetic understanding of the Commission's problem. The Commission possessed the Supreme Court's comforting assurance that the

---

[11] The Commission has held this to be the effect of the amendment of § 310(b) by the McFarland Act of 1952, § 8, 66 Stat. 716, 47 U.S.C. § 310(b) (1958), that any application for a transfer or assignment "shall be disposed of as if the proposed transferee or assignee were making application . . . for the permit or license in question; but in acting thereon the Commission may not consider whether the public interest, convenience, and necessity might be served by the transfer, assignment, or disposal of the permit or license to a person other than the proposed transferee or assignee." In St. Louis Amusement Co. v. FCC, 259 F.2d 202 (D.C. Cir.), *cert. denied*, 358 U.S. 894 (1958), the court questioned whether the amendment really went as far as the Commission thought, saying, "If this interpretation is correct, there may be a serious gap in the statutory scheme to which Congressional attention should be directed." 259 F.2d at 204. I wish I could find some basis for sharing the court's doubt; the language, particularly when read in the light of the committee reports, U.S. CODE CONG. & AD. NEWS, 82nd Cong., 2d Sess. 2245–46 (1952), and the contrast with the Commission's previous AVCO procedure, see 259 F.2d at 204 n.1, seems rather painfully clear. See Judge Danaher's dissent in Enterprise Co. v. FCC, 231 F.2d 708, 714 n.3 (D.C. Cir. 1955), *cert. denied*, 351 U.S. 920 (1956). See also note 58 *infra*.

[12] See McFarland Act of 1952, ch. 879, § 4, 66 Stat. 713 (1952), repealed by 75 Stat. 420 (1961), amending Communications Act of 1934, ch. 652, § 5(c), 48 Stat. 1069.

statutory standard was "as concrete as the complicated factors for judgment in such a field of delegated authority permit"; [13] but it had been clothed with little else. Nor has Congress seen fit to supply any more clothing over the years.[14]

So far as I can learn, the Commission has laid down only two definite nontechnological limitations as to the award of licenses, both embodied in the Multiple Ownership Rules.[15] One has the effect of limiting the number of stations under common control to a maximum of seven AM broadcast stations, seven FM stations, and seven television stations only five of which may be VHF. The other, the so-called duopoly rule,[16] forbids common control of more than one station of the same class serving the same area.

Beyond these, the Commission applies a number of so-called criteria, summarized by a former Chairman as follows:

> A list of the comparative criteria, which have been evolved and employed by the Commission in the comparative television cases, would include the following: Proposed programing and policies, local ownership, integration of ownership and management, participation in civic activities, record of past broadcast performance,

---

[13] FCC v. Pottsville Broadcasting Co., 309 U.S. 134, 138 (1940); see National Broadcasting Co. v. United States, 319 U.S. 190, 215-16 (1943).

[14] The conclusion of nearly a score of years ago, that "Neither the Congress as a whole nor the committees of the House and Senate concerned with radio legislation have ever produced a genuine 'policy' for radio-broadcasting," Friedrich & Sternberg, *Congress and the Control of Radio-Broadcasting II*, 37 AM. POL. SCI. REV. 1014, 1024 (1943), holds today. See Jaffe, Book Review, 65 YALE L.J. 1068, 1073 (1956).

[15] 47 C.F.R. § 3.35 (1958), as amended, 47 C.F.R. § 3.35 (supp. 1961) (standard broadcast stations), 47 C.F.R. § 3.240 (1958) (FM stations), and 47 C.F.R. § 3.636 (1958) (television). Perhaps one should add that the Chain Broadcasting Rules, 47 C.F.R. §§ 3.131–.138 (1958), also have some impact. The Multiple Ownership Rules contain an exception for "a showing that public interest, convenience and necessity will be served through such multiple ownership . . . ." 47 C.F.R. § 3.35(a) (1958). Literally this exception abolishes the rule since a showing would be mandatory in any event; save for legal doubts arising from the opinion in United States v. Storer Broadcasting Co., 351 U.S. 192, 204-05 (1956), it might better be eliminated.

[16] This was originally announced in Genesee Radio Corp., 5 F.C.C. 183, 186-87 (1938).

broadcast experience, relative likelihood of effectuation of proposals as shown by the contacts made with local groups and similar efforts, carefulness of operational planning for television, staffing, diversification of the background of the persons controlling, diversification of control of the mediums of mass communications.[17]

What strikes one about this list is not only the multiplicity of items and the contradictory character of some but the mingling of matters of high policy with mere pieces of evidence. As I review the decisions, there are only two true elements of policy — the community should have the programs best adapted to its needs, and this goal should be achieved in a manner that will avoid undue concentration of the media of mass communication, nationally, regionally, or locally. Most of the so-called criteria are simply a checklist of evidentiary items bearing, some directly and others indirectly, on an applicant's ability to achieve one or the other or both of these policy goals.[18]

Local Interest

Recognition of the spurious nature of many of the criteria at least blunts a few criticisms of the Commission's alleged inconsistency. Much has been made,[19] for example, of the Commission's alleged disregard of the "local ownership" criterion in its awards to a local newspaper in Tampa and to a subsidiary of the Travelers Insurance Company in Hartford, the stock of both of which was largely owned by nonresidents.[20] This overlooks that "local own-

[17] House Comm. on Interstate and Foreign Commerce, *Network Broadcasting* (report prepared by group headed by Dean Barrow), H.R. REP. No. 1297, 85th Cong., 2d Sess. 61–62 (1958) (letter to Committee from John C. Doerfer, Aug. 30, 1956).

[18] An examiner of the Commission seems on the right track when he says that " 'criteria' is the wrong word" and that it would be better to refer to the items as "specific areas of comparison." Irion, *FCC Criteria for Evaluating Competing Applicants*, 43 MINN. L. REV. 479, 481 (1959).

[19] See Schwartz, *supra* note 6, at 666–69.

[20] See Tribune Co., 9 RADIO REG. 719 (FCC 1954), *aff'd sub nom.* Pinellas Broadcasting Co. v. FCC, 230 F.2d 204 (D.C. Cir.), *cert. denied*, 350 U.S. 1007 (1956); Travelers Broadcasting Serv. Corp., 12 RADIO REG. 689 (FCC 1956).

ership" is simply one factor, and, particularly in view of the lack of restrictions on stock transfer, not necessarily a very reliable one, going to show that the applicant has the kind of association with the community that will afford fair assurance that the station will be responsive to local needs and will keep its promises as to programing. The proper test is not "local ownership" standing alone, but local "interest." This is surely what the Commission must have meant,[21] and there would have been less trouble if this had been what it said.[22] Realistically, what kind of entity would have more knowledge of and be more responsive to a city's problems than a local newspaper, whatever its stock ownership might be? There are other serious issues about such an award, which we will consider later, but lack of adequate local interest does not seem to be one. Again, how can anyone seriously doubt that, despite its nationwide stock ownership, the Travelers, with its officers and a multitude of employees residing in Hartford, where it had originated and been based for nearly a century, was quite as identified with Connecticut's capital as a new company whose "local" stockholders were free to sell their stock as soon as the application was granted? With respect to these criticisms the Commission thus has been to some extent the victim of its method of stating mere evidentiary items as ultimate criteria of choice; the result often seems defensible, although the tortuous argumentation wherein the opinion writer seeks to give the suc-

[21] At least three other "criteria" in the list — "integration of ownership and management," "participation in civic activities," and "relative likelihood of effectuation of proposals as shown by the contacts made with local groups and similar efforts," are wholly or partly related to this criterion of "local interest"; all these, and other items as well, must be weighed together in arriving at a judgment on that score.

[22] Professor Schwartz points out that local ownership in the true sense serves a purpose that the more general test of local interest would not, namely, "to make it harder for licensees to acquire multiple broadcast interests," *supra* note 6, at 662. However, so far as my reading goes, the Commission has not assigned this as a basis for the "local ownership" criterion — doubtless because it proposed to deal with the problem of multiple ownership directly.

cessful applicant a preference on every "criterion" (or at least to minimize its disadvantage) surely is not.[23]

However, the Commission does appear to have significantly altered its attitude concerning the importance of even what I have called the broader test of local interest, without adequate explanation. Until recently the preference for local interest was explicated on two bases. One of these, going all the way back to

[23] The other two cases mainly relied on by Professor Schwartz, *supra* note 6, at 666–67, to show "aberration" in the matter of local ownership are Indianapolis Broadcasting, Inc., 22 F.C.C. 421 (1957), *rev'd on other grounds sub nom.* WIBC, Inc. v. FCC, 259 F.2d 941 (D.C. Cir.), *cert. denied,* Crosley Broadcasting Corp. v. WIBC, Inc., 358 U.S. 920 (1958), and St. Louis Telecast, Inc., 22 F.C.C. 625 (1957).

The award in the *St. Louis* case was to CBS, which for 27 years had operated a 50 kw. station in St. Louis with great success and much featuring of local items. Of course, there was little "local ownership," but there was reason to think that, in view of its long habitation in St. Louis, this applicant was responsive to local needs and could be relied on to keep its promises quite as much as any of the others. Again, there may be different grounds for criticism — clearly the award runs counter to the early statement in Bamberger Broadcasting Serv., Inc., 3 RADIO REG. 914, 925 (FCC 1946), discussed p. 64 *infra,* but lack of "local" contact does not seem to be one. Perhaps also, as Professor Schwartz suggests, the decision, on its face, is hard to square with Westinghouse Radio Stations, Inc., 10 RADIO REG. 878 (FCC 1955), where Westinghouse lost to a local applicant in Portland, Oregon, but one would need to make a careful study of the relative qualifications of the successful Portland applicant and the unsuccessful St. Louis applicants to be sure the decisions are irreconcilable.

The *Indianapolis* decision cannot be upheld on the ground I have suggested with respect to the *Tampa, Travelers,* and *St. Louis* cases. Crosley, the successful applicant, had neither local ownership nor any other local affiliation; after the remand, the Commission awarded the license to a different applicant deemed less offensive on diversification grounds. 22 RADIO REG. 425 (FCC 1961). The other three cases claimed by Schwartz to instance disregard of the narrow local-ownership standard, Petersburg Television Corp., 10 RADIO REG. 567 (FCC 1954), Evansville Television, Inc., 11 RADIO REG. 411 (FCC 1955), and Scripps-Howard Radio, Inc., 11 RADIO REG. 985 (FCC 1956), are not only consistent with the broader criterion of local interest but do not even represent an overlooking of local ownership.

The more general approach to the question of local identification which I have proposed would not justify the Miami Channel 10 decision, WKAT, Inc., 22 F.C.C. 117 (1957), even apart from what was later revealed about the character of the decisional process, 258 F.2d 418 (D.C. Cir. 1958), *decision after remand,* 29 F.C.C. 216 (1960), *aff'd,* 296 F.2d 375 (D.C. Cir.), *cert. denied,* 368 U.S. 841 (1961).

the Commission's predecessor, was that the very fact of local interest would make the station a more useful public servant; "In a sense," the Federal Radio Commission had said, "a broadcasting station may be regarded as a sort of mouthpiece on the air for the community it serves . . . ." [24] The other basis was that local affiliation would give better assurance that the promises as to programming would be carried out. Both bases were stated as late as *WJR, The Goodwill Station, Inc.*, decided in 1954, where the Commission said: "We afford importance to such factors since, in our view, they lend assurance of a more complete and effective response to the needs of the community, and increase the probability that the promises and commitments advanced by the applicants will in fact be effectuated." But the very next sentence of the opinion continues: "However, where a record establishing the past performance of the applicants in this regard is available, such factors become less determinative." [25]

The swerve in this language is unmistakable. The swerve is censurable, not just because it was a swerve but because it was not acknowledged and because it failed to face up to the policy problems. There is much logic in saying that if X has operated a broadcast station elsewhere for a number of years and has kept his programming promises, the assurance this affords that he will keep similar promises in another city is at least as reliable as any assurance derivable from his residing there. Hence, under the new doctrine, one of the two purposes of the local interest requirement still is served. But there is no logic whatever in saying that a record of keeping promises in Keokuk makes an applicant as good a "mouthpiece" for Kalamazoo as a long-time Kalamazooan. Although no authority could support such a conclusion, the Commission's citation of *Hearst Radio, Inc.*,[26] not only does not

---

[24] *In re* Great Lakes Broadcasting Co., No. 4900, FRC, 1928, quoted in *Network Broadcasting, supra* note 17, at 124. Indeed, the Supreme Court has also spoken to this effect. See FCC v. Allentown Broadcasting Corp., 349 U.S. 358, 362 & n.5 (1955).
[25] 9 RADIO REG. 227, 260c–d (FCC 1954).
[26] 6 RADIO REG. 994 (FCC 1951).

advance the case, but rather emphasizes the disingenuousness of the opinion. *Hearst Radio* was a renewal proceeding, one of the few where a rival applicant has appeared as a challenger. When the Commission there said that "local ownership alone is of less import where an existing station has demonstrated its ability to operate in the public interest and to provide for the needs of the communities within its service area," [27] it was talking about an existing station which had been licensed to render and had rendered the very service at issue. Although Hearst's lack of local affiliation might have been a reasonable basis for denial of the original grant, refusal to renew on that ground after a period of satisfactory community service would indeed have been shocking; the decision in *Hearst Radio* did not say that local interest was "of less import" on an initial license, where no applicant could possibly have a record as to the service to be awarded and the Commission has a truly free choice.

Goodwill thus was new in stating that where the nonlocal applicant had a good record, local interests were "less determinative" than otherwise. In *Radio Fort Wayne, Inc.*,[28] only a few months later, this language was expanded into a statement that an applicant with a good record, to be sure in the same locality in that instance, would have to be *preferred* over one with more local affiliations "because of the less speculative nature of the presumption of satisfactory future performance." [29] This was pushed still further in *Indianapolis Broadcasting, Inc.*,[30] where the Commission found in an applicant, Crosley, having no connnection whatever with the locality, "the greatest assurance of effectuation of the proposals made in the public interest, due principally to the favorable record of past performance, its long years of experience in the broadcast industry, and the experience of the particular

[27] *Id.* at 1030–31.
[28] 9 RADIO REG. 1221, 1222g (FCC 1954).
[29] See to the same effect Scripps-Howard Radio, Inc., 11 RADIO REG. 985, 1042 (FCC 1956); and, in a dictum, Petersburg Television Corp., 10 RADIO REG. 567, 584–*l* (FCC 1954).
[30] 22 F.C.C. 421, 495–98, 516 (1957) (note 23 *supra*).

individuals that will be brought to the operation proposed." Nevertheless the local-interest refrain still resounds when the Commission wants to sing it.[31]

What I find distressing about this episode is not that the Commission changed its position as to local interest. There may be good reason for such a change — perhaps, for example, local interest is less important in television than it was in radio. If so, it is a commission's prerogative to change, especially when it operates under so vague a mandate and an alteration in policy for the award of new licenses, as distinguished from renewals, would do so little harm to any expectations reasonably created in the past. As the Court of Appeals for the District of Columbia has wisely said, "the Commission's view of what is best in the public interest may change from time to time. Commissions themselves change, underlying philosophies differ, and experience often dictates changes." [32] What gives concern is the manner, alas not atypical of the agencies, in which this change was made — slipped into an opinion in such a way that only careful readers would even know what had happened, without articulation of reasons, and with the prior authorities not overruled, so that the opinion writers remain free to pull them out of the drawer whenever the agency wishes to reach a result supportable by the old rule but not the new.

Concentration of Control

We must now leave local interest and see what the Commission has been doing as regards the policy favoring diversification of control of the media of mass communication.

Let me begin with brief reference to another example of the procedure I have just described, a procedure we will encounter again when we come to the Civil Aeronautics Board — a prece-

---

[31] See Sarkes Tarzian, Inc. 17 RADIO REG. 905, 922 (FCC 1959); Westinghouse Radio Stations, Inc., 10 RADIO REG. 878, 968 (FCC 1955).

[32] Pinellas Broadcasting Co. v. FCC, 230 F.2d 204, 206 (D.C. Cir.), *cert. denied*, 350 U.S. 1007 (1956).

dent apparently abandoned but not overruled. In 1946 the Commission announced in the *Bamberger* case: [33]

> The Commission is of the opinion that where there is a choice between two applicants, one of whom has a television station and another which does not, public interest is better served by granting a license to the newcomer . . . . Under this policy, it is possible for the maximum number of qualified people to participate in television and not have it restricted to a few large interests.

Contrast this with the *Indianapolis* decision in 1957, where one of the factors mainly relied on in favor of the award was Crosley's good record, not just in radio broadcasting, which might not be inconsistent with the *Bamberger* statement, but in operating "several television stations." [34] Perhaps it was time for a change; there may not be the same need for numbers, now that television has reached maturity in age, if not in excellence. If so, *Bamberger* should be put to rest; so far as I know, it has not been.

The most vexing problem in the diversification area has been the award of radio or television licenses to newspaper publishers. The dangers in such awards, at least when the number of papers or of available licenses in a given area is small, are apparent. In 1941 the Commission instituted an investigation to determine what statement of policy or rule, if any, should be adopted; [35] it decided not to formulate any policy but rather to consider newspaper ownership as only one factor in deciding among competing applicants.[36] The abandonment of the attempt to formulate a policy was unfortunate; the question was susceptible of answer, not indeed a universal aye or nay, since conditions differ from city to city, but one that would nevertheless have assisted in deciding many cases.

[33] Bamberger Broadcasting Serv., Inc., 3 RADIO REG. 914, 925 (FCC 1946).
[34] Indianapolis Broadcasting, Inc., 22 F.C.C. 421, 517 (1957) (note 23 *supra*). See also St. Louis Telecast, Inc., 22 F.C.C. 625, 737 (1957).
[35] FCC Order No. 79, 6 Fed. Reg. 1580 (1941); FCC Order No. 79-A, 6 Fed. Reg. 3302 (1941).
[36] Newspaper Ownership of Radio Stations, FCC Notice, 9 Fed. Reg. 702 (1944).

Perhaps one reason for the Commission's refusal to promulgate a policy was a fear that if the statement were to manifest an antinewspaper slant, Congress would legislate against it;[37] during the protracted proceedings leading up to the 1952 amendments, various attempts were made to secure an amendment that would prohibit the Commission from "discriminating" against newspaper owners.[38] Indeed, the bill passed by the House did contain a provision that no application should be denied solely because of any "interest in, association with, or ownership of any medium primarily employed in the gathering and dissemination of information." This was dropped because of the Commission's assurance that it did not and would not "discriminate" against newspaper applicants.[39] The assurance was scarcely candid; in fact the Commission had taken newspaper ownership very much into account in denying applications and had been sustained by the courts in doing so,[40] although in other cases it had awarded licenses to newspaper applicants. If Congress had enacted the provision of the House bill, the issue would have been settled —

[37] It has also been suggested that the Commission was concerned over Stahlman v. FCC, 126 F.2d 124, 127 (D.C. Cir. 1942), which, in sustaining the Commission's right to investigate, had said that "there is nothing in the Act which either prevents or prejudices the right of a newspaper, as such, to apply for and receive a license to operate a radio broadcast station." Heckman, *Diversification of Control of the Media of Mass Communication — Policy or Fallacy?*, 42 GEO. L.J. 378, 381 (1954).

[38] *Id.* at 390–93.

[39] MCMAHON, *op. cit. supra* note 3, at 159; WHDH, Inc., 22 F.C.C. 767, 879 (1957). The Conference Committee on the 1952 Act announced that the provision of the House bill "was omitted from the Conference substitute because the Committee of Conference felt that it was unnecessary. It is the view of the conference committee that under the present law, the Commission is not authorized to make or promulgate any rule or regulation the effect of which would be to discriminate against any person because such a person has an interest in, or association with, a newspaper or other medium for gathering and disseminating information." CONFERENCE REP. No. 2426, 82nd Cong., 2d Sess. 19 (1952).

[40] Scripps-Howard Radio, Inc., 4 RADIO REG. 525, 554 (FCC 1949), *aff'd*, 189 F.2d 677, 683 (D.C. Cir.), *cert. denied*, 342 U.S. 830 (1951); Central Broadcasting Co., 3 RADIO REG. 1151, 1157 (FCC 1947), *rev'd on other grounds sub nom.* Plains Radio Broadcasting Co. v. FCC, 175 F.2d 359 (D.C. Cir. 1949); Orlando Daily Newspapers, Inc., 3 RADIO REG. 624, 631 (FCC 1946).

not as many people would think it ought to have been, but settled none the less. *Per contra,* if the Senate had refused to go along, there would have been a clear failure to procure congressional limitation of the Commission's freedom of decision. As it was, the matter was left in the worst possible posture — the newspaper interests in a position to contend that Congress had really decided for them, the opposition able to rely on the lack of a vote to that effect,[41] and the Commission in the equivocal position of having prevented a congressional decision by an assurance that it would not "discriminate," which the newspapers can say it does if it turns down an otherwise best-qualified applicant solely because of a newspaper connection, and the opposition can say it does not if there are good public interest reasons for the denial in the particular case.

With this muddled background it is small wonder that the Commission's decisions since 1952 with respect to newspaper affiliation have been lacking in consistency. On some occasions the Commission has preferred a non-newspaper-owner, on grounds of diversification, over a newspaper applicant at least as well or better qualified.[42] On other occasions it has awarded licenses to newspaper-owning or -affiliated applicants despite the availability of other well-qualified contenders without newspaper affiliation.[43]

[41] See, *e.g.,* the statement in Levin, *Broadcast Regulation and Intermedium Competition,* 45 VA. L. REV. 1104, 1133 n.93 (1959): "Equally pertinent, however, is the fact that Congress has thus far chosen not to amend the Communications Act to prevent discrimination against newspapers as radio-television licensees, notwithstanding powerful pressures towards that end."

[42] McClatchy Broadcasting Co., 9 RADIO REG. 1190, 1220i–j (FCC 1954), *aff'd,* 239 F.2d 15, 18 (D.C. Cir. 1956), *modified on rehearing,* 239 F.2d 19 (D.C. Cir. 1956), *cert. denied,* 353 U.S. 918 (1957); Enterprise Co., 9 RADIO REG. 816, 818q (FCC), *rev'd,* 231 F.2d 708 (D.C. Cir. 1955), *cert. denied,* 351 U.S. 920 (1956). Loyola Univ., 12 RADIO REG. 1017, 1111–13 (FCC 1956). *Accord,* Tampa Times Co., 10 RADIO REG. 77, 138–39 (FCC 1954), *aff'd,* 230 F.2d 224, 227 (D.C. Cir. 1956); KTBS, Inc., 10 RADIO REG. 811, 876a (FCC 1955); Northeastern Indiana Broadcasting Co., 9 RADIO REG. 261, 317–18 (FCC 1953). In Radio Fort Wayne, Inc., 9 RADIO REG. 1221, 1222i–m (FCC 1954), the decision against the newspaper applicant was based on particular competitive practices it had followed.

[43] Biscayne Television Corp., 11 RADIO REG. 113 (FCC 1956) (two leading

On still other occasions it has chosen between applicants both of which had heavy dosages of newspaper affiliation — and of radio broadcasting as well.[44]

Such inconsistency is intolerable. The Commission must develop enough courage to penetrate the fog it has helped create. It could say, for example, that experience since 1952 had shown that the promises it then gave Congress about newspaper applicants were too broad; that newspaper applicants occupying a dominating position in a city would no longer be granted standard broadcast or VHF licenses as against other qualified applicants — or perhaps even when there were none [45] — and that even where there was no such domination, qualified non-newspaper applicants not presenting a diversification problem would be preferred. If Congress thought this wrong, the promulgation of such a policy statement ought to precipitate legislation to set matters right. Alternatively, the Commission could do the exact opposite and say that review of its promises to Congress in 1952 had convinced it that it must altogether shut its eyes to newspaper affiliation. If the advocates of diversification have correctly weighed the public will, this should be a sufficient irritant to provoke legisla-

---

stockholders of successful applicant controlled two dominant Miami newspapers); WHDH, Inc., 22 F.C.C. 767 (1957) (applicant owned two important Boston newspapers).

[44] In Radio Wisconsin, Inc., 10 RADIO REG. 1224 (FCC 1955), the Commission preferred an applicant with heavy regional newspaper and radio affiliations over one with more intense local concentrations. In Tribune Co., 9 RADIO REG. 719 (FCC 1954), aff'd sub nom. Pinellas Broadcasting Co. v. FCC, 230 F.2d 204 (D.C. Cir.), cert denied, 350 U.S. 1007 (1956), the Commission preferred an applicant owning one of the four papers in Tampa and a radio broadcasting station there over another whose owner controlled the morning paper in St. Petersburg and a radio station there. I cannot agree with Professor Schwartz, supra note 6, at 686–87, that the Tribune decision is necessarily inconsistent with those in note 42 supra; I do agree that those in notes 42 and 43 supra are inconsistent with each other.

[45] A Note in 66 YALE L.J. 365, 375–76 (1957), suggests this would have been the proper disposition of Radio Wisconsin, Inc., supra note 44. Levin, supra note 41, at 1124, looks with some favor on "delayed authorization" through initial denial, at least "where markets are already blanketed with one or more services."

tion. Doubtless other courses, less drastic and more politic, are available. What is essential is that the Commission do *something* so that a policy will emerge.

Although the newspaper problem should be the beginning of the definition of standards in the diversification area, it should not be the end. I doubt that the problem can be handled quite as simply as Professor Schwartz proposes, by legislative stipulation that "in deciding comparative cases, the Commission shall give priority to applicants who are superior on the criteria of diversification itself, local ownership and integration of ownership and management . . . ."[46] To me the answer is not clear enough to warrant so high a degree of definiteness. I am not persuaded that a newly organized "local" company with no experience in television is superior *semper et ubique* to one that has successfully operated a television station in a city of similar size five hundred miles away and is going to move its assistant manager into the town; and I find it hard to believe that this type of affiliation creates any great danger of "1984." On the other hand, one can readily think of cases where a somewhat less rigid proposal would lead to a good result, and it is surely unfortunate that, as has been said, "the current approach to the comparative decision, wherein diversification becomes just another of numerous factors to be considered, . . . seemingly has encouraged the Commission to accord ever-diminishing significance to this factor . . . ."[47] Even though many of the horses have escaped, it is not too late for a statement on this subject in the manner of Judge Cooley, carefully analyzing the objectives the diversification policy is designed to attain and the degree to which different forms of concentration offend them.

As I see it, the policy has three, possibly four, objectives, some interrelated: prevention of undue control over thought and opin-

---

[46] *Supra* note 6, at 695.
[47] *Network Broadcasting, supra* note 17, at 124. See St. Louis Telecast, Inc., 22 F.C.C. 625, 735 (1957); Pinellas Broadcasting Co. v. FCC, 230 F.2d 204, 206 (D.C. Cir.), *cert. denied*, 350 U.S. 1007 (1956).

ion, locally, regionally, or nationally; preservation of independent stations from impairment or destruction by the economic power of multi-medium or multi-station operators; prevention of the exercise of undue economic power on advertisers or undue preference to the large advertiser against the small; and, possibly, although I am not sure this is any longer valid, maximizing the number of persons in the industry. Various forms of concentration offend these objectives in varying degrees. The newspaper problem is one thing, an AM and FM broadcaster seeking the television license in the same town another,[48] the owner of a single television station seeking a license in another city still another, and the owner of a chain of stations seeking an added license different still. Moreover, the problems will differ with the power of the particular applicant, ranging, in the newspaper field, for example, from a case where a sole newspaper that already controls the sole radio station seeks the sole television license,[49] to a case, at the other end of the spectrum, where one of a dozen newspapers in a large city applies for one of a number of FM licenses. Because of these variations it is impracticable to frame a sentence, or even a pair of sentences, that will solve all cases. Still, the permutations are hardly more numerous than those with regard to the long-and-short-haul clause on which Judge Cooley shed so much light in so little time; and a careful policy statement as to the degree and the effect of detrimental assessment in various typical patterns would promote administrative consistency and intelligibility, and also facilitate congressional action if Congress desired to act.

Still other expedients would seem available. Revision of the Multiple Ownership Rules might make these a more useful regulatory tool. Seven AM, seven FM, five VHF, and two UHF stations are a rather considerable number if the stations are located

---

[48] Recent decisions on this problem seem quite inconsistent. *Compare* Sucesion Luis Pirallo-Castellanos, 16 RADIO REG. 113, 138–39 (FCC 1959), *with* Veterans Broadcasting Co., 19 RADIO REG. 339, 339g (FCC 1960).
[49] See Levin, *supra* note 41, at 1111.

in the nation's largest markets or are concentrated in a single region; a new formula reducing for the future the number of permitted stations in such instances might itself answer many diversification problems. Also it would seem that the Commission could avoid some decisional problems with respect to concentration by standard terms and conditions in a license — for example, forbidding arrangements whereby an advertiser is required to use one medium as a condition to his use of another, or is offered discounts for utilizing several media under common control.[50]

Some Final Thoughts

The mass communication problem is thus susceptible of handling by better definition of standards. But the Commission will still have many licensing cases that are not. These are the proceedings that require a choice among applicants with no demerit for other mass-communication interests or among applicants with

[50] Such action might be questioned on the grounds that §§ 307 and 308 of the Communications Act do not contain the language, usual in federal licensing statutes, empowering the Commission to "attach to the issuance of the certificate such terms and conditions as in its judgment the public convenience and necessity may require." 41 Stat. 478 (1920), 49 U.S.C. § 1(20) (1958); *cf.* 49 Stat. 552 (1935), 49 U.S.C. § 308(a) (1958); 49 Stat. 553 (1935), 49 U.S.C. § 309(b) (1958); 54 Stat. 942 (1940), 49 U.S.C. § 909(d) (1958); 56 Stat. 84 (1942), 15 U.S.C. § 717f(e) (1958), and that there are limits to the authority conferred even by such a grant, United States v. Chicago, M., St. P. & P.R.R., 282 U.S. 311 (1931). *But see* Atlantic Ref. Co. v. Public Serv. Comm'n, 360 U.S. 378, 391–92 (1959). On the other hand, § 303(r) authorizes the Commission to "make such rules and regulations and prescribe such restrictions and conditions, not inconsistent with law, as may be necessary to carry out the provisions of this chapter . . . ." The Supreme Court referred to this clause in sustaining the Commission's Chain Broadcasting Regulations, NBC v. United States, 319 U.S. 190, 215–19 (1943), but in that case there was also § 303(i) which specifically authorized the Commission "to make special regulations applicable to radio stations engaged in chain broadcasting." United States v. Storer Broadcasting Co., 351 U.S. 192 (1956), sustained the validity of the Multiple Ownership Rules under 47 U.S.C. §§ 154(i) and 303(r).

The problem is a shade on the academic side, since if the Commission lacks power to impose conditions, it can accomplish nearly the same result by announcing that breach of certain standards would be regarded as a seriously disqualifying factor on an application for renewal.

equal but not altogether damning ones.[51] Perhaps the best the Commission can do here is to narrow the field of eligible contenders and then apply to recommendations of its examiners a rule akin to the "not clearly erroneous" doctrine that federal appellate courts use in reviewing a judge's finding of fact,[52] unless, indeed, some competitive bidding procedure is to be legislatively authorized.[53] Indeed, it would seem advantageous for the agencies to follow rather generally a practice of upholding examiners in areas where no policy determination has been made and there is no real ground for thinking that decision by a commission, probably divided, will be better than that of the man who heard the witnesses and has spent more time on the problem than the members possibly can. These are the cases where the absence of any sound basis for choice renders "pressure" on the commission most likely; the examiner's civil service status makes him an ideal lightning rod.[54]

The suggested narrowing of the field could be accomplished by a rule raising the "minimum" qualifications, at least for important channels; this might have avoided the débâcle of the Miami Channel 10 litigation, where the award ultimately went, although only for a limited period, to an applicant clearly inferior from a public service standpoint to any of the other three.[55] These qualifications might well include requiring a specified amount of training or experience on the part of the proposed station manager, together with a condition that any successor must be similarly qualified. Detailed examination of program proposals strikes me

[51] See p. 67 & notes 44 & 45 *supra*.

[52] See FED. R. CIV. P. 52(a); for the practice in admiralty, see McAllister v. United States, 348 U.S. 19, 20 (1954).

[53] The case for this is powerfully presented in Coase, *The Federal Communications Commission*, 2 J. & L. ECON. 1, 17–40 (1959), and in Levin, *Regulatory Efficiency, Reform and the FCC*, 50 GEO. L.J. 22–45 (1961).

[54] On the other hand, to take the time of examiners to formulate recommendations on policy matters which the members will necessarily decide for themselves is a waste of valuable human resources. See Friendly, *A Look at the Federal Administrative Agencies*, 60 COLUM. L. REV. 429, 443–44 (1960).

[55] WKAT, Inc., 29 F.C.C. 216 (1960), *aff'd*, 296 F.2d 375 (D.C. Cir.), *cert. denied*, 368 U.S. 841 (1961).

as a good deal of an exercise in futility, especially in view of the Commission's recognition that "we would be deluding ourselves and the public, if we concluded that the program proposals will be produced exactly as represented." [56] Indeed, too much stress on the details of program proposals may be positively harmful, since the entire area is so spongy as to make this an all-too-easy method for masking a decision reached on other grounds. I wonder also whether the Commission is really wise enough to determine that live telecasts — of local cooking lessons, for example — so much stressed in the decisions, are always "better" than a tape of Shakespeare's Histories. Would it not be as well to specify broad program norms to which applicants for different types of licenses would be expected to conform, demand promises that they will, insert these requirements in the license, and utilize the powers of cease and desist orders, revocation, and nonrenewal [57] to obtain compliance? The one legislative change that seems vital is an alteration of the transfer provision, section 310(b), to end the present absurd spectacle wherein a considered selection of the applicant who can best serve the public interest, made after much travail and expense, can be rendered nugatory by private arrangements among the very persons who have submitted themselves to the Commission's determination.[58] Although

[56] Tribune Co., 9 RADIO REG. 719, 770f (FCC 1954) (note 20 *supra*).

[57] 66 Stat. 716 (1952), 47 U.S.C. § 312(b) (1958); 48 Stat. 1086 (1934), 47 U.S.C. § 312(a) (1958); 48 Stat. 1083 (1934), 47 U.S.C. § 307 (1958). The Commission has recently refused to renew the license of a station in Pasadena, Calif., Eleven Ten Broadcasting Corp., 32 F.C.C. 706 (1962).

[58] St. Louis Amusement Co. v. FCC, 259 F.2d 202 (D.C. Cir.), *cert. denied*, 358 U.S. 894 (1958), tells the story of what happened after St. Louis Telecast, Inc., 22 F.C.C. 625 (1957). The Denver story is equally disheartening. See Aladdin Radio & Television, Inc., 9 RADIO REG. 1 (FCC 1953); Denver Television Co., 10 RADIO REG. 771 (FCC 1954); Aladdin Radio & Television, Inc., 10 RADIO REG. 773 (FCC 1954). The parties in Enterprise Co., 9 RADIO REG. 816 (FCC 1955), moved too quickly; a remand to consider the changed situation resulted, 231 F.2d 708 (D.C. Cir. 1955), *cert. denied*, 351 U.S. 920 (1956). The Commission, however, was intransigent, and affirmed its original grant. 17 RADIO REG. 48 (FCC 1958), *rev'd on other grounds*, 265 F.2d 103 (D.C. Cir. 1959), *original grant again reaffirmed*, 19 RADIO REG. 67 (FCC 1960), *aff'd*, 295 F.2d 165 (D.C. Cir. 1961). The need for amendatory legislation is emphasized in STAFF REPORT 26-27, 36-38.

experts can probably find much wrong in the details of these suggestions, to me they suffice to demonstrate that, uncharted as was the course that Congress set, the Commission need not have drifted quite so helplessly for twenty-eight years.

The Commission has now adopted a rule, § 1.365, requiring hearings on a transfer within three years of acquisition save in exceptional cases, and declaring that ordinarily "transfer or assignment of a broadcast license held for a short time is prima facie inconsistent with the duties of the licensee and the public interest." 32 F.C.C. 689, 690, 702–03 (1962).

V

Competitive Domestic Air Route Certification

HOWEVER baneful in its effect on the fair name of the administrative process the FCC's performance may have been, it might be hard to show any causal relation between it and today's rather spare diet on the air waves. On the other hand, a good case can be made that the inability of the CAB to develop and adhere to intelligible standards of convenience and necessity in the issuance of competitive certificates [1] has imposed higher costs on the traveling public, and needless and serious losses on airline investors. I shall limit my comments to the domestic scene, not because the Board's handling of the somewhat different problems presented in "overseas" and, more particularly, in international cases is beyond criticism, but because I participated in so many of them that my judgment could hardly be unbiased.

Few administrative agencies have begun their careers under such favorable auspices. In contrast to bodies that have been handed eggs already badly scrambled — the Motor Carrier Act of 1935 [2] is an example — the Board was entrusted with regulation of a "mere speck in the sky." [3] The entire domestic air network in 1938 consisted of but 37,000 route miles [4] and pas-

---

[1] As Professor Jaffe has put it, the Board "in the course of its very short history has shown an almost incredible flexibility in moving toward and away from competition." Jaffe, Book Review, 65 YALE L.J. 1068, 1074 (1956).

[2] 49 Stat. 543 (1935), as amended, 49 U.S.C. §§ 301-27 (1958).

[3] *Hearings on H.R. 2531 Before the House Committee on Interstate and Foreign Commerce*, 76th Cong., 1st Sess., pt. 1, at 28 (1939) (ICC Commissioner Splawn).

[4] See Westwood, *Choice of the Air Carrier for New Air Transport Routes*, 16 GEO. WASH. L. REV. 1, 2–3 (1947). For a more detailed account of much that follows, see these articles, 16 GEO. WASH. L. REV. 1, 159 (1947–48), the classic review of the Board's performance of its certificating function during its first decade.

senger revenues amounted to only $25,000,000.[5] Tremendous growth in this new mode of transport was inevitable — enough to permit a fair degree of administrative error to escape undetected, or perhaps even to be tolerated.[6] Although the Board indulged from the beginning in the moaning on the score of overwork which is evidently deemed required for admission to the administrative social club, and somehow did manage to accumulate a sizable backlog, the workload in its first decade was exceedingly small.[7]

The Civil Aeronautics Act [8] applied to this truly infant industry the scheme of regulation embodied in the Motor Carrier Act — a derivation which the Board has repeatedly acknowledged.[9] Section 2 directed the Board to consider "as being in the public interest, and in accordance with the public convenience and necessity" a number of factors, subsections (a) through (c), which had almost precise parallels in section 202(a) of the Motor Carrier Act. However, as the Board emphasized in an early case,[10] the Civil Aeronautics Act included in its list of desiderata another provision, section 2(d), having no counterpart in the Motor Carrier Act, as follows: "Competition to the extent necessary to as-

[5] CAB, REPORT SUBMITTED TO THE SUBCOMMITTEE ON MONOPOLY, SENATE SELECT COMM. ON SMALL BUSINESS, 82ND CONG., 2D SESS., THE ROLE OF COMPETITION IN COMMERCIAL AIR TRANSPORTATION 8 (Comm. Print 1952).

[6] Domestic passenger miles grew from 480,000,000 in 1938 to 29,233,000,000 in 1960; passenger revenues climbed from $25,000,000 to $1,756,000,000. The Board frequently uses such figures to defend its record. See, e.g., Comments of the CAB on the Hector Memorandum to the President 7 & n.3, March 29, 1960, a good example of *post hoc non ergo propter hoc*.

[7] A convenient bench-mark as to the small size of the Board's workload is that the well-known Docket No. 3500, National Airlines Route Investigation, Order No. E-2025, was initiated on September 28, 1948, a month after the Board's tenth birthday. This means an average of 350 cases on the formal docket per year. Actually the number of proceedings was very much less, in view of the consolidation of many applications and the abandonment of others.

[8] 52 Stat. 973 (1938) (now Federal Aviation Act of 1958, 72 Stat. 731, 49 U.S.C. §§ 1301–1542 (1958)).

[9] See Acquisition of Marquette by TWA — Supplemental Opinion, 2 C.A.B. 409, 412 (1940); American Export Lines, Control of American Export Airlines, 4 C.A.B. 104, 107 (1943); American President Lines, Ltd., Petition, 7 C.A.B. 799, 804 (1947); Continental Charters, Tariff Rule, 16 C.A.B. 772, 777 (1953).

[10] American Export Airlines, Inc., Trans-Atlantic Service, 2 C.A.B. 16, 30 (1940).

sure the sound development of an air-transportation system properly adapted to the needs of the foreign and domestic commerce of the United States, of the Postal Service, and of the national defense."

But for section 2(d), established principles would have suggested, if not demanded, that the Board follow in its certificate decisions the rather restrictive interpretation which the Interstate Commerce Commission had given the certificate section of the Motor Carrier Act in pre-1938 decisions such as *Pan American Bus Lines Operation* [11] and *Clark Common Carrier Application*,[12] in the latter of which the Commission had said that "the maintenance of sound economic conditions in the motor-carrier industry would be jeopardized by allowing new operators to enter a field in competition with existing carriers who are furnishing adequate, efficient, and economical service." The crucial question, therefore, was how far section 2(d) permitted or required the Board to depart from these ICC precedents, modified perhaps by what the Commission later characterized "as an exception or qualification," namely, "that an additional service may be required in the public interest even though an existing operator is supplying in quantum what appears to be a sufficient service, where there is lacking any worthy competitor of such operator in its own field and where the available business is ample to support another operation." [13]

[11] 1 M.C.C. 190, 203 (1936). In Delta Air Corp., Additional Service to Atlanta and Birmingham, 2 C.A.B. 447, 452 (1941), the Board paraphrased the Commission's formulation in the *Pan American Bus* case, with the added factor, "whether any cost of the proposed service to the Government will be outweighed by the benefit which will accrue to the public from the new service," called for by the subsidy provisions of the Civil Aeronautics Act, § 406.

[12] 1 M.C.C. 445, 448 (1937). See Hale & Hale, *Competition or Control III: Motor Carriers*, 108 U. PA. L. REV. 775, 780 (1960).

[13] Santa Fe Trail Stages, Inc., Common Carrier Application, 21 M.C.C. 725, 749 (1940).

The ICC's handling of motor carrier certificate cases over the years seems not to have caused great satisfaction. The STAFF REPORT says, at 59–60: "On their face, the decisions of the ICC do not appear to follow consistently any ascertainable standards in determining whether public convenience and necessity require the

Legislative history afforded only a little light. Section 2(d) had its origin in a bill, prepared by a committee representing various government departments in the fall of 1937, wherein the corresponding clause read, "The preservation and encouragement of competition among persons operating airlines to the extent necessary to assure the sound development of air transportation . . . ."[14] This was slightly altered to the present language in the bill introduced by Representative Lea.[15] The provision appears to have been a compromise between those who thought that air transport needed effective protection against freedom of entry even at that early stage, and those who, like the Department of Commerce,[16] were fearful of imposing certificate regulation on an industry so undeveloped and then so generally lacking in direct competition.[17]

There would seem to be but three readings of section 2(d) in any way meriting consideration; as we shall see, the Board, at various times, has employed them all, and perhaps others as well. The most liberal reading would be that Congress directed

---

service which an applicant proposes to render. . . . It is possible . . . that the apparent differences in results reached in different cases may be justified but if so, the opinions do not make clear why one result is reached in one case and the opposite result in another."

[14] Westwood, *supra* note 4, at 167 n.34.

[15] H.R. 9738, 75th Cong., 3d Sess. § 401(d), introduced March 4, 1938. Remarks by Mr. Lea on the floor indicate that he personally could not have intended the clause to have a very broad effect. See 83 CONG. REC. 6407 (1938). And Representative Randolph said that "the industry has reached the point where unbridled and unregulated competition is a public menace" and that one of the major aims of the bill was protection against cutthroat competition. *Id.* at 6507. For a full and critical summary of the legislative history, see William K. Jones, *Antitrust and Specific Economic Regulation: An Introduction, Appendix II, Domestic Air Transport and the Legislative History of the Civil Aeronautics Act of 1938*, A.B.A., SECTION OF ANTITRUST LAW (August 8, 1961).

[16] See *Hearings on S. 2 Before a Subcommittee of the Senate Committee on Interstate Commerce*, 75th Cong., 1st Sess., pt. 1, at 89 (1937).

[17] Direct competition in 1938 was "limited to the business between a few main centers such as New York–Chicago, New York–Los Angeles, New York–Washington, Chicago–Dallas, Chicago–St. Louis, and Chicago–Kansas City." Westwood, *supra* note 4, at 164.

competition to the fullest extent compatible with the sound development of an air transportation system. But that is not what Congress enacted, and such a reading would be quite inconsistent with what was said in 1938 both by proponents and by opponents of the bill. The most conservative reading would be to insert "but only" between "Competition" and "to the extent." That also would be to supply a phrase which Congress could readily have used, but whose insertion might have revived opposition the compromise had stilled. A middle reading is that the clause, surprisingly, meant just what it said: Congress favored competition "to the extent necessary to assure," etc. Under this central reading, proof that competition is necessary is something an applicant must establish by factual evidence in order to meet the burden, imposed by section 401(d)(1), of showing "that such transportation is required by the public convenience and necessity; otherwise such application shall be denied."

What was needed initially was a comprehensive opinion, like Judge Cooley's of 1887, laying down the Board's understanding of the statutory language. Needed later would be continuing careful study of how duplicate, triplicate, and even higher multiples of competition were in fact working and how they could be expected to work. The Board produced neither.

The Early Years, 1938–1943

The Board's handling of its first case in this area, a proposed service between the Twin Cities on the one hand and Kansas City and St. Louis on the other,[18] was a promising start. Mid-Continent Airlines held a grandfather certificate from the Twin Cities to Kansas City via Omaha. It wished an alternate route through Des Moines both to Kansas City and to St. Louis. Braniff and Northwest also applied for part or all of the proposed new routes. The Board noted that "The fact that Mid-Continent already has a service between the Twin Cities and Kansas City

---

[18] Mid-Continent Airlines, Inc., Twin Cities–Des Moines–Kansas City–St. Louis Operation, 2 C.A.B. 63, 93 (1940).

might suggest the desirability of entrusting an alternative service between those points by a different route to another carrier." Having made the suggestion, the Board rejected it. Looking to the future, it envisioned nonstop service between the Twin Cities and Kansas City; if two different carriers were operating, nonstop privileges should be open to both, with consequent "duplication of nonstop service where there may be a comparatively early justification for such service by one carrier, but not, at least for a much longer time, by two." The process of decision conformed precisely to the statute. Applying expert judgment to the characteristics of the particular route, the Board not only found competition not "necessary to assure the sound development" of the air transport system but inconsistent therewith.[19]

The next significant decision,[20] only five months later, evidences some blurring. Like the *Twin Cities* case, this did not involve paralleling but rather an entirely new service, between Houston and Memphis, which might provide competition because of a junction with service already authorized; the question of competition thus arose only in the choice of a carrier. One applicant, Chicago & Southern, already had a route connecting Memphis and Chicago; Braniff, also an applicant, held a certificate from Houston to Chicago via Kansas City and thus would be subjected to competition for Houston–Chicago traffic if the Houston–Memphis route went to Chicago & Southern. By a three-to-two vote the Board picked Chicago & Southern. Braniff, the majority pointed out, would not be interested in routing Houston–Chicago business through Memphis when it would get a longer haul via Kansas City, whereas Chicago & Southern "may be expected to seek to develop the maximum traffic on the new route regardless of its ultimate destination." The considerations concerning the effect of duplication on the early inauguration of

---

[19] The decision had scant permanent importance, Mid-Continent being merged with Braniff. See Braniff–Mid-Continent Merger, 15 C.A.B. 708 (1952).
[20] Braniff Airways, Inc., Houston–Memphis–Louisville Route, 2 C.A.B. 353, 386 (1940).

nonstop service, regarded as so persuasive only five months before, went unmentioned.[21] Instead the majority contented itself with saying: "That healthy competition is presumed to be beneficial to the public may be inferred from various Congressional expressions." They made no analysis of the one expression directly relevant, and added the scarcely illuminating commonplace that competition "represents the economic philosophy underlying the antitrust acts" — which, of course, are inconsistent with *any* limitation upon entry and from which, in certain areas, the Board is permitted to exempt.[22] Unsatisfactory as the opinion is, one ought not to be overcritical. The considerations where the competition issue arises only incidentally in selecting a carrier for a wholly new service admittedly required are different from those where the provision of some or more competition is the sole or the principal factor relied on for a new certificate on a route already served; the Board might well have pointed this out more clearly.

Further development was postponed by the temporary freeze on certificate hearings imposed after Pearl Harbor. Although resumption of certificating activity was justified in order to permit the carriers to make postwar plans, one would have supposed that an expert agency would have steeled itself against the influence of abnormal wartime conditions.[23] Seats were at a premium owing

[21] Six years later the Board refused both carriers certificate amendments that would permit nonstop service because the available traffic sufficed only for one daily DC-4 schedule and it would be wrong to hurt either carrier — but help the traveling public — by giving the authorization to one alone. See Braniff Airways, Inc., Chicago & Southern Air Lines, Inc., Route Consolidations, 7 C.A.B. 831, 835-36 (1947).

[22] 72 Stat. 770 (1958), 49 U.S.C. § 1384 (1958).

[23] It was only after the war that the Board, in denying an application, recognized that "the war-swollen revenues of the air carriers, which reflect the intensive use of equipment and the tremendous growth in air travel occasioned in large part by wartime activities that are not yet liquidated, are more than likely to afford a distorted basis for predicting the peacetime conditions in air transportation which we are not yet able to discern with any degree of clarity." West Coast Case, 6 C.A.B. 961, 972 (1946). When granting applications during the war, the Board had found no such mist in its crystal ball. See Northeast Airlines, Inc., Additional Service to Boston, 4 C.A.B. 686, 691 (1944).

to the combined effect of the traffic boom and the diversion of equipment to military contract services, which bore a considerable part of the carriers' overhead. Obsolescence of equipment, an economic factor of prime importance in this industry, was largely suspended by the Government's takeover of the four-engined equipment that would otherwise have been going into airline use. Yet all these conditions were sure to be temporary; when the war ended, equipment of larger size, greater range, higher speed, and heavier plane-mile cost would soon be available. Even the ultimate advent of the jets was plainly to be foreseen; the jet engine was used on military aircraft during the war and its commercial application could be only a question of time.[24]

The Rise and Fall of the Presumption in Favor of Competition, 1943–1944

The case in which the Board was forced to make its first policy pronouncement as to section 2(d) was *Transcontinental & Western Air, Inc., Additional North–South California Services*.[25] There were two decisions, one in May, the other in August, 1943; the pronouncement came only in the latter. The route was Los Angeles–San Francisco, theretofore a monopoly of United which that carrier sought to retain.[26] The applicants were TWA, which

[24] See Whittle, *The Aircraft Gas Turbine and Civil Aviation, With Special Reference to Development in Great Britain*, IATA BULL. 86–96 (Dec. 1948).

[25] 4 C.A.B. 254, 264, 276 (1943), 4 C.A.B. 373 (1943) (supplemental opinion).

[26] United's argument that it was entitled to be protected against any competition went beyond all bounds. No such monopolistic contention had ever been made before; the argument against further certification in the international cases had been that foreign competition would fill the bill. Some of the Board's statements on the latter subject are rather painfully amusing today. The basic one is in American Export Airlines, Inc., Trans-Atlantic Service, 2 C.A.B. 16, 32 (1940): "Moreover, fundamental differences in background and technique between United States and foreign flag air carriers may tend to distinguish their respective services by essentially noncompetitive basic characteristics, rather than by those differences of degree which stimulate progress through competition." Although later opinions acknowledged that foreign competition would be a factor, the Board was unduly influenced by the preeminence of American-flag lines immediately after World War II, due to the destruction of most of the European lines. One member thought "the open-field opportunities" thus created could be utilized to preempt

had a transcontinental route to Los Angeles, with a fork diverging to San Francisco from Winslow, Arizona, and Western, whose then operations were solely between San Diego, Los Angeles, and Salt Lake City. The initial opinion granted TWA's application, with a restriction limiting Los Angeles–San Francisco service to flights originating or terminating at or east of Albuquerque, on the basis that TWA needed this to enable it to compete effectively with United for transcontinental traffic to San Francisco, as well as to provide single-plane service to San Francisco from points on its transcontinental route not enjoying such service theretofore.[27] Western's application to conduct a purely local service in competition with United was denied. There had been "no showing of inadequacy in the United service between Los Angeles and San Francisco and although certain benefits might be expected to accrue to the local traffic from Western's service over that of TWA, such benefits are . . . outweighed by the advantages of the TWA service to through traffic." Western's argument that award of the route would fortify "its efforts to function as a strong independent carrier in the area west of the Rocky Mountains"[28] won no converts. Without expressing any view whether this argument would warrant competitive certification as a matter of law, the Board rejected it as a matter of fact; Western would be under a great disadvantage in competing with United and a still greater one in competing with both United and TWA.[29] The Board believed it was not "either necessary or desirable to attempt to lay down at this time a rule for general application with respect to the inauguration of new air services which may involve competition with existing routes."[30] It did not say why, although Member Branch, concurring, wisely suggested that such a statement "even though subject to later revision

---

a large part of the field for the American flag. See Northwest Airlines, Inc., Pacific Case, 7 C.A.B. 209, 244 (1946).

[27] See 4 C.A.B. at 265.
[28] Id. at 266.
[29] Ibid.
[30] Id. at 264.

and reappraisal, seems to me necessary today in order to permit intelligent planning by all those interested in the future development of our domestic air transportation system."

If the Board had made such a statement, this surely would have been altogether different from the one it was to make a few months later, when, on Western's petition for reconsideration, it unanimously executed a complete *volte-face*. The Board's predicament in justifying its new decision was much greater than if it had certificated Western on the first round. It would have been quite easy to write an opinion supporting this, on the basis, already indicated, that effective competition for local traffic was desirable on so heavily traveled a route and that TWA's restricted authorization would not provide it.[31] However, all that had been quite as evident in May as in August; since the facts had not altered, the change in decision had to be based on a new view of the law. After some unexceptionable remarks that adequacy of the existing service was not an absolute bar to duplicating competition, the Board edged on to say, "The Act thus implies the desirability of competition in the air transportation industry when such competition will be neither destructive nor uneconomical," and then took the following leap:

> While no convenient formula of general applicability may be available as a substitute for the Board's discretionary judgment it would seem to be a sound principle that, since competition in itself presents an incentive to improved service and technological development, there would be a strong, although not conclusive, presumption in favor of competition on any route which offered sufficient traffic to support competing services without unreasonable increase of total operating cost.[32]

---

[31] Of course, the opinion would also have had to say why the solution was not to give TWA an unrestricted authorization; the predominantly long-haul character of TWA's operations and TWA's then preoccupation with a proposed round-the-world service would have made such an explanation entirely plausible.

[32] Transcontinental & Western Air, Inc., Additional North-South California Services, 4 C.A.B. 373, 375 (1943).

"Competition to the extent necessary" thus became "competition is necessary unless proved to be unnecessary" — moreover not simply competition between two, which might be easily defensible, but, in this instance, among three — subject only to the proviso that the traffic be sufficient "to support competing services without unreasonable increase of total operating costs," a proviso which the Board's continued failure to define its terms or to make serious cost studies rendered almost meaningless.

The "presumption" language was soon repeated, again unanimously, in *Colonial Airlines, Inc., Atlantic Seaboard Operation*,[33] where the Board certificated National to provide competition for Eastern on the heavily traveled New York–Miami route, a decision rather clearly right on its facts — at the same time, however, declining to establish a service competitive to Eastern on the less dense route between New York and New Orleans. This was shortly followed by the portion of the *Northeast Airlines, Boston Service* case relating to the route between Boston and New York.[34] Like San Francisco–Los Angeles, this was an extremely dense segment theretofore served by a single carrier, in this instance American. Eastern's case for extension of its Miami–New York route to Boston was overwhelming: "The record shows that there is a heavy flow of passenger traffic between Boston and points south of New York which would be provided single-carrier service under the Eastern proposal."[35] Competition by Eastern was thus "necessary," and, even with the absence of significant cost data usual in Board proceedings, the ability of the New York–Boston route to sustain two operations could hardly be doubted. The serious question, largely elided in the opinion, was whether there should be still another competing carrier. The Board prepared the way for the latter by restricting Eastern's New York–Boston service to flights originating or terminating south of Richmond, Virginia, or west of Charleston, West Virginia, then slid

---

[33] 4 C.A.B. 552 (1944).
[34] Northeast Airlines, Inc., Additional Service to Boston, 4 C.A.B. 686 (1944).
[35] *Id.* at 694.

on to the question whether Colonial or Northeast should be the third carrier, and picked Northeast.[36]

There are two extraordinary things about this decision. One is its failure to give serious consideration to the question whether the need for competition could not be better met by an unrestricted authorization to Eastern than by a restricted one to Eastern and an unrestricted one to Northeast. Perhaps the reason the question was not asked was that it could not have been honestly answered in the manner the Board wanted. Eastern was experienced in competing with American in a very similar, and contiguous, market, New York–Washington; moreover, everything said in the first *North–South California* opinion about Western's difficulties in competing with both United and TWA applied a fortiori to Northeast.[37] Yet, in contrast to the restriction on TWA in the *California* case, the restriction imposed on Eastern, although probably as severe as the public interest permitted,[38] was not severe enough to shelter Northeast from Eastern's competition.

The other extraordinary item is the concurring opinion of Members Branch and Ryan. They thought the majority opinion, "while expressly reaffirming its belief in the soundness of the presumption doctrine, offers an interpretation of that doctrine

[36] Nothing in the opinion suggested that Northeast's service was needed to convenience traffic from points on its routes north of Boston.

[37] A dozen years later Northeast was to admit that it had been forced to withdraw from competition with American and Eastern in the local Boston-New York market. See New York-Florida Case, 24 C.A.B. 94, 102 (1956); *id.* at 127-28 (separate opinion). Only in the late 1950's did Northeast attain a significant role in this market, apparently, if one may judge from current reports, without beneficial economic effects.

[38] The Board may have been warranted in requiring the flights to originate and terminate south of Washington on the basis that American already met the need for turnaround service between Boston and Washington; on the other hand, moving the restriction still further south, *e.g.*, to North Carolina and Georgia points, would have had little or no practical effect. The junction of Eastern's two routes from the south at Washington almost inevitably permitted it to operate about as many New York–Boston flights under a restriction as it would have wished to fly without one, although, of course, under some competitive handicap, especially northbound. The restriction was ultimately removed. See New York–Florida Case, 24 C.A.B. 94 (1956).

which, in our view, would seem to render it largely meaningless." This, they considered, left the question "in an unsatisfactory state of confusion and uncertainty." Their solution was to overrule the doctrine. They thought "the Board should not presume the answer to the question of the need for competition by creating a prima facie case based solely upon the availability of sufficient traffic to permit economical operation; it should search for the answer among the facts of record developed in public hearing in accordance with established principles of administrative law and procedure." It is easy to understand why these two members took this sound view of the law; what is hard to comprehend is how they could have joined, in August 1943 and in February 1944, in something they rightly deemed so offensive in June 1944, or what they found in the "facts of record" to show that competition among three carriers between New York and Boston was needed rather than competition between two.

A Period of Drift, 1944–1951

The Board could scarcely have looked back with much satisfaction on this first bout with section 2(d). Within ten months after putting forth the presumption doctrine, the majority had restated it in a manner which the minority claimed made it meaningless; and the minority had not merely repudiated the doctrine but acted as if they had not been around when they had joined in formulating it. No further progress in developing an understandable criterion was made in the next important case, *Northwest Airlines, Inc., Chicago–Milwaukee–New York Service*,[39] although the results may have been sound enough. There the Board, among other things, denied applications of Braniff and Chicago & Southern to compete on the Chicago–Detroit route which was already served by American and PCA (later Capital), and for which United was certificated subject to a long-haul restriction, saying:

The mere fact that a particular route develops a large volume of

[39] 6 C.A.B. 217 (1944).

traffic does not of itself afford sufficient justification for a finding that the public convenience and necessity require establishment of an additional competitive service exactly duplicating an existing operation.[40]

We are left to speculate how this was to be reconciled with the "strong, although not conclusive, presumption in favor of competition on any route which offered sufficient traffic to support competing services without unreasonable increase of total operating cost." If the distinction was that two unrestricted services had already been authorized, it was not made. Confusion as to the continued life of the presumption doctrine was further confounded when an application by Colonial to become a second carrier on a route served only by American was denied, not because of traffic insufficient even under the presumption doctrine, as it could well have been, but because "parallel competition is not justified unless some substantial benefit to the public can be expected as a result of such service" and the record failed to establish any.[41]

A year and a half later the Board returned to the Pacific Coast. Again the journey was not to be a happy one. This time Western was seeking to break United's monopoly on the San Francisco–Portland–Seattle route segment, just north of that where it had ultimately succeeded before. Decision took a course now familiar; Western lost the first round,[42] only to prevail a year later on petition for reconsideration.[43]

The task of the first opinion was to reconcile the denial of Western's application to become a second carrier north of San Francisco with the previous superimposition of Western over both United and a restricted TWA service to the south. It was hard to say that the route did not offer "sufficient traffic to support competing services without unreasonable increase of total oper-

[40] *Id.* at 228. A similar statement with respect to a route proposal by PCA is made at 236–37.
[41] *Id.* at 232.
[42] West Coast Case, 6 C.A.B. 961 (1946).
[43] West Coast Case, 8 C.A.B. 14 (1947) (supplemental opinion).

ating cost" — although the Board had neither examined to what extent competition increases costs nor defined "unreasonable," and has not to this day. Another course would have been to overrule the presumption doctrine — and conclude that no sufficient "need" had been shown. However, to admit explicitly that the presumption doctrine had been an aberration would have violated the Board's dogma of its own infallibility.

The Board took a less ingenuous method of escape. The opinion paraphrased section 2(d) and added statements that the act "leaves to this Board the determination of the question whether competition is required on a particular route" and that this "should be decided upon the facts of record and should be considered together with any other factors of public interest which in the particular case may point in the opposite direction." [44] This is perfectly sound, if a bit trite, and worlds away from the presumption doctrine, which, however, was not overruled. The opinion writer went on to say that competition was "not mandatory in relation to any particular route or service," since it was "a fact well-known to the Congress at the time of the enactment of the Civil Aeronautics Act . . . that every route operated by a single air carrier has not been insulated against the emulating spirit to which in the field of commerce we give the name of competition, but that on the contrary the benefits of the competitive incentive frequently spread to routes that do not have direct competing service." [45] That was the argument made by United in the *North–South California* case [46] and there rejected; it is not merely inconsistent with the presumption doctrine but nearly the opposite. Still the writer was not satisfied; the opinion explained that if a need for competition on the route exists, "the present record does not reveal it; and it is reasonable to assume that if United's service . . . were not of that quality which is commonly attributable to the competitive incentive, Western would have

[44] 6 C.A.B. at 970.
[45] *Ibid.*
[46] 4 C.A.B. 254, 264 (1943).

offered evidence in support of such fact as it did in support of its application for its Los Angeles–San Francisco route which this Board granted." [47] The author would have fared ill if this last statement had been required to meet the test of section 11(a) of the Securities Act.[48] For although it was literally true that Western had "offered evidence" in the earlier case to show that United's service between Los Angeles and San Francisco was inadequate, the larger truth was that the Board had there found "the record does not sustain the contention that United's service has been inadequate." [49]

A year later, on a petition for reconsideration by Western, the Board again turned about, thereby creating more trouble for its opinion writers. The differing descriptions of the route in the two opinions are amusingly revealing. The writer for denial in 1946 considered San Francisco–Portland–Seattle a route whose traffic flow "is not as great as that enjoyed by many other United States domestic routes, a number of which are served by a single carrier"; [50] by 1947 the selfsame route had become one which "still stands out among the few major route segments . . . that are served by a single carrier." [51] The writer of 1947 thought the 1946 denial had rested on the Board's then inability "to conclude that the indicated future traffic volume over the route would be of such magnitude as to minimize the resultant financial effect on United," [52] and that the May 1947 Board could see a shape of things to come not perceptible to its predecessor a year before. However, the Board's earlier opinion had not proceeded on the basis of lack of traffic; it had "recognized," quite specifically, "that United's route No. 11 has in the past enjoyed substantial traffic and offers promise of future traffic development." [53] More-

---

[47] 6 C.A.B. at 969.
[48] 48 Stat. 82 (1933), as amended, 15 U.S.C. § 77k (1958).
[49] 4 C.A.B. at 264.
[50] 6 C.A.B. at 972.
[51] West Coast Case, 8 C.A.B. 14, 20 (1947), *modifying* 6 C.A.B. 961 (1946).
[52] *Id.* at 22.
[53] 6 C.A.B. at 972.

over, the "development" found in the 1947 opinion ought to have been rather readily foreseeable in May 1946, especially since the traffic figures used in the second opinion were for September 1946 — indeed, the dissent in the earlier case had correctly "anticipated that this traffic will increase substantially in the immediate future."[54] Again, whereas the May 1946 denial had heavily emphasized United's unfavorable financial showing in "February 1946, the latest month for which data are available,"[55] the later opinion relied on the supposed improvement starting in April 1946, but then had to explain away United's unfavorable showing "in the last 2 months of 1946 and the first 2 months of 1947," on the basis of what surely could not have been a secret a year before, that "these winter months generally reflect a seasonal drop in the air transportation industry . . . ."[56] Curiously the 1947 opinion failed to mention a truly significant fact, the desperate financial condition of Western which, as the Board was to say a few months later, "could have resulted in receivership or bankruptcy" but for a rescue operation in which United made ad-

---

[54] *Id.* at 1005 (concurring and dissenting opinion).
[55] *Id.* at 971.
[56] 8 C.A.B. at 23. It should be noted that neither United's unfavorable financial showing in February 1946, emphasized in the first opinion, nor the supposed improvement beginning in the spring of that year, relied on in the second, could possibly have been the subject of testimony at the hearings; these data became cognizable only because of stipulations, signed generally in CAB proceedings, which permit the Board to take note of carrier reports and Board traffic surveys up to the date of final decision. All too often, owing to the delays in proceedings, decision is predicated on the data thus made available by stipulation rather than on that which was subjected to cross-examination at the hearing but had aged by the date of decision. This makes one wonder what the long hearing really accomplishes; there have been all too many instances of decisions thus made on the basis of stipulated post-hearing data which the losing party could have shown to be unreliable if it had had an opportunity. See Friendly, *A Look at the Federal Administrative Agencies*, 60 COLUM. L. REV. 429, 432–33 (1960). This problem is not peculiar to the CAB; the Administrative Conference (*supra* p. 4 & note 19) will be rendering an important public service if it can devise procedures whereby the interval between the hearing and the decision will be so shortened that the former serves a more useful purpose. Perhaps some sort of "show-cause" procedure would help.

vances under an agreement whereby Western would transfer to United its Los Angeles–Denver route and related property.[57]

My objection is not to the result ultimately reached in the *West Coast* case; it is quite unthinkable that United should have been left forever with a monopoly of this heavily traveled route. My quarrel is with the decisional process and the opinion writing. If most airline executives and lawyers thought that the Board had no standards as to the grant or denial of competitive certificates, that the elaborate hearings had almost no effect on the outcome, that the factors truly motivating decision were quite other than those stated, that, as was later to be said by one of the wisest of airline counsel, "instead of the decision of a case being based upon the findings of fact and determinations of policy disclosed in the agency opinion, the findings and determinations are based upon the decision," [58] the two *West Coast* opinions amply warranted such views. The Task Force of the Hoover Commission understated the fact when it reported that "in granting new route cases . . . the Civil Aeronautics Board provides little real help in understanding its governing principles"; and that its "handling of the domestic route pattern . . . has proceeded largely on an ad hoc basis." [59]

The Brief Life of the Presumption Against Competition, 1951–1954

The optimistic conclusion that the airlines had turned the corner, so loudly voiced in the second *West Coast* opinion, proved a poor piece of expertise. Instead of 1947's marking an improve-

---

[57] United Air Lines, Inc.-Western Air Lines, Inc., Acquisition of Air Carrier Property, 8 C.A.B. 298, 302 (1947).

[58] Westwood, *The Davis Treatise: Meaning to the Practitioner*, 43 MINN. L. REV. 607, 613 (1959). See also RICHMOND, REGULATION AND COMPETITION IN AIR TRANSPORTATION 108 (1961).

[59] COMMISSION ON ORGANIZATION OF THE EXECUTIVE BRANCH OF THE GOVERNMENT, TASK FORCE REPORT ON REGULATORY COMMISSIONS (APPENDIX N) 40, 41–42 (1949).

ment over 1946, the losses of the domestic carriers trebled.[60] Owing to the long time taken in processing new route cases, the impact of this financial crisis was reflected in a Board decision only after the crisis had ceased. In the first opinion in the *Southern Service to the West* case [61] in 1951, the Board swerved from a presumption in favor of competition to a presumption against it — without, however, overruling its earlier statements, sharply brought to its attention by a dissent.[62]

The swerve was all the greater because, in contrast to the two cases on the Pacific Coast or the *Miami–New York* case or Northeast's application for New York–Boston, the applications in the *Southern Service to the West* case offered important elements of public convenience in addition to those claimed for competition alone. The case, as the Board said, "presents the question of the need for through service between points in the southeastern and southern parts of the United States and points on the west coast," [63] a need thought to have become so compelling a decade later that the Board certificated not one but two carriers.[64] Nevertheless, the Board denied all the new route applications and proposed that the needed through plane service be provided by equipment interchange.

The discussion of competition began with a quotation of section 2(d) — this time with the words "to the extent necessary" italicized.[65] It continued with the theme of the beneficent influence of competition spreading to routes without direct competition, sung in the first *West Coast* opinion of 1946, although the

[60] Adams, *The Air Route Pattern Problems*, 17 J. AIR L. & COM. 127, 128 (1950).
[61] 12 C.A.B. 518 (1951).
[62] *Id.* at 574, 587.
[63] *Id.* at 522.
[64] Southern Transcontinental Service Case, 1A Av. L. REP. (Av. Cas.) ¶ 21131 (CAB March 13, 1961), *rev'd in part and remanded*, Braniff Airways Inc. v. CAB, D.C. Cir., May 24, 1962. A recent text justifiably characterizes this proceeding, stretching over a decade, as epitomizing "the worst features of administrative procedure; endless delays and repeated reversals of prior findings." FULDA, COMPETITION IN THE REGULATED INDUSTRIES 235 (1961).
[65] 12 C.A.B. at 532.

Board had not found the song so sweet when United had sung it in the *North–South California* case of 1943 and was unable to hear it when the *West Coast* case was redone in 1947. Again, striking the minor key of the first *West Coast* case and ignoring the crashing D-major chords of the second, the Board expressed some dismal thoughts:

> It would be short-sighted indeed were we to organize our air transport route system on the assumption that conditions in this industry will always be favorable. We know from the experience of the last 4 years that air transportation can pass with surprising abruptness from relatively sound conditions to conditions of grave crisis, even when the circumstances of the general economy are favorable. In formulating policies and reaching decisions in the discharge of our regulatory and developmental tasks, we take the chance of committing fatal error if we close our eyes to the warning lessons of this experience.

Then, after announcing that interchange arrangements would "provide adequately the improved through services that are found to be needed on the present record," the Board made this statement:

> We would be less than helpful if, at this time, we did not express our considered opinion that further route expansion in our domestic trunk-line network would present problems of serious difficulty in view of the conditions which presently and during the postwar period have existed in this industry. Certainly the task of proving public convenience and necessity in satisfying the statutory requirements would place a difficult, if not insurmountable, burden upon the air carriers which would undertake to sponsor further route extensions of any substantial character.[66]

Here was a policy for the future, certainly different from that of the past although not acknowledged to be,[67] and hard to recon-

---

[66] *Id.* at 533–34.

[67] In 1952 the Board informed Congress that "In authorizing new competitive services point-to-point competition has been avoided other than in unusual circumstances where it has been necessary to make extensions of existing lines to

cile with the language of the statute, but a policy all the same. It was not to last long. Some three years later, a badly split Board adopted another opinion in the same case saying, for all the world as if the prior opinion had never been written:

> We need not detail the advantages of competition, nor to prove them again in each case. An objective reading of the Civil Aeronautics Act leaves no doubt that the lawmakers considered competition to be [a] desirable objective which should be established whenever it is economically feasible and will contribute to the development of a sound national air transportation system.[68]

True, the later opinion dealt with a competitive interchange rather than with a new certificate, but any practiced eye could see that the lone dissent in the first *Southern Service to the West* case was in the way of becoming the majority view.

The Decisions of 1955 and Later Years

The deluge was not long in arriving. A series of decisions starting in 1955, under a new Chairman who, in his tenure of only thirteen months, often furnished the deciding vote, remade the nation's airline map.[69] By 1958 "twelve routes had five or more

---

common gateways for the establishment of through long-haul connections." CAB, REPORT SUBMITTED TO THE SUBCOMMITTEE ON MONOPOLY, SENATE SELECT COMM. ON SMALL BUSINESS, 82D CONG., 2D SESS., THE ROLE OF COMPETITION IN COMMERCIAL AIR TRANSPORTATION 10 (Comm. Print 1952). Apparently Los Angeles–San Francisco, Miami–New York, New York–Boston, San Francisco–Portland–Seattle, and many other cases, were all such "unusual circumstances"!

[68] Southern Service to the West Case, Reopened, 18 C.A.B. 790, 799–800 (1954).
[69] The principal ones are Reopened Milwaukee–Chicago–New York Restriction Case, 21 C.A.B. 760 (1955); Southwest–Northeast Service Case, 22 C.A.B. 52 (1955); New York–Chicago Service Case, 22 C.A.B. 973 (1955); Denver Service Case, 22 C.A.B. 1178 (1955); and New York–Florida Case, 24 C.A.B. 94 (1956). The last resulted in the certification of Northeast, for a five-year period, as a third carrier on the Miami–New York route, largely for the purpose of strengthening Northeast; press reports indicate that up to the present time this action, while sapping the strength of Eastern and National, has not greatly benefited the newcomer. The trend continued at least until 1958 when Northwest was placed as a third carrier in the Chicago–Florida market. See Great Lakes–Southeast Services Case, 27 C.A.B.

carriers and one route, New York to Washington, had nine."[70] Everything said in the initial *Southern Service to the West* case was repudiated in action, although, true to form, not in words. Although some decisions merely added a second carrier whose certification could have been justified on traditional grounds,[71] most went far beyond that. I shall give only a few examples. By a three-to-two vote, Continental's Denver–Kansas City route was extended east to Chicago and west to Los Angeles, with a nonstop authorization paralleling the services already offered by three transcontinental carriers — at the same time that additional competition was being created at both Denver and Kansas City by placing the former, previously with transcontinental service only by United, on TWA's transcontinental certificate, and the latter, previously having such service only by TWA, on United's.[72] In another case Capital was authorized to compete on the New

---

829, 843 (1958), *aff'd sub nom.* Eastern Air Lines, Inc. v. CAB, 271 F.2d 752 (2d Cir. 1959), *cert. denied*, 362 U.S. 970 (1960).

[70] Hale & Hale, *Competition or Control IV: Air Carriers*, 109 U. PA. L. REV. 311, 318 (1961). Some of the certificates had long-haul restrictions.

[71] Among these were Braniff's certification to compete against American on the Dallas–New York route and Delta's to compete with Eastern on the Houston–New Orleans–Atlanta–New York route. See also St. Louis–Southeast Service Case, 27 C.A.B. 342 (1958).

[72] Denver Service Case, 22 C.A.B. 1178 (1955). The Examiner had recommended in favor of the certification of Continental but against the changes in TWA's and United's certificates, since "Denver and Kansas City would obtain advantages from competitive service without disrupting the present competitive balance between United and TWA . . . ." *Id.* at 1294. The majority approved his recommendation while destroying its basis, saying merely: "As we have recently noted, competitive air service offers greater assurance that the public will receive the quality and quantity of air service to which it is entitled." *Id.* at 1184. No explanation was made why, if the reason for certificating Continental was to improve service for Kansas City and Denver, Continental should not have been restricted to flights stopping at one or the other of these cities, particularly since, in rejecting another application for Chicago–Los Angeles service, the Board said: "Insofar as the Chicago–Los Angeles market is concerned, we are unable to find a need at this time for an additional nonstop service in this market, and our awards to Continental are not predicated upon such a need." *Id.* at 1189–90. The majority did discuss the point in denying reconsideration, *id.* at 1306, but not in any satisfying way.

York–Atlanta–New Orleans route at the same time that Eastern's service on that route was being duplicated by Delta.[73] Northwest was placed in the New York–Chicago market as a fifth carrier (with a long-haul restriction), not because of any public need for the service but because "we will be remedying a major weakness in Northwest's route structure and enable it to become a more effective competitor with United in transcontinental service."[74] At the same time the Board removed a long-haul restriction on Northwest's New York–Detroit certificate since "in our judgment, the size and potential of the New York–Detroit market will now support three turnaround services rather than merely one heretofore operated by American";[75] the basis for this "judgment" was not disclosed. In the same case the Board concluded "that the public convenience and necessity require virtually all the authorizations proposed by Capital,"[76] for routes paralleling those already served by one, two, or three carriers. The chief, indeed almost the sole, reason was:

> While the Civil Aeronautics Act seeks the development of a sound national system, and not the advantage of an individual carrier as such, we find that this case is one where the strengthening of an individual carrier is required for the sound development of the national system of which it is a part.[77]

---

[73] Southwest–Northeast Service Case, 22 C.A.B. 52, 63–68 (1955).
[74] New York–Chicago Service Case, 22 C.A.B. 973, 979 (1955).
[75] *Ibid.*
[76] *Id.* at 977.
[77] *Id.* at 978. A separate essay would be needed to trace the Board's backings and fillings on this question whether the "need" of a carrier or ability to render superior public service is the dominant criterion for selection. See Hector, *Problems of the CAB and the Independent Regulatory Commission*, 69 YALE L.J. 931, 940–41 (1960). The Board's authorization of multiple competition in order to decrease the dominance of the "Big Four" — American, United, Eastern, and TWA — proved relatively unsuccessful. Reviewing the figures, Fulda concludes: "The Big Four thus maintained, by and large, the same position of dominance they enjoyed at the inception of federal regulation, in spite of the fact that the route maps of the Small Eight were expanded almost beyond recognition." *Op. cit. supra* note 64, at 212.

The Lack of Standards and of Studies

This series of cases must mark the nadir. Decisions that would vitally affect the economics of the domestic airline industry for a generation were taken in a tone of gay abandon more suggestive of the Lord Chancellor's "one for thou and one for thee" than of what ought be expected of a responsible regulatory agency. Seventeen years after its creation the Board had arrived at no understandable criteria governing its most important activity. When a committee of the Senate asked the direct question how the Board interpreted "public convenience and necessity," the best its staff was able to do was to fill half a page with a quotation of section 2 and then add this truly succulent piece of gobbledygook:

> An examination of the congressional policy against the overall statutory plan as revealed by the various sections of the act taken as a whole establishes that in determining whether a particular proposal is in accordance with the public convenience and necessity the Board must apply the specified standards so as to maintain an appropriate equilibrium between the two major policies of the act — that of controlling the air transport industry along the traditional lines of public utility regulation and that of fostering and promoting air transportation.[78]

The Board's Chairman put the matter both more crisply and more candidly when he told a House Committee: "You know, we keep talking about philosophy. We keep talking about the philosophy of the Board. Well, the philosophy of the Civil Aeronautics Board changes from day to day. It depends who is on the Board as to what the philosophy is. You cannot say that the Board as a

---

[78] CAB, Materials Relative to Competition in the Regulated Civil Aviation Industry, 1956, Transmitted to the Select Senate Comm. on Small Business 7–8 (Comm. Print 1956). Why the two "policies" should have been deemed antithetical, so that an "equilibrium" had to be maintained between them, escapes me; I should have supposed that Congress imposed controls for the precise purpose "of fostering and promoting air transportation."

whole has a fixed philosophy for any very fixed period of time because as the members come and go, and they do come and go pretty fast down there." [79]

Board members have often sought to place blame for decisions such as those just reviewed on the airlines, which made uneconomical route proposals.[80] This would be fair enough if the Board had developed and adhered to any standards as to what an uneconomical route proposal was. Without that, when one airline was confronted with what it deemed such a proposal by another to parallel, or to enter a community on, its route, it could have no assurance that a purely negative stance would protect it against unwarranted diversion; hence it retaliated with a "defensive" proposal to compete with the applicant, very likely hoping that this might focus the Board's attention on the economics and that both applications would be denied. What happened in the 1955 series of cases was that instead both were usually granted! The Board, and administrative agencies generally, ought to make better use of the legend President Truman is said to have kept on his desk — "The buck stops here."

Probably a majority of the Board's opinions have professed adherence to what I have called the central — and correct — reading of section 2(d), namely, that whether competition is "necessary" is an issue of fact for determination in each case under standards defined by it; but the Board not only has failed to explicate this but has confused the problem by often indulging in other readings. Perhaps as close an approach as the Board has made to a reasoned statement on competition is in the 1952 report to the Small Business Committee of the Senate.[81] There it indicated that competition (1) had stimulated improvement in equipment ("although it is perhaps inevitable that, apart from competitive considerations, the largest carriers would have led

---

[79] *Hearings on Monopoly Problems in Regulated Industries Before the Antitrust Subcommittee (Subcommittee No. 5) of the House Committee on the Judiciary*, 84th Cong., 2d Sess., ser. 22, pt. 1, at 153 (1956).

[80] For a recent example see note 96 *infra*.

[81] *Supra* note 67, at 10–15.

the way in equipment advances," as they did); (2) had improved schedules (although "an analysis of the interrelation between competition and flight schedules is an exceedingly difficult one due to the variables that must be considered and the factors other than competitive influences that play an important part in the decisions of management with respect to its flight schedules"); and (3) had increased the variety of views as to the proper fare level. Taking all three positions as established (with the qualifications the Board had added), the statement shows simply the need for some competition, which no one would deny; it fails to deal with the more significant questions of what determines the need for it on a particular route and, particularly, what creates a need for multiple competition. Deficient as this was, confusion was added by the Board's report to the same Small Business Committee four years later. This pointed out that "modern equipment purchased for competitive reasons is not restricted to use over competitive segments only, and because of the complex interrelationships between fares, lower fares produced by competitive pressure on one route or segment generally must be applied to noncompetitive segments as well" [82] — language generally used in denying need for competition. But in answer to the question "What weight does the Board assign to competition as a component of the public interest?" the Board said that this was "a major element," that the Board "has consistently regarded effective competition as a necessary and practical means of assuring the maintenance of a higher quality of service," and that it "has pursued a policy of authorizing the maximum amount of competition consistent with the sound development of the air transportation system." [83] Evidently there were some new writers at work and the Board had forgotten what it had told the same Committee four years before; [84] eclecticism had truly run riot.

Equally or more serious has been the Board's failure to make

[82] *Supra* note 78, at 9.
[83] MATERIALS, *supra* note 78, at 8.
[84] See note 67 *supra*.

any significant studies to determine either the benefits of multiple competition or its cost,[85] or even to take a position with respect to investigations made by others. Its opinions reflect almost complete disregard of such private studies as Gill and Bates' demonstration that competition by more than two carriers had generally proved detrimental rather than advantageous to good service,[86] Bluestone's criticism of the statistics purporting to show how additional competition had increased traffic,[87] and his thesis that "the cost of competition due solely to load factor losses" approximated 10.7 per cent of expenses.[88] I do not assert

[85] Bluestone's article, *The Problem of Competition Among Domestic Trunk Airlines — Part II*, 21 J. AIR L. & COM. 50, 69 (1954), states that in 1948 the Board "directed its staff to prepare a comprehensive and complete analysis of the domestic route pattern, which finally became a study of cost standards by which to measure route changes." This is CROZIER, COST STANDARDS — DOMESTIC SCHEDULED AIR CARRIERS (1950), Supplemental Report, July 1951. Starting from the basic proposition "that traffic-unit costs tend to vary in inverse ratio to volume of traffic," the study seeks to predict the levels which such costs will reach with various changes in traffic volumes and route characteristics. The report notes, at 278, that "during the past ten years there has been a great expansion in the traffic and routes of the scheduled domestic air transport system, . . . accomplished partly by the extension of routes into areas not previously served, partly by establishing or increasing multiple-carrier services in areas already served, and partly by traffic increase consequent to growing public acceptance," but that this expansion has been "accompanied by a trend of increased total requirements for government financial aid." It suggests as a remedy "the merging of carriers whose routes can be efficiently integrated, particularly mergers of the strong and the weak, and the elimination of services which do not appear to be justified by either quantitative or qualitative values." These teachings were scarcely heeded in the decisions of 1955-1956. If it be said that the study taught the need of increasing the size of the smaller carriers, the answer is that although it showed a tendency of unit costs to decrease with size, it could hardly have meant that a multiplication of carriers that would seriously impair load factors would benefit anyone — indeed the implications were quite to the contrary.

Since September 1954, the Board has periodically released figures showing the division of competitive traffic. Although these may afford the basis for some conclusions as to the workings of competition, none have been drawn.

[86] GILL & BATES, AIRLINE COMPETITION 506-07, 628, 630-31 (1949).

[87] Bluestone, *The Problem of Competition Among Domestic Trunk Airlines — Part I*, 20 J. AIR L. & COM. 379, 391-94 (1953).

[88] *Id.* at 384-91.

that the conclusions of these experts were right; I do assert that an agency charged with the duty of authorizing competition "to the extent necessary" and not otherwise, which had failed to discharge its duty of preparing studies of its own, should have given some heed to such research by experienced and disinterested analysts. Doubtless the Board would try to excuse its failure to make studies on a plea that conditions in the industry have never been sufficiently "normal" to permit definitive work. This might have been a good answer for the Board's first decade; but conditions since 1948 have been as "normal" as can be expected in an era when abnormality has become the norm.

The results of the series of decisions starting in 1955 were what might have been anticipated. Just as "the whole series of very important domestic new route cases from the end of 1942 up to the *West Coast* case in May 1946 can be scanned in vain for any expressed appraisal of future traffic reflecting any thought other than an indefinite continuation of carrying capacity in DC–3 terms," [89] so the opinions of 1955, stemming from records made years before, betray no examination of the wholly new scheduling and load factor problems to be created by the jets, the initial orders for which were but a year away. Introduction of these new airplanes, highly economical if well filled, devastatingly costly if not, reduced domestic trunk line profits to a return of 2.86 per cent on investment in 1960 and produced losses estimated to approximate thirty million dollars in 1961,[90] and these despite fare increases in 1958 and another in 1960 aggregating 25 per cent.[91] A report recently furnished the President gloomily con-

[89] Westwood, *Choice of the Air Carrier for New Air Transport Routes*, 16 GEO. WASH. L. REV. 159, 226 (1948).

[90] TASK FORCE ON NATIONAL AVIATION GOALS, REPORT, PROJECT HORIZON, FEDERAL AVIATION AGENCY 157 (1961).

[91] Orders No. E-12203, Feb. 25, 1958; No. E-13066, Oct. 14, 1958; CAB Press Release 60–13, June 17, 1960. By Order No. E-17885, Dec. 28, 1961, the Board, by a 3–2 vote, permitted another 3% increase avowedly only for six months, during which "a series of steps will be undertaken to resolve the underlying economic problems." As the end of the six months approaches, there is no sign that any really significant steps have been taken. In its order, the Board noted "a declining

cludes: "The present low level of earnings of the industry, if continued, threaten its entire financial structure." [92] One can sympathize with the plaintive remark of a present Board member, in no way responsible for the 1955 decisions: "The heart of the matter is that competition between airlines which appears to be reasonable when medium capacity, medium speed piston aircraft are utilized, may be unreasonable or uneconomic when high capacity, high speed jet aircraft are substituted." [93] Yet surely all this ought to have been foreseeable to a body presumptively endowed with expertise.[94] As a crowning irony, the multiple-competitive routes awarded to Capital in 1955, almost solely in order to strengthen it against larger lines, were allowed in 1961 to pass into the hands of United, thereby making United the country's largest air carrier.[95] Yet if any official *peccavimus* has come

---

trend of earnings experienced during the last six years," notwithstanding fare increases, "attributable largely to the sharp decline in passenger load factor," arising from an increase in capacity "at a faster rate than traffic." One wonders just how this came about!

[92] PROJECT HORIZON, *supra* note 90, at 153. The report states also "that if the 1960 pattern of earning prevails throughout the decade, the industry could be in serious trouble and individual carriers could be in bankruptcy." *Id.* at 159.

[93] Gillilland, Address before American Bar Association, Section of Public Utility Law, Washington, D.C., August 29, 1960. PROJECT HORIZON, *supra* note 90, at 159, also comments that much of the excess capacity that has drastically impaired earnings "may stem from the fact that levels of competition, which were perhaps economical with the smaller piston equipment, cannot be profitably maintained with large jet equipment."

[94] The CAB Staff Analysis and Evaluation of the Hector Memorandum to the President, at 37, revealed that the Board had under way "a jet study, the results of which may, among other things, have a significant relationship to policies relating to route structure, fares, and the economics of route development." If the reference was to Staff Research Report No. 2, General Characteristics of Turbine-Powered Aircraft, Feb. 1960, this was a considerable overbilling; I have seen nothing since that fits the description. In any event a study now comes much too late.

[95] The Board ruefully announced it had "decided to approve the merger of Capital and United because it has no practicable alternative," since "Capital is financially *in extremis* and will not survive if the merger is disapproved." It feared to condition approval on the withdrawal of any significant part of Capital's authority because of the statement of United's president "that the carrier is not interested in acquiring Capital if its route system is substantially curtailed." See United-

from the Board, I have not heard it; the Board or, perhaps more accurately, its staff, seems unwilling to admit it has ever erred.[96] It is not hard to see today what the Board should have done to discharge its task — indeed, it was not hard to see at the time. The Board ought early to have enunciated in some detail what it thought section 2(d) meant, indicating the standards it would apply in different situations that were sure to arise, and to have revised this as experience required. It is no answer to take refuge in such clichés as that "no mechanical formula exists whereby statistics can be fed into a machine and an ultimate route decision obtained" — as if anyone had ever contended that it did — and that "the outcome depends upon a balancing and weighing" of many factors such as "diversion, subsidy, cost, need for service, strengthening of weak carrier, competitive balance, [and] adequacy of existing service."[97] The Board ought to have been able to say *something* as to *how* these factors would be weighed —

Capital Merger Case, 1A Av. L. Rep. (Av. Cas.) ¶ 21132 (CAB April 3, 1961), aff'd sub nom. Northwest Airlines, Inc. v. CAB, 2 Av. L. Rep. (Av. Cas.) 17809 (D.C. Cir. 1962).

[96] The *New York Times*, Sept. 24, 1961, § 3, p. 1, col. 8, reports a meeting to be held between airline presidents and the new Chairman of the Board, which "is said to be receptive to mergers that would reduce competition where that competition has meant three or four lines operating in the red instead of one or two lines making money." Such a call to the airlines to join routes the Board had put asunder, and thereby remedy the Board's mistakes — of course not called such — is reminiscent of the late 1940's. See O'Connell, *Legal Problems in Revising the Air Route Pattern*, 15 J. Air L. & Com. 397, 401–02 (1948). Again, on November 3, 1961, Chairman Boyd "called . . . for mergers among the domestic airlines to reduce excess competition" and said "that if the eleven trunk airlines did not act soon toward reducing their number the board should study the situation and make its own recommendations." He put the blame on "miscalculation and overoptimism of airline management, together with impatience on the part of the public"; the Board had been guiltless, as usual. N.Y. Times, Nov. 4, 1961, p. 36, col. 1. See also N.Y. Times, Feb. 4, 1962, § 10, p. 1, col. 8.

This has been written too soon to know the Board's reaction to the first, and doubtless unexpected, fruit of the invitation for mergers — that proposed by American and Eastern. See N.Y. Times, Jan. 24, 1962, § 1, p. 1, col. 8.

[97] Comments of the CAB on the Hector Memorandum to the President 21, March 29, 1960.

which were more important and which less — and to develop some useful tests of these and other factors through careful economic study. A considered statement of this kind ought to have prevented such divagations as the presumption doctrine of the second *North–South California* opinion in one direction, and the "difficult, if not insurmountable, burden" language of the first *Southern Service to the West* opinion in the other. In contrast, as we have seen with respect to the FCC, such an undifferentiated list of criteria leaves the agency free to decide any case any way it wishes; Mr. Justice Bridlegoose's method would provide results quite as good, and with far less expense and delay.

No true effort to explicate having been made, and the Board having strayed, it should have had the courage and candor to repudiate its aberrations and return to the straight path. It should have recognized the significant differences between cases involving the certification of a second carrier, where the general desirability of competition would be enough to carry the day on any route with traffic plainly sufficient to "support" two carriers, and cases where the Board was asked to authorize a third or fourth, whose added competitive spur should not have been needed if the initial choice had been well made. If such few studies as exist are anywhere near right, the Board should have set itself rather resolutely against such multiple certification save where this would provide public advantages in the shape of needed new service, as contrasted with just more competition or the supposed strengthening of a weak carrier, and even there it should have imposed restrictions requiring the service to be tailored to the found need. To be sure, stamina was needed to resist the clamor that more competition is always good; but the proper control of competition in the public interest was the very reason for the Board's creation. Eschewing the easy temptation to rationalize results by using data for short and unrepresentative past periods, of which the two *West Coast* case opinions are sufficient examples,[98] the Board should have conducted regular studies of the benefits and costs

[98] *Supra* pp. 87–91.

of competition and then utilized the experience of the past as a guide to what might reasonably be anticipated with the traffic and equipment of the future. Above all it should have written clear, consistent, reasoned opinions or policy statements — facing up to problems rather than sweeping them under the bed, and regularly informing the Congress, the industry, and the public just what it was doing with the nation's air route structure and why, rather than being all things to all men and ultimately satisfying none except itself — if, indeed, it really did that.

The Board's history is a prime example of how an agency's failure to grasp the nettle can make a relatively easy problem hard.

VI

The Minimum-Rate Power of the Interstate Commerce Commission

MY initial plan to content myself with these four case histories provoked a comment that I had simply demonstrated the impossibility of definition of standards in licensing, as against its feasibility in other regulatory areas. This criticism suggested the desirability of a further area of study, outside the licensing field. I selected the minimum-rate power of the Interstate Commerce Commission,[1] both because of its intrinsic interest and because it again illustrates, this time in a far less happy fashion, the interplay of administrative and legislative action discussed in relation to the fourth section of the Interstate Commerce Act.

My critic might say that, in picking this subject, I had not gotten away from licensing save in a formal sense. For whereas the grant of radio or television licenses or of airline certificates of convenience and necessity determines who may enter a

---

[1] Other possible areas of study would have been, on the side of a generally successful definition of standards, the performance of the SEC under § 11 of the Public Utility Holding Company Act, 49 Stat. 820 (1935), 15 U.S.C. § 79k (1958), see RITCHIE, INTEGRATION OF PUBLIC UTILITY HOLDING COMPANIES (1954), reviewed by Forer, 69 HARV. L. REV. 585 (1956), and, on the other side, the FPC's handling of the natural-gas rate problem. See LANDIS REPORT 54–58; Note, *FPC Regulation of Independent Producers of Natural Gas*, 75 HARV. L. REV. 549 (1962).

Another interesting subject would have been the FTC's failure to arrive at clearer definitions of "unfair methods of competition . . . and unfair or deceptive acts or practices," whether by case-to-case decision or by rulemaking; that body is a long way from having realized the hope, expressed by John Dickinson in 1927, that "the run of the decisions may, however, in time cause standardized competitive methods to be pronounced once and for all as either 'fair' or 'unfair' . . . ." ADMINISTRATIVE JUSTICE AND THE SUPREMACY OF LAW 237. See also President Wilson's Message of January 20, 1914, 51 CONG. REC. 1962–64.

business, the minimum-rate power may largely decide who shall stay in it; indeed, for that reason, pressures on the agency may be even greater here than in initial licensing. Yet, in a deeper sense, the problems are quite different. In licensing, the best that can be hoped for is a clearer definition of the criteria determining whether a license will be issued, and, if so, to whom; particularly as to the latter question, which in the FCC's case is almost the only question, there will be many instances where several applicants qualify and the choice among them could be made about as well by the simpler methods used on the football field or in the auction room. In contrast, the minimum-rate power has raised a series of substantive questions, with the opposing forces in the kind of direct conflict with which courts are familiar — questions that were, and still are, susceptible of yes or no answers. It should have been possible for the Commission to develop a series of propositions within the broad congressional directives, as these have changed from time to time, such as we have seen done by the Labor Board — propositions that would have pretty well determined most cases and therefore ought altogether to have eliminated a great many of them. To be sure, the task was an agonizingly hard one. All too often the Commission was not supplied with the cost tools needed for the job, and its decisions were bound to have a literally vital effect on transport companies with large investments and many employees, not to speak of the shipping and consuming public, whose interest often seems to have been rather neglected in the heat of intermodal rivalries. But, whatever the anguish of decision, the fruits of indecision have proved more bitter still; the Commission's drifting among the minimum-rate shoals has submerged it in waves of proceedings that definition would have avoided, and has provoked criticisms from all the modes of transportation the Commission regulates and from many disinterested sources as well.[2]

---

[2] The literature is too large for any approach to complete citation. See, *e.g.*, Huntington, *The Marasmus of the ICC: The Commission, the Railroads, and the Public Interest*, 61 YALE L.J. 467 (1952); Langdon, *The Regulation of Com-*

It would be impossible here to present anything like a complete survey of what the Commission has done in this area — Professor Williams' study, in 1958, comprehended 900 cases in the rail-motor field alone.[3] Such an effort would also be unrewarding; even a sampling of the reports is sufficient to validate the comment of an articulate railroad critic that "any attempt to reconcile the ICC decisions on this subject would be futile."[4] Rather, with not merely a risk but a certainty of oversimplification, what I shall try to do is this: passing somewhat rapidly over the initial grant of the minimum-rate power and its early years, I shall explain how the growth of competing modes of transportation gave it an importance unforeseen when the locomotive was king, and how Congress endeavored to update the grant in the Transportation Act of 1940. Survey of some relevant Commission cases and a mercifully short journey through the fog of "costs" will bring us to the most significant problem in this area — the prohibition of even a fully compensatory rate proposed by one mode of transport which would harmfully affect another. A detour through the Supreme Court decisions often argued to control Commission action will be followed by examination of the course of agency decision since 1940, the development of the Janus-faced amendment of 1958, a summary of what has happened since, and some consideration of where we go from here.

The Initial Grant

It is exceedingly doubtful that when Congress endowed the Commission with the minimum-rate power in Transportation

---

petitive Business Forces: The Obstacle Race in Transportation, 41 CORNELL L.Q. 57, 61 (1955); DOYLE REPORT 398; and the statements by Professors Williams and Fulda, quoted in notes 72, 73, 97, 98, *infra*. For a somewhat more generous view of the Commission's performance, see Jaffe, Book Review, 65 YALE L.J. 1068, 1072-73 (1956).

[3] WILLIAMS, THE REGULATION OF RAIL-MOTOR RATE COMPETITION (1958).

[4] Langdon, *supra* note 2, at 61. He adds that the decisions "cannot be fitted into a consistent pattern. Every case, or so it seems, has been handled on an individual basis, with varying standards, and the chances have been good that,

Act, 1920, anyone had any real conception of what lay ahead. True, the Commission had drawn attention, as far back as 1888, to the damage to the railroads and the public from unreasonably low rates and its inability to prevent these under section 3 of the act, for one reason because the carrier could remove an unlawful discrimination by reducing the higher rate rather than by raising the lower;[5] and the Commission had sought the minimum-rate power as early as 1893.[6] When this was granted twenty-seven years later, the House Committee made the not very illuminating comment that it was being given to enable the Commission to "prevent a rail carrier from reducing a rate out of proportion to the cost of service," and "from destroying water competition between competitive points."[7] Apparently Congress thought that if the Commission had been able to fix reasonable maximum rates, as the Commission had been doing with some success since the Hepburn Amendment of 1906, it ought to be able to fix minimum ones just as well. The distinction that the former resolved a conflict between individual shippers and monopolistic or oligopolistic power, a process with a tradition reaching back for many centuries into the common law, whereas the latter would limit the permissible bounds of competition among railroads and, as was later to become even more important, between railroads and other modes of transportation, seems not to have been adequately appreciated either by Congress or by the Commission. Indeed, in one of the first cases in which the minimum-rate power was invoked, the Commission, in seeking to ex-

---

once decided, the ICC report has not been cited as a precedent more than once or twice, if that often." *Ibid.*

[5] 2 ICC Ann. Rep. 19–24 (1888).

[6] 7 ICC Ann. Rep. 38–39 (1893), expressing the somewhat optimistic view, "We can anticipate no opposition to such legislation . . . ." The recommendation was repeated in the annual reports for 1897, 11 ICC Ann. Rep. 142–43 and 1898, 12 ICC Ann. Rep. 23–27, which brought out an additional reason why the Commission could not deal with the problem under § 3, namely, that the unduly low rate was often charged by a carrier not a party to the higher one.

[7] H.R. Rep. No. 456, 66th Cong., 1st Sess. 19 (1919).

plain why cost studies were not required, made what now appears the rather smug and somewhat naive statement that

> there is nothing in the act which either directs or implies that we should use tests of different general character in the determination of reasonable minimum rates than those which we have consistently and uniformly applied for many years, with the tacit consent and sanction of the Congress and the express approval of the courts, in fixing maximum reasonable rates.[8]

Until 1920 Congress had not instructed the Commission what it meant by "just and reasonable" rates. Simultaneously with the grant of the minimum-rate power, it enacted section 15a,[9] directing the Commission to establish

> such rates so that carriers . . . will, under honest, efficient and economical management and reasonable expenditures for maintenance of way, structures and equipment, earn an aggregate annual net railway operating income equal, as nearly as may be, to a fair return upon the aggregate value . . .

of their property, with the Commission having "reasonable latitude to modify or adjust any particular rate which it may find to be unjust or unreasonable." In 1933 this standard, which had never been attained, was altered; Congress directed the Commission to give

> due consideration, among other factors, to the effect of rates on the movement of traffic; to the need, in the public interest, of adequate and efficient railway transportation service at the lowest cost consistent with the furnishing of such service; and to the need of revenues sufficient to enable the carriers, under honest, economical, and efficient management, to provide such service.[10]

---

[8] Salt Cases of 1923, 92 I.C.C. 388, 410 (1924), *aff'd sub nom.* Jefferson Island Salt Mining Co. v. United States, 6 F.2d 315, 319 (N.D. Ohio 1925) (specifically approving this language).

[9] Transportation Act, 1920, ch. 91, § 422, 41 Stat. 488.

[10] Emergency Railroad Transportation Act, 1933, § 205(2), 48 Stat. 220 (now 49 U.S.C. § 15a(2)(1958)).

When motor carriers were brought under the Commission's jurisdiction two years later, the Commission was given a similar rate-making directive with respect to them.[11]

Intermodal Competition and the Transportation Act of 1940

Changes in the transport scene were to give the minimum-rate power an importance its framers had not surmised. For an analysis, we cannot do better than turn to the Commission's annual report for 1938 and, more particularly, to that for 1939, a year in which Mr. Eastman was Chairman and the report for which is rather clearly his work. The Commission told Congress of the new problems resulting from the "transportation revolution" which the country had "experienced . . . in a very short space of time," a revolution in which "the automotive highway vehicle has been the principal factor" but which had also included new water transportation, the extension of pipe lines, and the birth of air transport, and had been "characterized, also, by a tremendous growth of private transportation, as distinguished from common carriage for the public."[12] To the extent that the railway rate structure had been built on the principle of charging what the traffic will bear, more euphemistically described as "value of service,"[13] and had thereby "resulted in rates disproportionately high from a cost standpoint, it has provided opportunities for competitors that might not otherwise have existed."[14] Where "railroad freight rates have been considerably higher than cost of service would justify . . . the trucks and water lines have not been slow in availing themselves of these opportunities" to compete. In such cases the rails

[11] Motor Carrier Act, 1935, § 216(i), 49 Stat. 560, 49 U.S.C. § 317 (1958).
[12] 52 ICC Ann. Rep. 17 (1938).
[13] To me the former term has no invidious connotation, for reasons splendidly expressed in 1 ICC Ann. Rep. 30–31 (1887). See generally 3–B Sharfman 425–32; Locklin, Economics of Transportation 158 (4th ed. 1958).
[14] 52 ICC Ann. Rep. 19 (1938).

can make large reductions in their rates to meet the competition without going below full cost of service. On the other hand, they frequently make or propose reductions, particularly when competing on long hauls with water carriers or on less-than-carload traffic with trucks, where their only hope is to cover so-called out-of-pocket expense and perhaps a trifle more.[15]

The Commission described its problem as being

use [of] the minimum-rate power, so far as the law permits, to the best advantage for the purpose of eliminating the more destructive aspects of the competition and stabilizing the situation in such a way that, without injustice to any of the carriers, those whose operation is economically justified will have a better chance of earning a fair return.[16]

To permit this, "the best possible knowledge of full costs of service and also so-called out-of-pocket expense is essential."

However, as the Commission noted, in a masterpiece of understatement: "It is no simple thing to approximate the cost of a particular railroad service on a particular commodity . . . ." Although the railroads had not only resisted the attempt but declared it impracticable, the Commission had created and was expanding a cost-finding unit to that end. Yet "adequate knowledge of service costs . . . will not in itself determine how the minimum-rate power should be exercised." To allow one carrier always to meet the lower rates of another, which covered the latter's full costs of service, so long as the higher-cost carrier earned something over out-of-pocket costs, would mean that "most carriers would earn no more than a reasonable return on part of their traffic and much less on the rest." On the other hand, to prohibit all rates that did not meet full costs "would normally leave one type of carrier in possession of the traffic and exclude the other," which "would cause a rather high degree of carrier mortality."[17] The Commission ended on this note:

[15] 53 ICC Ann. Rep. 26–27 (1939).
[16] *Id.* at 27.
[17] *Id.* at 27–28.

We shall endeavor to the best of our ability to develop wise policies in the handling of these matters through the careful consideration of each particular situation as it comes before us for action. It may be that to some extent what is wise can only be determined through the process of trial and error.[18]

In the Transportation Act of 1940, which also brought interstate water carriers under the Commission's jurisdiction,[19] Congress endeavored to supply further guidance. It did so in three ways. The declaration of ratemaking principles as to rail and motor carriers, sections 15a(2) and 216(i), was amended in a significant respect, likewise embodied in the corresponding section, 307(f),[20] relating to water carriers — namely, that whereas the rail and motor sections had theretofore directed the Commission to consider "the effect of rates on the movement of traffic," the 1940 act added "by the carrier or carriers for which the rates are prescribed."[21] Second, the rail and motor sections dealing with discrimination and prejudice, 3(1) and 216(d), were amended and the corresponding water section, 305(c), was enacted, so as to include a proviso "that this paragraph shall not be construed to apply to discrimination, prejudice or disadvantage to the traffic of any other carrier of whatever description," the legislative history showing, as indeed the language makes sufficiently clear, that these sections did not forbid rates, otherwise proper, simply because they hurt a rival form of transportation.[22] Finally, the act was preceded by the *National Transportation Policy*;[23] charac-

---

[18] *Id.* at 29.
[19] 54 Stat. 929 (1940), 49 U.S.C. § 901 (1958).
[20] 54 Stat. 938 (1940), 49 U.S.C. § 907(f) (1958).
[21] 54 Stat. 912, 925, 938 (1940), 49 U.S.C. §§ 15a(2), 316(i), 907(f) (1958).
[22] 54 Stat. 902, 924, 935 (1940), 49 U.S.C. §§ 3(1), 316(d), 905(c) (1958). Professor Oppenheim points out that these amendments, like those to the ratemaking sections, "grew out of the insistent demands of the water carriers for safeguards against nullification of their inherent advantages by forcing their rates to the level of competing rail rates." THE NATIONAL TRANSPORTATION POLICY AND INTER-CARRIER COMPETITIVE RATES 51 (1945).
[23] 54 Stat. 899 (1940), 49 U.S.C. § 257 (1958):
  It is hereby declared to be the national transportation policy of the Con-

teristically, the *Policy* announces so many different and sometimes inconsistent goals as seriously to impair its usefulness. Still, the combination of the two changes in the specific provisions with the correlative mandate in the *National Transportation Policy* "to recognize and preserve the inherent advantages of each" [24] mode of transportation, leaves little doubt that a primary purpose was to protect each mode in exploiting its own peculiar abilities, surely among the most important of which is to offer a lower price to the shipper that yet will cover the carrier's costs.

There is, of course, a ghastly oversimplification in thus speaking of "costs" as if that term had some clear and unmistakable meaning. With respect to the rails, the definitions of costs claimed to be relevant for minimum-rate purposes spread over an enormous range. On the low side is the position, now rather rarely advanced and almost never upheld, that the only costs properly to be taken into account are those that would clearly not have been incurred if the particular shipment had not been hauled. Next come various more reasonable theories of "short-run added-cost" which include some share of direct, but common, operating expenses. In the middle of the spectrum is the "long-run out-of-pocket cost" of the Commission's Bureau of Accounts and Cost

---

gress to provide for fair and impartial regulation of all modes of transportation subject to the provisions of this Act, so administered as to recognize and preserve the inherent advantages of each; to promote safe, adequate, economical, and efficient service and foster sound economic conditions in transportation and among the several carriers; to encourage the establishment and maintenance of reasonable charges for transportation services, without unjust discrimination, undue preferences or advantages, or unfair or destructive competitive practices; to cooperate with the several States and the duly authorized officials thereof; and to encourage fair wages and equitable working conditions; — all to the end of developing, coordinating, and preserving a national transportation system by water, highway, and rail, as well as other means, adequate to meet the needs of the commerce of the United States, of the Postal Service, and of the national defense. All of the provisions of this Act shall be administered and enforced with a view to carrying out the above declaration of policy.

The legislative history of the *Policy* is set forth in OPPENHEIM, *op. cit. supra* note 22, at 4–15.

[24] This mandate is also expressed in the ratemaking section for motor carriers, Motor Carrier Act, 1935, § 216(i), 49 Stat. 560, 49 U.S.C. § 317 (1958).

Finding. To me this phrase is a poor piece of description, whether the economics underlying it be poor or good; the formula includes many items that ordinary minds would not consider "out-of-pocket" and omits only a few needed for a full distribution. At the upper range of the spectrum is a complete allocation of all costs, including taxes and a full return on investment, and sometimes even the deficit on other traffic that does not pay its way.[25] The range is much less in the case of motor transportation, since the relatively minor investment in fixed facilities and the comparatively small size of the vehicle generally cause added volume to be accompanied by an almost proportionate increase in expense. Still, as Commissioner Eastman said, "trucks and ships find plenty of opportunities for applying the . . . [added cost] theory, particularly in securing return loads when traffic preponderates in one direction." [26]

There has been fair uniformity in the use of the minimum-rate power, both before and after the Transportation Act of 1940, in at least one situation — some would say it is the only one. The Commission will not allow rates to be established or maintained "unless they cover, and more than cover, the out-of-pocket expenses of providing the service in question." [27] When only short-

[25] See generally U.S. Bureau of Accounts and Cost Finding, ICC, Explanation of Rail Cost Finding Procedures and Principles Relating to the Use of Costs, Statement No. 2–48 (1948). The DOYLE REPORT, at 410, states:
Rail form A long-run out-of-pocket cost has been defined to include 80 percent of operating expenses, rents, and taxes, and includes, in addition, an allowance for return at 4 percent on 50 percent of road property and on 100 percent of equipment. In other words, an allowance of 2 percent on the total value of road property and 4 percent on the total value of equipment is provided for.
This formula does not include a small "non-variable" portion of operating expenses, rents, taxes, and return, or the deficits on losing operations, notably the passenger service. For a helpful summary of the Commission's costing techniques, one of the few ever attempted by the courts, see Judge Hincks's opinion in the *Sea-Land* case, New York, N.H. & H.R.R. v. United States, 199 F. Supp. 635, 647–48 (D. Conn. 1961).
[26] Eastman, *The Adjustment of Rates Between Competing Forms of Transportation*, 7 I.C.C. PRAC. J. 190, 193 (1940).
[27] Locklin, *Rates and Rate Structure*, in U.S. NATIONAL RESOURCES PLANNING

run out-of-pocket costs are meant, the reasons are too obvious to require discussion. However, the Commission has gradually transformed this standard to refer to "long-run out-of-pocket costs" and these, I must reemphasize, include much more than that phrase would convey to the uninitiated.

What if the rate exceeds long-run out-of-pocket costs but fails by an appreciable margin to meet fully distributed costs? In one leading case the Commission refused to outlaw such rates, saying:

> Rates that are depressed to meet competition, as is here the case, when they cover much more than the out-of-pocket costs, may, because of the traffic they attract, make a greater contribution toward the indirect or constant costs than higher rates that would meet the fully distributed costs. In other words, a small contribution per unit on a large volume of traffic may yield greater revenue than a large unit contribution on a small volume.[28]

BD., TRANSPORTATION AND NATIONAL POLICY 87, 108 (1942), citing Cocoanut Oil From Pac. Coast to Eastbound Transcontinental Destinations, 167 I.C.C. 599 (1930), and Ex-Lake Grain to No. Atl. Ports, 235 I.C.C. 415 (1939). See generally Commissioner Eastman's statement dissenting in Pick-Up and Delivery in Official Territory, 218 I.C.C. 441, 492 (1936). Perhaps one should add, as another clear case, that rates which themselves are not below reasonable minima will be proscribed "if they result in the creation of undue preference and prejudice or unjust discrimination." Locklin, *supra* at 109.

With respect to motor carriers the Commission takes a dim view of rates yielding only added costs, even for back-hauls; although carriage of such traffic might appear beneficial for the individual trucker, "an unbalanced condition of truck traffic, because of the greater number of operators [than the railroads], is apt to be somewhat of an individual matter" and use of such a rate by all operators "might well result in a break-down of the rates in both directions." Refrigerator Material From Memphis, Tenn., to Dayton, Ohio, 4 M.C.C. 187, 189 (1938). The only exception is "that if the railroads are hereafter to be allowed to apply this [added cost] theory in competing with the trucks, the latter must fairly be allowed equal leeway." *Id.* at 190. The "equal leeway" theory was applied in Stoves From Ala. & Tenn. to Interstate Points, 4 M.C.C. 641, 649 (1938), along with an admonition "that the railroads and motor carriers should put their houses in order and avoid this destructive competition."

[28] Petroleum Haulers of New England, 269 I.C.C. 6, 20 (1947); see International Minerals & Chem. Corp., 269 I.C.C. 611, 625 (1948).

In other cases it appears to have taken a radically different view.[29] Perhaps, however, the decisions may not really be so inconsistent as they seem; close analysis might show that some apparent differences in result actually reflect only differences in cost terminology or failures in proof. The issue is important since the railroads maintain that their ability to handle traffic at more than out-of-pocket costs, although at considerably less than fully distributed costs, not only without impairment of their general financial position but with some improvement in it, is an "inherent advantage" the Commission is bound to recognize under the *National Transportation Policy*;[30] however, I cannot tarry over this, since the "inherent advantage" area presents another problem even more intriguing, and more readily intelligible to lawyers. This is whether the Commission may and, if it may, should forbid a proposed reduced rate that covers even fully distributed costs, either because the reduction will hurt other modes of transport too much, or because in its view this traffic should absorb a larger proportion of the deficits of other forms. The typical case is when

[29] Thus, in Middle Atl. States Motor Carrier Conference, Inc., 232 I.C.C. 381, 391 (1939), the Commission said: "Whatever validity the added-traffic theory of rate-making may have had some years ago, we think it has very little today," in view of the great volume of traffic "moving at submaximum rates" established "to stimulate traffic or to prevent its diversion to other forms of transportation." The statements in this case were quoted and followed in All Commodities, Less Than Carloads, Between Me., Mass., & N.H., 255 I.C.C. 85, 88 (1942). It may be significant that both these cases dealt with "all-freight" or "all-commodity" rates. See generally Eastman, *supra* note 26, at 193; Roberts, *The Regulation of Transport Price Competition*, 24 LAW & CONTEMP. PROB. 557, 560–64 (1959).

[30] Note, *Minimum-Rate Regulation by the Interstate Commerce Commission*, 73 HARV. L. REV. 762, 766–68 (1960), agrees with this. In Lumber From Cal. & Ore. to Cal. & Ariz., 308 I.C.C. 345 (1959), decided after the Transportation Act of 1958, discussed pp. 131–136 *infra*, the majority disapproved certain rates that were less than out-of-pocket costs "restated" to include "the variable portion of all taxes" and a 4% return on the "variable portion" of investment, to-wit, 50% of road property and 100% of equipment. *Id.* at 362–63. Three Commissioners dissented from this upward adjustment, which increased out-of-pocket costs by 23% to 26%. See also WILLIAMS, *op. cit. supra* note 3, at 38. The injunction in the *Sea-Land* case was only against the cancellation of rail rates "which return at least the fully-distributed cost of carriage." 199 F. Supp. at 646.

a railroad seeks to reduce its tariffs on high-rated traffic that is being or is threatened with being lost, sometimes to another mode of transport regulated by the act and sometimes to a mode that is not.

Supreme Court Opinions

A survey of some Supreme Court opinions is a desirable preliminary to an inquiry into this problem. For the Commission's exercise of the minimum-rate power in this controversial area has been conditioned by judicial pronouncements claimed to have decided far more than they did, and by what seems an administrative tendency to consider that the power may wisely be exercised whenever the Commission thinks the courts would think it might lawfully be.

The Supreme Court first spoke on the minimum-rate power in 1933, when it said, in a case relating to port differentials, that where the evidence failed to show that proposed rates "were not compensatory" and "the Commission refused to find that they were so low as to cast a burden on other traffic," there was "no basis for an order fixing minimum reasonable rates." [31] Properly enough, there has been little attempt to argue from these vague statements. The rates were not claimed to be less than reasonable minima, and the opinion said: "The parties agree that authority for the order must be found in § 3(1)." Since the majority was only laying a ghost to rest, it was not required to use a very sharp blade.[32]

---

[31] Texas & P. Ry. v. United States, 289 U.S. 627, 633 (1933). This language seems opposed to the decision in Jefferson Island Salt Mining Co. v. United States, 6 F.2d 315, 318–19 (N.D. Ohio 1925), and to some statements, although not to the decision, in Anchor Coal Co. v. United States, 25 F.2d 462, 471–72 (S.D.W. Va. 1928), rev'd as moot, 279 U.S. 812 (1929). It was followed in New York Cent. R.R. v. United States, 99 F. Supp. 394, 398 (D. Mass.), aff'd per curiam, 342 U.S. 890 (1951).

[32] 289 U.S. at 633. Perhaps the majority thought the reference necessary because of Mr. Justice Stone's statement in dissent, 289 U.S. at 669:

And now that the Commission has power under § 15(1) to fix a minimum rate it may equally command the removal of the discrimination by directing

The next relevant Supreme Court opinion, if opinion it can be called, is *Scandrett v. United States*,[33] dealing with the Commission's much-debated report, rendered in 1939, in *Petroleum Between Wash., Ore., Idaho, Mont.*[34] There the Commission had refused to allow the railroads to establish a 25-cent rate per 100 pounds on petroleum products from North Pacific ports to interior points, found to be "compensatory, considering all costs," which the rails had proposed in order to meet river-truck competition. Defining its problem as being "to determine what incentive the rail lines must afford . . . to create that equality of opportunity which should fairly apportion the traffic between the rail lines and the river-truck routes," [35] the Commission required the rail carriers to increase the rate to the level, 28.5 cents, which it considered to be the minimum reasonable rate that river-truck competition would ultimately charge. The report included the thought that the agency's "duty in the exercise of that [minimum-rate] power is not done . . . if we allow competitive rates to gravitate to the lowest possible level." [36]

A three judge court denied an injunction by a two-to-one vote. Each judge wrote a separate opinion. Circuit Judge Haney con-

---

a rate to be raised, just as where the carrier maintains discriminatory practices the Commission may direct the modification of one and not the other, and is not bound to allow the carrier a choice.

However, this was directed to the contention that the Commission lacked power to act because the carriers alleged to be in violation of § 3(1) did not "control" the joint rates; see Central R.R. of N.J. v. United States, 257 U.S. 247 (1921). The three-judge court, whose decision upholding the order was reversed, had not relied on the minimum-rate power. See 42 F.2d 281 (S.D. Tex. 1930).

[33] 312 U.S. 661 (1941), *affirming per curiam* 32 F. Supp. 995 (D. Ore. 1940). The Court had meanwhile dealt with the minimum-rate power in United States v. Chicago, M., St. P. & P. R. Co., 294 U.S. 499 (1935), and in Youngstown Sheet & Tube Co. v. United States, 295 U.S. 476 (1935), but these cases did not present the type of problem here considered.

[34] 234 I.C.C. 609 (1939). For discussion of the Commission and court decisions, see Locklin, *supra* note 27, at 119–20, and OPPENHEIM, *op. cit. supra* note 22, at 91–93.

[35] 234 I.C.C. at 624.

[36] *Id.* at 637.

sidered that, in view of the policy declared in section 500 of Transportation Act, 1920, "to foster and preserve in full vigor both rail and water transportation" and in section 202 of the Motor Carrier Act, the Commission could use the minimum-rate power to prevent the railroads from destroying water-truck competition and to equalize "by differentials, the prospects or opportunities for procuring traffic"; however, his opinion also relied on the absence of any finding that the twenty-five cent rate would yield a fair return "and therefore a conflicting public interest does not appear." [37] District Judge McColloch, concurring, went further; he thought no one could

> question the Commission's power under the statutory mandate to coordinate transportation by rail and truck, to attempt an equitable apportionment of the traffic involved between the railroads and the trucks, even though this results incidentally in help and protection of a decisive nature to intermediate unregulated water carriers.[38]

Such a negative prediction is always dangerous; in a vigorous dissent Judge Fee, then a district judge, did precisely what his colleague thought no one ever could.

The Supreme Court affirmed per curiam. The only clues to its reasons are references to "Interstate Commerce Act, §§ 15(1); 15a(2)," and to "*United States* v. *Louisiana*, 290 U.S. 70, 75–77; *Florida* v. *United States*, 292 U.S. 1, 9." The cited decisions do not go to the basic issue, although relevant to a subsidiary point. Insofar as one can glean anything from the section references, it would be that the Court, although not impressed with the equalization-of-opportunity argument, for which other sections would have had to be mentioned, was picking up Judge Haney's final suggestion with respect to fair return; in other words, that, un-

---

[37] 32 F. Supp. at 998, 999, 1000. I am unable to follow the "therefore"; I should think the public had a legitimate interest in lower rates, yielding some margin over all costs, which the rail carriers were willing to establish even though they could not have been compelled to do so.

[38] 32 F. Supp. at 1001. (Footnote omitted.)

der the act as it stood before 1940, the Commission could lawfully set as a minimum any rate not higher than what it could lawfully set as a maximum.

Apologists for the Commission might say that with this cavalier treatment of a report that had provoked so much debate among the *cognoscenti* and such division in the court below, it is no wonder the Commission floundered. Doubtless one reason for the Supreme Court's failing to write more fully was that, by the time *Scandrett* reached it, the Transportation Act of 1940 had become effective. The changes in the ratemaking and discrimination sections made by that act, noted above, weakened the case for action by the Commission like that under review; Professor Oppenheim thinks the *National Transportation Policy* made it stronger, or at least left it as strong.[39] To me that is not so plain; one needs to ask just what element in the *Policy* gave the power to proscribe a rate more than covering all costs, in terms sufficiently clear to overcome the thrust of the changes in the rate and discrimination sections. One element in the *Policy*, as already noted, appears to work in the same direction as those changes; the ability to carry the traffic at the desired rate and still cover all expenses, with something left over, would seem an "inherent advantage" of the carrier proposing the rate, especially, although perhaps not only, when it is the low-cost carrier on a fully allocated cost basis.[40] Taking other elements in the *Policy*, I find it hard to see why such a rate fails "to promote safe, adequate, economical, and efficient service and foster sound economic conditions in transportation and among the several carriers," or "to encourage the establishment and maintenance of reasonable charges for transportation services," unless "reasonable" means that even under the revised ratemaking section,

---

[39] *Op. cit. supra* note 22, at 90–93. He lists five "Theories and Methods of Inter-Carrier Rate Adjustments Presumptively Compatible with National Transportation Policy," and four "Presumptively Incompatible." See *id.* at 83–88.

[40] See Locklin, *supra* note 27, at 117; New York, N.H. & H.R.R. v. United States, 199 F. Supp. at 639–40 (D. Conn. 1961).

15a(2), the Commission may require a rate that not only will cover all expenses but will yield a full return in theory even though the carrier justifiably believes a lesser rate will yield a larger return in fact, in which event section 15(1) does the job alone without the need of help from the *Policy*, as the enigmatic *Scandrett* per curiam may be argued to indicate. Neither is it easy to conclude that a rate more than covering all expenses is a "destructive competitive practice." As Judge Hincks has recently said for the District Court for Connecticut in the *Sea-Land* case, although "It well may be that for the higher-cost mode to jeopardize the continued existence of the lower-cost mode by setting rates below the costs of each, could be characterized as a 'destructive competitive practice' . . . ,"[41] that can hardly be so when the challenged rates are compensatory and the proponent is the low-cost mode.[42] Hence we reach the question whether the final exhortation that all powers are to be used "to the end of developing, coordinating, and preserving a national transportation system by water, highway, and rail, as well as other means" adequate for the nation's needs, is itself a grant conditioning or even superseding all that has gone before.[43]

The Supreme Court has not yet been required to decide this, although perhaps it shortly will be, on review of the *Sea-Land* decision.[44] *Eastern-Central Motor Carriers Ass'n v. United*

---

[41] *Id.* at 641.

[42] *Id.* at 644–45. *But cf.* New York Cent. R.R. v. United States, 194 F. Supp. 947 (S.D.N.Y. 1961), *aff'd per curiam*, 368 U.S. 349 (1962), affirming the Commission's proscription of a compensatory rate which had the additional factor of what came near to being a tying clause.

[43] Professor Oppenheim argues that it is precisely that, *op. cit. supra* note 22, at 53–54. A contrary view is indicated by Judge Hincks's comment, in *Sea-Land*, that the final statement is not one of "an operative policy or means" but rather "only . . . the hoped-for 'end' of the operative policy-factors previously enumerated." 199 F. Supp. at 645 (D. Conn. 1961).

The *Scandrett* case was cited, after the 1940 act, in New York v. United States, 331 U.S. 284, 345–46 (1947).

[44] Lower court decisions, antedating *Sea-Land* and not making Judge Hincks's characteristically thorough analysis, gave a broad interpretation to the Commission's power under the *National Transportation Policy*. See Pacific Inland Tariff

States,[45] on which Professor Oppenheim placed primary reliance for a broad construction of the effect of the *National Transportation Policy*, hardly supports all he draws from it. The Commission had there rejected reduced motor carrier rates based on a 30,000 pound minimum, admittedly compensatory and within the zone of reasonableness,[46] on the bases that the motor carriers had shown no savings at the 30,000 pound level to warrant the differential below a higher rate at a 20,000 minimum which was the carrying capacity of the trucks, and that the reduction would thus discriminate against truck shippers in the range between 20,000 and 30,000 pounds. The Court held the Commission was not justified in doing this without considering whether the reduced rates were not needed to permit truckers to compete with railroads at the 30,000 pound level. One may readily agree that the logic of *Eastern-Central* would not compel the Court to prohibit the Commission from prohibiting a railroad's establishing a rate, covering all costs, that would hurt truckers or water carriers too much. But it requires alchemy more powerful than mine to transmute a decision disapproving the prohibition of a compensatory rate under the circumstances there presented into an authority approving such a prohibition in others. Despite the discursiveness of the opinion, about all that was held was that the Commission could not proscribe a rate as discriminatory between shippers without considering whether the discrimination was warranted because of competition from other types of transport; that was hardly an epoch-making pronouncement.[47]

Bureau v. United States, 129 F. Supp. 472 (D. Ore. 1955); Cantlay & Tanzola, Inc. v. United States, 115 F. Supp. 72 (S.D. Cal. 1953); Atlanta & St. A.B. Ry. v. United States, 104 F. Supp. 193 (M.D. Ala. 1952); *cf.* Columbia Transp. Co. v. United States, 167 F. Supp. 5 (E.D. Mich. 1958).

[45] 321 U.S. 194 (1944).
[46] 321 U.S. at 199.
[47] The case had a rather inglorious ending, being dismissed as moot on a showing by the respondents that they no longer had rates subject to a 30,000 pound minimum. Rugs and Matting from the East to Western Trunk Line Territory, 43 M.C.C. 540 (1944).

Neither is the Commission's power to proscribe a fully compensatory rate in any way decided by the oft-cited opinion in *ICC v. Mechling*,[48] outlawing higher joint-rail rates east of Chicago for ex-barge than ex-lake or ex-rail grain. The mere statement should suffice to show that the case did not involve the minimum-rate power — the case was one where the Court disapproved the Commission's approval of a rate the Court thought too high, not one where the Court either approved or disapproved the Commission's action as to a rate claimed to be too low. The bases for the Court's action lay in section 2,[49] forbidding different charges for "a like and contemporaneous service in the transportation of a like kind of traffic under substantially similar circumstances and conditions," and in section 3(4),[50] forbidding a carrier to discriminate in "rates, fares, and charges between connecting lines," which had been amended specifically to include water carriers. All this would have seemed almost too clear for argument but for the provision in section 307(d) [51] authorizing the Commission to "prescribe such reasonable differentials as it may find to be justified between all-rail rates and the joint rates in connection with such common carrier by water." The majority held this was not a charter to raise the rail portion of a joint rail-water rate so as to deprive the barge line of the advantage stemming from the lower cost and rates on its portion.[52] Again any bearing of the

---

[48] 330 U.S. 567 (1947).
[49] 24 Stat. 380 (1887), as amended, 49 U.S.C. § 2 (1958).
[50] 54 Stat. 903–04 (1940), 49 U.S.C. § 3(4) (1958).
[51] 54 Stat. 937 (1940), 49 U.S.C. § 907(d) (1958). Mr. Justice Jackson dissenting, 330 U.S. at 584, also argued that the majority was flouting the new mandate in 54 Stat. 938 (1940), 49 U.S.C. § 907 (f) (1958), directing the Commission to consider "the effect of rates upon the movement of traffic by the carrier or carriers for which the rates are prescribed." The majority did not deign to make the fairly obvious answer that charging the same ex-barge as ex-rail or ex-lake rate would not affect the carriers east of Chicago, whose portion of the rate was at issue; its effect would be on the rail and lake carriers west of Chicago.
[52] In Alabama G.S.R.R. v. United States, 340 U.S. 216 (1951), the Court sustained the Commission in prescribing through barge-rail rates lower than the through all-rail rates, with the barges absorbing the differential so that the rail carrier received the same rate ex-barge as ex-rail, *Mechling* being distinguished

case on our problem is not in the decision but in the language, where the Court said it was "not within the province of the Commission to adjust rates . . . to protect the traffic of railroads from barge competition," since "Congress left the Commission no discretionary power to approve any type of rates which would reduce the 'inherent advantage' of barge transportation . . . ."[53] Naturally this is sweet music to the water carriers, who read it, quite exaggeratedly it seems to me, as giving the Commission almost unlimited power to proscribe competitive rail rates. However, the rails find comfort in it too, simply substituting "motor or water carriers" for "railroads" in the first quotation and "railroad" for "barge" in both. Since in *Mechling*, one type of carrier, the railroads, was trying to deprive a second, the barge lines, of the latter's "inherent advantage" by a discriminatorily higher rail rate on ex-barge grain rather than to realize on their own inherent advantages as in proposed reductions in rail rates, the second quotation has to be rewritten, in order fully to perform the railroads' office, to say that Congress "left the Commission no discretionary power to [dis]approve any type of rates which would reduce the 'inherent advantage' of [rail] transportation." Whether the Court would go along with such a revision remains to be seen.

My conclusion is that not only did the Supreme Court never decide whether, under the 1940 act, the Commission had power to proscribe a rate that was fully compensatory and otherwise lawful, solely because of its adverse effect on another form of transportation, but that there is not even a dictum that would in any way have restrained the Court's freedom of decision.[54] Although such a harvest may seem meager, perhaps, in view of all that has been written about these cases, it is not entirely barren.

---

on the basis that "Here the question is whether the barge lines may charge less than the railroads for the different service they render." *Id.* at 227.

[53] 330 U.S. at 579.

[54] The later cases in the area, Dixie Carriers, Inc. v. United States, 351 U.S. 56 (1956), and Arrow Transp. Co. v. United States, 176 F. Supp. 411 (N.D. Ala. 1959), *aff'd per curiam sub nom.* State Corp. Comm'n v. Arrow Transp. Co., 361 U.S. 353 (1960), do not require discussion.

Unlike the Court, the Commission has had to grapple with the problem; let us see what it has done.

The Commission's Decisions Under the 1940 Act

The Commission's first important decision under the 1940 act was the *Seatrain* case.[55] There the Commission, modifying a decision taken prior to 1940,[56] refused to permit the continuation of differentially higher rates for the rail portion of a rail-water service wherein cars were placed directly on the ship than for a break-bulk service, the differential being sought to compensate for other costs to shippers incident to the break-bulk service and its consequent lower "value." Noting that since its earlier decision the ratemaking rules had been modified so as to require it to consider "the effect of rates upon the movement of traffic *by the carrier or carriers for which the rates are prescribed* . . . ," the Commission said that the meaning of the amendment

> supported also by the legislative history, seems to be that no carrier should be required to maintain rates which would be unreasonable, judged by other standards, for the purpose of protecting the traffic of a competitor.[57]

This language seemed, indeed, a victory for the position of the railways; perhaps they read into it more than was warranted.[58] To permit a railroad to charge a higher price for exactly the same service when rendered in connection with Seatrain than with the break-bulk water carriers would have been strong medicine; this was the very kind of discrimination that *Mechling* later required the Commission to prevent.[59] Moreover, the Commission's phrase, "which would be unreasonable, judged by other stand-

---

[55] Seatrain Lines, Inc., 243 I.C.C. 199 (1940) (opinion by Commissioner Eastman).
[56] Seatrain Lines, Inc., 226 I.C.C. 7 (1938).
[57] 243 I.C.C. at 214.
[58] See Langdon, *The Regulation of Competitive Business Forces: The Obstacle Race in Transportation*, 41 CORNELL L.Q. 57, 61–63 (1955).
[59] See pp. 124–125 *supra*.

ards," may not mean what it seems at first to mean. To be sure, a rate covering all costs is generally not "unreasonable," but the question whether "other standards" may not allow the Commission to hold a rate unreasonably low if the rate does not also include a fair return on investment or obtain the highest reasonable contribution from the particular traffic [60] is often the very point at issue when the Commission is asked to proscribe a "compensatory" rate.

However, the pronouncement against "umbrella" ratemaking which the railroads thought the Commission had made in *Seatrain*, it apparently did seek to make five years later, in *New Automobiles in Interstate Commerce*.[61] The issue was whether the rails should be required to increase, to the truck level, rates for new automobiles which yielded something between out-of-pocket and fully distributed costs — a course that would divert further traffic to the trucks because of the latter's generally more convenient service; the answer was "No." The context makes clear that *New Automobiles* was intended to be an important policy pronouncement — to do for the minimum-rate power in 1945 what Judge Cooley had done for the fourth section in 1887. Unhappily the performance did not approach the standard Judge Cooley set.

The discussion begins by saying that "what constitutes a minimum reasonable rate is a matter to be determined in the light of the facts of record in each individual case, avoiding arbitrary action and keeping within statutory and constitutional limitations . . ." — the sort of invocation that is not usually the harbinger of much enlightenment in the sermon to come. There follows a comprehensive list of factors to be considered in fixing minimum rates, some debatable and several contradictory. The Commission next traced the history down to the 1940 act, which it

---

[60] Commissioner Aitchison, concurring, carefully preserved the latter point: "But the worth of the service to the user must always be given serious consideration." 243 I.C.C. at 223.

[61] 259 I.C.C. 475 (1945). For much that follows, see *id.* at 530–40.

characterized as having brought about the "fundamental changes in policy" described in *Seatrain*. That decision and two cases in which the Commission refused to increase the rates of contract motor carriers above their costs in order to benefit common carriers [62] were cited to show the Commission's "views respecting the policy of the law subsequent to the Transportation Act of 1940." It was recognized that "there have been occasional deviations" of differing degrees of culpability; [63] other cases were cited as properly following *Seatrain*.[64] After quoting from a motor carrier case [65] which had said that "the predominant element to be considered" with respect to rates challenged as below a reasonable minimum is "whether they are reasonably compensatory" and defining the latter term to mean a rate "which is remunerative, i.e., covers the out-of-pocket costs, as hereinbefore defined, of handling the particular traffic under consideration, including a proper return on investment," the Commission stated, in a passage to be much quoted thereafter, that "the rates of

---

[62] Contract Minimum Charges From & to Baltimore, Md., 32 M.C.C. 273, *modified on reconsideration*, 41 M.C.C. 435 (1942); New England Motor Rate Bureau, Inc., 30 M.C.C. 651 (1941).

[63] Most of these were explained as resulting from the change, made by the 1940 act, placing on the carrier who proposed a reduced rate the burden of showing it was just and reasonable; it is not clear why, if the carriers had failed to meet the statutory burden, such decisions were a "deviation." Similarly confusing is the listing as "deviations" of a case, Petroleum Prods. Between Kan., Okla., Ark., Mo., & Colo., 245 I.C.C. 617 (1941), in which the carriers threatened "to destroy a reasonable rate structure, and failed to show that such reduced rates were compensatory," and another, All Commodities, Less Than Carloads, Between Me., Mass., & N.H., 255 I.C.C. 85 (1942), in which the reduced rates ordered to be cancelled were "in most instances considerably lower than the costs on a fully distributed basis, without return on investment, and in all instances were below such costs including a return on the freight portion of the valuation." Still another case, Petroleum From So. Atl. Ports to Southeast, 245 I.C.C. 23 (1941), was branded as a deviation, relapsing to the decision affirmed by the Supreme Court in *Scandrett* and without extenuating circumstances.

[64] Automobiles From Memphis to Ark. & La., 245 I.C.C. 334 (1941); Automobiles From Evansville, Ind., to the So., 245 I.C.C. 339 (1941).

[65] Freight, All Kinds, Between Lincoln, Omaha, & Neb. Points, 32 M.C.C. 339, 344 (1942).

each . . . agency should be determined by us in each case according to the facts and circumstances attending the movement of the traffic by that agency" and rejected the motor carriers' plea that it prescribe rates for one form of transportation necessary to preserve "the inherent advantage in respect of service" of another form.[66]

Apart from the confusing remarks already noted, *New Automobiles* suffered from a congenital schizophrenia. How was the final pronouncement "that the rates of each . . . agency should be determined by us in each case according to the facts and circumstances attending the movement of the traffic by that agency" to be reconciled with the prelude listing a number of other issues that might require consideration, especially whether the proposed rate "represents competition that is unduly destructive to a reasonable rate structure and to the carriers . . . ."?[67] Quite naturally, the railroads said the conclusion overcame the introduction;[68] just as naturally, the water and motor carriers contended the conclusion applied only to the particular case.[69] Although the Commission's evident intent to say something important made the rails' argument more persuasive, there was enough in the opposition's case so that the lesson thought to have been taught by *New Automobiles* was soon eroded.

The principal eroding agent was the resurgence of the "not lower than necessary" principle, which had often been applied prior to 1940, *e.g.*, in the *Petroleum* decision giving rise to *Scandrett*.[70] This was that a rate should not be reduced to a level

---

[66] 259 I.C.C. at 538–39. Eastern-Central Motor Carriers Ass'n v. United States, 321 U.S. 194 (1944), relied on by the motor carriers, was turned against them by the Commission. See *id.* at 540.

[67] *Id.* at 534.

[68] See, *e.g.*, Langdon, *supra* note 58, at 66.

[69] Ames, *The Transportation Act of 1958*, 26 ICC PRAC. J. 656, 666–68 (1959).

[70] The concept seems to have originated in cases applying the 1920 amendment to § 4 forbidding the Commission to permit a lower rate for the longer haul "not reasonably compensatory for the service performed." See pp. 33–34 *supra*. It has been argued that whether or not this was a reasonable interpretation in the light of the special purposes of § 4, it was an error to carry this over into the

lower than necessary "to regain or to retain a fair share" of the traffic, although an even lower rate, still "remunerative" as defined in *New Automobiles*, would get a larger share — such action was said to constitute "an unfair and destructive practice."[71] Another eroding factor has been the occasional disposition of the Commission to refuse to sanction a lower but fully compensatory rate on what had been high-rated traffic, simply on the ground that the reduced rate "would place an undue transportation burden on [the carrier's] other traffic," *i.e.*, that the Commission thought the railroads could get more.[72]

Assuming without deciding — to use a familiar and useful phrase — that both these doctrines lay within the Commission's power, they defy the canon that a principle of administrative adjudication ought be susceptible of intelligible statement and uniform application. Each gave rise to a host of subsidiary

---

field of minimum rates in general. See Langdon, *The Regulation of Competitive Business Forces: The Obstacle Race in Transportation*, 41 CORNELL L.Q. 57, 87–89 (1955).

[71] See, *e.g.*, Scrap Tobacco From Newark, N.J., to Selma, Ala., 293 I.C.C. 427, 428–30 (1954); Pig Lead From Tex. to E. St. Louis & St. Louis, 292 I.C.C. 797 (1954). In Petroleum Prods. in Ill. Territory, 280 I.C.C. 681, 691 (1951), the Commission insisted on rail rates which, for longer distances, were well above fully distributed costs, since the lower rates proposed "would reverse the present situation and deprive the tank-truck operators of a fair opportunity to compete with the respondents," and "being lower than necessary to meet the competition, . . . would result in an undue burden upon the respondents' other traffic." In Petroleum Prods. in Cal. & Ore., 284 I.C.C. 287, 304 (1952), it disapproved reductions conceived to be "lower than necessary to meet the competition encountered" although covering direct costs and contributing "substantially to the overhead burden and profits." Many similar decisions could be cited. See, *e.g.*, Aluminum Articles From Tex. to Ill. & Iowa, 293 I.C.C. 467 (1954); Scrap Rails From So. Ports to Chicago, 283 I.C.C. 357 (1951); Tobacco From N.C. Points to So. Points (Rail), 280 I.C.C. 767, 773 (1951).

[72] See, *e.g.*, Manufactured Tobacco From Va. & N.C. to Official Points, 293 I.C.C. 133, 141–42 (1954). Professor Williams criticizes this decision in THE REGULATION OF RAIL-MOTOR RATE COMPETITION 199 (1958):

> The proposition of avoiding depressed earnings and burdens upon other traffic has no relation to the rail carriers where, as here appears, a highly remunerative traffic was rapidly deserting them. . . . The loss of the traffic necessarily casts a burden upon other traffic which would be avoided at a compensatory rate sufficiently low to secure a good portion of the business.

questions, perhaps unanswerable in any understandable fashion and surely unanswered. How low is "necessary"? Is it the same rate as the rival carrier's, a lower rate which takes account of the latter's service advantages, or a higher rate which allows for service advantages of the proponent? Must it allow for such advantages in full or only in part? The Commission has been on all sides.[73] How much more than a fully compensatory rate may the Commission require simply because it believes the traffic will bear this? Does not the cry of interference with management prerogatives, which the railroads have surely sounded too often, here ring true? Is not the Commission's policy questionable from a public interest standpoint — by what right does it deny a shipper a lower rate, voluntarily offered, that will yield the carrier all costs and even some return? If the answer be that the Commission has a responsibility to maximize profits for the transportation system as a whole, at least that ought to be articulated and the necessary findings made. Hardest of all, what share of the traffic is "fair"? Is it an existing but very likely depressed share, a former higher share, a fifty-fifty share? A king whose name has become synonymous with wisdom presumed to make such a decision only with good assurance he would not have to go through with it; the Commission might have been wiser to follow his lead.

The Transportation Act of 1958

Although, in customary administrative fashion, the Commission's journey away from *New Automobiles* and back to the *Petroleum* decision there condemned, was unacknowledged, it was not unrecognized. The railroads made the swerve a prime subject of complaint to the Presidential Advisory Committee on

---

[73] See *id.* at 44:
   The attitude of the Commission has not been fixed and certain. In some instances it has ignored service differences and insisted upon rate parity, or at least disapproved rail reductions below the motor-carrier basis. In other instances it has permitted differentials. And in a number of cases it has permitted rail rates below motor rates by the amount of the proved added costs to the shipper of using rail service.

Transport Policy and Organization, headed by the Secretary of Commerce, whose report in 1955 [74] led ultimately to the Transportation Act of 1958.[75] The evolution is most instructive.

The Advisory Committee recommended:

> The declaration of policy should be revised to make it clear (1) that common carriers are to be permitted greater freedom, short of discriminatory practices, to utilize their economic capabilities in the competitive pricing of their service, and (2) that in all such matters the regulatory Commission is expected to act as an adjudicator, not a business manager.[76]

This was pretty vague; somewhat more precision was afforded in a supplemental memorandum:

> Under the proposed rule of ratemaking, the Commission would not be entitled to declare that such a rate was unlawful merely because it fell below rates currently in effect in the tariffs of competitors, or merely because it might have adverse effects upon competitors. Indeed, the Commission would not be entitled to take into consideration at all the level of rates of competitors or the effect of the proposed rates upon competitors.[77]

Ultimately these views were crystallized in a proposed addition to section 15a of the Interstate Commerce Act, colloquially termed the "three-shall-nots." [78] This provided that in determining whether a proposed rate was less than a reasonable minimum, the Commission shall not consider (1) "the effect of such charge

---

[74] See *Hearings on the Report of the Presidential Advisory Committee on Transport Policy and Organization Before the Subcommittee on Transportation and Communications of the House Committee on Interstate and Foreign Commerce*, 84th Cong., 1st Sess. 3-15 (1955).

[75] 72 Stat. 568 (codified in scattered sections of 49 U.S.C.).

[76] *Hearings on the Report of the Presidential Advisory Committee on Transport Policy and Organization*, supra note 74, at 8. The Advisory Committee stated its belief that "rates are unreasonably low when not compensatory, i.e., when they fail to cover the direct ascertainable cost of producing the service to which the rates apply." *Id.* at 9.

[77] *Id.* at 53.

[78] See H.R. 6141, 6142, 84th Cong., 1st Sess. (1955).

on the traffic of any other mode of transportation"; (2) "the relation of such charge to the charge of any other mode of transportation"; or (3) "whether such charge is lower than necessary to meet the competition of any other mode of transportation." Here was sunlight for the railroads; the storm was not long in coming.

Before the thunder had ceased, the Secretary of Commerce had reconsidered the "three-shall-not" rule and decided "that it goes too far"; [79] he recommended that instead Congress should restrict the Commission's power to consider the effect on a competitor in fixing a minimum rate to cases "where its effect might be substantially to lessen competition or tend to create a monopoly in the transportation industry or where the rate was established for the purpose of eliminating or injuring a competitor." [80] Congress did not accept this proposed alternative. The next move came in 1958 from a subcommittee of the Senate Committee on Interstate and Foreign Commerce headed by Senator Smathers. It also was "not convinced that the record before it justifies approval of the railroads' proposal"; [81] the subcommittee said it believed the policy of Congress was "that each form of transportation should have opportunity to make rates reflecting the different inherent advantages each has to offer" but "that such ratemaking should be regulated by the Commission to prevent unfair destructive practices" — unspecified in nature; that the Commission "has not been consistent in the past in allowing one or another of the several modes of transportation to assert their inherent advantages in the making of rates" although the Commission had discerned the true path in *New Automobiles*; and that it was "necessary to amend the act only so as, in effect, to admonish the Commission to be consistent in following the

---

[79] H.R. REP. No. 1922, 85th Cong., 2d Sess. 13 (1958).

[80] *Hearings on Problems of the Railroads Before the Subcommittee on Surface Transportation of the Senate Committee on Interstate and Foreign Commerce*, 85th Cong., 2d Sess., pt. 4, at 2353 (1958).

[81] S. REP. No. 1647, 85th Cong., 2d Sess. 2, 18 (1958).

policy enunciated in the Automobile case . . . ." The proposed amendment dealt solely with rail minimum rates; it provided that "in a proceeding involving competition with another mode of transportation, the Commission . . . shall consider the facts and circumstances attending the movement of the traffic by railroad and not by such other mode." [82] This left the motor and water carriers apprehensive that although the subcommittee had rejected the three-shall-nots in form, it had adopted them in fact, simply putting all three pills in one capsule; more pulling and hauling resulted in a further compromise.

The report of the House Committee on Interstate and Foreign Commerce begins by echoing the nice things the Smathers subcommittee had said about inherent advantages, the disagreeable things about the unmentionable unfair destructive practices, and the admiring reference to *New Automobiles*, which was now thought to have been further sanctified by the Supreme Court's language in the *Schaffer* certificate case.[83] The inherent-advantage theme of the Senate subcommittee then reenters, but over a new and subtle melody in the bass, devised by a skillful hand:

> The committee believes that the Commission consistently should follow the principle of allowing each mode of transportation to assert its inherent advantages, whether they be of cost or service, *giving due consideration to the objectives of the national transportation policy declared in the Interstate Commerce Act.*[84]

For anyone with a modicum of experience in the ways of Washington it is easy to visualize the scene — the motor and water interests wondering whether they had even yet extracted all the fangs from the Advisory Committee's report, but hesitating to press for more for fear they might emerge with less; the railroads debating whether to accept this watered-down version of the three-shall-nots or risk not getting even that; the

---

[82] *Id.* at 18.
[83] Schaffer Transp. Co. v. United States, 355 U.S. 83, 91 (1957).
[84] H.R. REP. No. 1922, *supra* note 79, at 14. (Emphasis added.)

legislators highly pleased because although none of the carriers could be altogether pleased, none could be altogether displeased. The amendment to section 15a embodied in the Transportation Act of 1958 [85] followed the line proposed by the House Committee. Its first sentence took the Senate subcommittee's language, generalized it to apply to all forms of transport, but then omitted the single surviving "not." To make up to the railroads for the omission, the second sentence gave them a half-not. It starts as if it were about to sanction their slogan against "umbrella" ratemaking by providing that "rates of a carrier shall not be held up to a particular level to protect the traffic of any other mode of transportation," only, however, to add, with a bow to the motor and water carriers, the pregnant postscript taken from the report of the House Committee, "giving due consideration to the objectives of the national transportation policy declared in this Act." In order to appreciate the full beauty of the ambiguity introduced by the postscript, one must look back to the final sentence of the 1940 *National Transportation Policy* which directed that "All of the provisions of this Act shall be administered and enforced with a view to carrying out the above declaration of policy." The railroads can thus say that repetition meant nothing, or at least added nothing, whereas the motor and water carriers can respond that everything said in 1958 was qualified by what had been said eighteen years before.

The legislators had tackled a tough problem, had looked long and hard at it, and then, caught between conflicting pressures, had come up with a whimper.[86] Indeed, the Government was

---

[85] The full text of § 15a(3) of the Interstate Commerce Act, 72 Stat. 572, 49 U.S.C. § 15a(3) (1958), is as follows:

In a proceeding involving competition between carriers of different modes of transportation subject to this Act, the Commission, in determining whether a rate is lower than a reasonable minimum rate, shall consider the facts and circumstances attending the movement of the traffic by the carrier or carriers to which the rate is applicable. Rates of a carrier shall not be held up to a particular level to protect the traffic of any other mode of transportation, giving due consideration to the objectives of the national transportation policy declared in this Act.

[86] The DOYLE REPORT, at 399, says, somewhat gloomily, but surely accurately:

later to contend in the *Sea-Land* case that Congress had simply emulated the King of France and managed, after great travail, to leave everything precisely as it had been before. More likely, as the district court there held, a glimmer of legislative purpose had penetrated the murk. I shall finish my story by recounting a little of what has since happened in the Commission and the courts. Of course, the legislative battle was not ended; having blunted the rail offensive, the motor and water carriers pressed a bill to amend the new section 15a(3) in a manner that would place the Commission's power to consider the effect of a proposed rate on all forms of transportation beyond doubt.[87]

Recent Developments

Paint & Related Articles in Official Territory [88] was supposed to test what, if anything, the legislative labors of four years had accomplished. Counsel for the railroads said he "would rather lose this case than to get a decision which allows the rates to go in but under conditions which still leave us up in the air"; the National Industrial Traffic League hoped the decision would inform everyone "where the Commission stands and where transportation stands in pricing its service"; and the motor carriers also "expected this proceeding to produce a landmark decision." [89] They were all to be disappointed. The Commission apparently concluded that the proposed reduced rates would cover out-of-pocket costs and make some contributions to fully distributed costs; that regaining only a very small amount of the potential traffic would recoup the loss from the drastically re-

---

The discussions leading up to the legislation of 1958 brought out the uncertainty of the existing law. The 1958 amendment is so worded that its meaning is also uncertain. The manner in which this amendment is to be applied and its longrun implications are likewise uncertain.

See the discussion in New York, N.H. & H.R.R. v. United States, 199 F. Supp. 635, 642 (D. Conn. 1961).

[87] S. 1197, 87th Cong., 1st Sess. (1961).
[88] 308 I.C.C. 439 (1959).
[89] 308 I.C.C. at 451 (concurring opinion).

duced rates; and that retrieving the proportion which was envisaged would contribute large sums above out-of-pocket costs. Dealing with the motor carriers' contention that the rates would constitute an unfair or destructive competitive practice, it found, after some carefully guarded reference to court decisions, that "because of service advantages, the motor carriers may be able to continue to compete for this traffic without any reduction in their rates," but that in any event "there is no indication that the proposed rates will have an adverse effect upon the protestants in such manner as to constitute an unlawful practice" — whatever that may mean.

One must agree with a concurring Commissioner that the report raised more questions than it answered. Did the Commission think it was deciding differently from the way it would have before the 1958 amendment? If it did, why did it not say so? Was the amendment the reason for the absence of reference to "not lower than necessary"? Did the Commission think that on some occasions rates that are "reasonably compensatory" may constitute an unfair or destructive practice?[90] All this was left uncertain.[91]

[90] *Cf.* U.S. Dep't of Commerce, Federal Transportation Policy and Program 17–18 (1960).

[91] Neither is any great illumination afforded by two other rather lengthy reports in the same volume. In Sugar From Gulf & So. Atl. Ports to Ohio River Crossings, 308 I.C.C. 167, 185 (1959), the Commission declined to require "rail rates which substantially exceed full cost to be differentially higher than water costs . . . ."; I should hardly have thought it would have done so before the 1958 amendment. In Lumber From Cal. & Ore. to Cal. & Ariz., 308 I.C.C. 345, 377 (1959), the Commission again suggested that under some circumstances "reasonably compensatory" rates, there allowed to go into effect, might "constitute a destructive competitive practice" under other circumstances. Other decisions indicating little difference in result under the 1958 act from theretofore are Gasoline & Fuel Oil From Friendship to Va. & W. Va., 299 I.C.C. 609 (1957), *aff'd as modified*, 305 I.C.C. 673 (1959); Tobacco From N.C. to Cent. Territory, 309 I.C.C. 347 (1960); and Foodstuffs Between Mich. & Pa. & From Pa. to N.J. & N.Y., 310 I.C.C. 343 (1960); *cf.* Georgia Pub. Serv. Comm'n, 310 I.C.C. 225 (1960). The Doyle Report, at 405, concludes that "the Commission in its written decisions and its statements to congressional committees provides the best documentation of the thesis that the meaning of minimum rate policy is less certain and its application more confusing than before the addition of section 15a(3)."

More light as to the Commission's views of the 1958 act, of a kind not liked by the railroads, was shed by the decision known in the Commission as *Commodities — Pan-Atlantic S.S. Corp.*,[92] and in the courts, because of a change in the water carrier's name, as the *Sea-Land* case. The Commission phrased the issue as whether, in attempting to meet the competition of Pan-Atlantic, which, with cooperating motor carriers, offered a ship-truck service in transferable highway containers, and of Seatrain Lines, which moved loaded freight cars,

> the railroads may establish compensatory rates which are on a parity with the rates of those competitors, or whether the rate-making provisions of the Interstate Commerce Act, interpreted in the light of the national transportation policy, under the facts here presented, require that the rail rates on this traffic be maintained differentially higher than the rates of those competing modes.[93]

A majority answered "No" to the first question and "Yes" to the second. Addressing itself to the "umbrella" provision of section 15a(3), it said that in the light of the proviso,

> the prohibition does not mean that rates which fail to meet other standards of lawfulness in the act, interpreted in the light of the national transportation policy, must be approved because an effect of their disapproval might be to protect the traffic of a competing mode.[94]

The problem having thus been put back about where it would have been before the 1958 amendment, the Commission concluded that

> the objectives of the national transportation policy require the establishment and maintenance of a differential relationship . . . which will allow these water carriers operating in the coastwise

---

[92] 313 I.C.C. 23 (1960), *rev'd in part sub nom.* New York, N.H. & H.R.R. v. United States, 199 F. Supp. 635 (D. Conn. 1961).
[93] *Id.* at 25.
[94] *Id.* at 46–47.

trade to maintain rates that will enable them to continue efficient and economical coastwise service.[95]

The district court's reversal of this decision to the extent that the Commission had proscribed rail rates yielding fully distributed costs [96] will inevitably produce further uncertainty pending Supreme Court review. Even that Court's decision can determine only the legal limits of the Commission's minimum-rate power; wise setting of policy guidelines within those limits will still be required.

Granted the difficulty of the minimum-rate problem, the record of the past forty years is not inspiring. We have seen the power conferred by Congress, with relatively little thought how it was to be used, in the days of what was close to a railroad monopoly. We have noted how it came to be increasingly utilized by the Commission during the competitive traffic struggle of the great depression, in somewhat confused and disparate ways and with a failure adequately to define the various cost standards or to explicate the rationale for using a particular one.[97] We have seen it

---

[95] *Id.* at 49–50. A later decision, by a sharply divided Commission, reached a different conclusion where the protesting carriers were found not to have presented adequate cost evidence. Various Commodities From or to Ark. & Tex., 314 I.C.C. 215 (1961). See also Drugs, Brass, Bronze, Copper Pipe, Wire From N.J. to Tex., 314 I.C.C. 420 (1961); Machinery & Brass, Bronze, Copper Articles From E. to Tex. & La., 314 I.C.C. 363 (1961); Pig Iron From Neville Island, Pa., to Louisville, Ky., 313 I.C.C. 771 (1961); Cigars From Jacksonville to Kansas City, 313 I.C.C. 633 (1961).

[96] New York, N.H. & H.R.R. v. United States, 199 F. Supp. 635 (D. Conn. 1961). The injunction was qualified to the extent that if the Commission should later find that the joint land-water service was the low-cost mode and that value-of-service considerations so demanded, the Commission might require rail rates higher than fully distributed rail costs but not higher than fully distributed costs of the competing service. *Id.* at 646–47.

[97] The situation has not improved. "Regrettably," a recent treatise rightly states, "one searches in vain for an unambiguous pronouncement of general policy with respect to the various measures of compensativeness. Indeed, the reading of the decisions creates the impression that the Commission selects whichever theory appears best to fit the case at hand." FULDA, COMPETITION IN THE REGULATED INDUSTRIES *Transportation* 370 (1961).

supposedly brought up to date by Congress in 1940, with language so encompassing as to create as many contradictions as were dissipated, on the eve of a war that so heavily taxed all forms of transport as to postpone the need for more accurate definition. We have examined how it was reformulated by the Commission in a policy pronouncement which contained serious ambiguities and never became a true norm of decision,[98] and how it was revised in the 1958 legislation that took with one hand much of what was given with the other. It was fair enough for Commissioner Eastman to suggest a "process of trial and error" in 1939; [99] something more in the way of definition should have been attained by 1962. The chief reason it has not been is that neither the Commission nor the Congress has been willing to face up to the basic policy decisions long seen to have been needed.[100] The issues have again been presented in a report the Senate has commissioned and, more importantly, in a message from President Kennedy recommending general exemption of bulk and agricultural commodities from minimum-rate regulation; [101] one can only hope that with the further stimulus that Supreme Court opinions in the *Sea-Land* case may give — I venture into the dangerous domain of prophecy just far enough to use the plural — Congress will find the time, and acquire the resolution, to take some firm decisions.

[98] It is hard to disagree with Professor Williams' conclusion, *op. cit. supra* note 72, at 208–09:
> The treatment of the declaration of policy both by the Commission and by the courts, therefore, leaves in doubt the nature of the general objective toward which the Commission should work. In effect the average case is decided without reference to any such objective. In those few instances in which construction of the policy seems almost unavoidable care is taken to skirt the edges; to reach an acceptable decision in the instant case, but one which may not be relied upon as a guide to the decision of future cases.

[99] See p. 113 *supra*.

[100] In addition to the Commission's own 1939 analysis, the problems were fully explored in Professor Locklin's penetrating essay, *Rates and Rate Structure,* in U.S. NAT'L RESOURCES PLANNING BD., TRANSPORTATION AND NATIONAL POLICY 87 (1942).

[101] DOYLE REPORT 407–44; H.R. DOC. No. 384, 87th Cong., 2d Sess. 4 (1962).

VII

The Road to Improvement

HAVING thus surveyed the administrative process in action, we have earned the right — indeed incurred the obligation — to consider the final question: how can a better job be done in defining the standards by which the agencies live? I shall take up first the role of the agency, then that of the executive, next that of Congress, and, finally and very briefly, that of another set of institutions which may seem surprising.

That fourth set, I should say straightaway, is not the judiciary. The courts have their function in marking out the allowable limits of agency action.[1] Moreover, the thoughtful reading of a statute by a careful judge may help an agency even within its permitted confines, just as a hasty or ill-expressed one will do the opposite, and a reversal for lack of adequate findings may force an agency to focus on the issues more closely and to define its standards more sharply.[2] Doubtless the courts can do better than they have in performing these and other roles in the administrative scheme.[3] But the tastes of a variety of fields of administrative adjudication that we have had must surely have made it clear that the task of defining substantive standards cannot possibly be transferred to the courts either in whole or in any significant part.

---

[1] The existing definition of the scope of review seems to me quite satisfactory; if I were to make an exception, it would be the so-called doctrine of Gray v. Powell, 314 U.S. 402 (1941) — at least if this were pressed to extremes, which however, later decisions such as Social Security Bd. v. Nierotko, 327 U.S. 358 (1946), and NLRB v. Highland Park Mfg. Co., 341 U.S. 322 (1951), declined to do.

[2] See, e.g., United States v. Chicago, M., St. P. & P.R. Co., 284 U.S. 499, 510–11 (1935); Secretary of Agriculture v. United States, 347 U.S. 645 (1954); Braniff Airways, Inc. v. CAB, D.C. Cir., May 24, 1962.

[3] See the serious criticisms in DAVIS, *Preface* at iii–x.

The Role of the Agency

Platitude though it be to say so, the best agency to improve agency performance is the agency itself. The essential first step is for each commission to recognize what the student of the senior one has termed the "need of a more carefully articulated enunciation of majority views on basic matters, in the interest of clarifying policy, not only to outsiders, but to the Commission itself." [4] Our study has demonstrated how vital it is that such recognition come early and be oft repeated; we can contrast the momentum Judge Cooley gave the ICC,[5] not only as to the fourth section but in other areas, with the sufferings the CAB inflicted on itself by deliberately refusing to make a considered statement of policy as to competitive route certification in its early days, and then being forced to justify *ad hoc* decisions by a series of inconsistent pronouncements.[6]

Many proposals now current can contribute to the process of better definition of standards by the agencies and to other objectives as well. Among these are the appointment of commissioners of higher intellectual power and moral courage,[7] establishing a longer term and pursuing a tradition of reappointment,[8] affording

---

[4] 3-B SHARFMAN 764.

[5] See pp. 28–31 *supra*; see also note 64 *infra*.

[6] See pp. 82–105 *supra*.

[7] Eastman, *A "Credo" as to the Judicial Functions of Administrative Tribunals*, 30 A.B.A.J. 266–67 (1944); LANDIS REPORT 66–68; Friendly, *A Look at the Federal Administrative Agencies*, 60 COLUM. L. REV. 429, 444–46 (1960).

[8] This serves a variety of purposes — promoting the recruiting of able commissioners by enhancing the attractiveness of the posts, capitalizing on the skill which only experience can give, and bolstering the courage "to make a decision or take a position which may react seriously in some way upon the one who makes or takes it." Eastman, *supra* note 7, at 266–67. Agency members who have forgotten the reprisal meted out by the Senate to Commissioner Esch in 1928 for his vote in Lake Cargo Coal Rates, 1925, 101 I.C.C. 513 (1925), 126 I.C.C. 309 (1927) (see 2 SHARFMAN 462–64), may recall more recent examples. See HARRIS, THE ADVICE AND CONSENT OF THE SENATE 178–94 (1953) ("The Rejection of Leland Olds"), and the letter of a number of professors of administrative law on the failure to reappoint Federal Power Commissioner Connole, N.Y. Times, Apr. 28, 1960, p. 34, cols. 7–8. The Senate Committee on the Judiciary has recom-

the commissioners more opportunity for study and reflection by freeing them from the multitude of routine tasks that now encroach so heavily upon their time,[9] and enforcing individual responsibility for opinions.[10] All these have been canvassed so thoroughly in recent months, and, save perhaps for the last, are so generally agreed upon, that no further discussion of them here is needed.

There is less accord as to the medium whereby agency crystallization of standards is to be realized. Historically, policy has evolved mainly from a case-by-case approach. The Board of Investigation and Research, although recognizing some merit in

---

mended "that legislation should be enacted to increase the terms of regulatory agency members to uniform terms of 10 years, together with an annual increment in salary and with strengthened provisions for pension rights." S. REP. NO. 168, 87th Cong., 1st Sess. 6 (1961). (All italicized in original.) Senator Dirksen favored a fifteen-year term. See *id.* at 18, and S. 3410, 87th Cong., 2d Sess., introduced June 13, 1962.

[9] See Hector, *Problems of the CAB and the Independent Regulatory Commission*, 69 YALE L.J. 931, 937 (1960). Some "time charts" of members of the ICC and the NLRB will be found in GELLHORN & BYSE, ADMINISTRATIVE LAW, CASES AND COMMENTS 1076–79 (4th ed. 1960). "One commissioner recently testified that he had made 18,000 decisions in 5 years, and another said he had to make a decision every 5 minutes of each workday." S. REP. NO. 168, *supra* note 8, at 15 (individual views of Senator Dirksen); Senator Dirksen suggests a division of function between the making and the application of policy, with the commissioners left free for the former. *Id.* at 16–17, and S. 3410, 87th Cong., 2d Sess., introduced June 13, 1962. Although I doubt the feasibility of altogether divorcing policy making from decision making, some means must be found for giving the members of an agency more time for those decisions whence policy will emerge. Agencies like the FTC, which can determine what proceedings shall come before them, ought to be peculiarly able to stem the flood of trivia. See Exposition Press v. FTC, 295 F.2d 869, 876–77 (2d Cir. 1961), *cert. denied*, 8 L. Ed. 2d 496 (1962); Gimbel Bros., FTC Docket No. 7888, Feb. 23, 1962 (dissenting opinion of Commissioner Elman).

[10] See pp. 1, 4 & note 20 *supra*; LANDIS, THE ADMINISTRATIVE PROCESS 106 (1938); Hector, *Problems of the CAB and the Independent Regulatory Commission*, 69 YALE L.J. 931, 947–48 (1960); Hector, *Government by Anonymity: Who Writes Our Regulatory Opinions?*, 45 A.B.A.J. 1260 (1959); N. L. Smith, *The Administrative Process*, 64 PUB. UTIL. FORT. 549, 554–55 (1959). For a defense of the "institutional opinion," see Comments of the CAB on the Hector Memorandum to the President 26–27, March 29, 1960, and 2 DAVIS, ADMINISTRATIVE LAW TREATISE § 11.07 (1958).

this method, was more struck with its disadvantages: its accidental character, the possible inadequacy of the record in the crucial case, the appearance — perhaps, indeed, the reality — of rather snail-like progress, and, finally, that

> indefinite or conflicting standards of decision are easily maintained so long as situations are dealt with separately; one case may be decided by a rule that points east, and the next by a rule that points west, which leaves those who look to the decisions for guidance without any rule on which they may confidently rely.[11]

This last deficiency is surely not inherent; if the work has been properly done, there will not be cases looking east and west on similar facts, although, as with the courts, there may be some looking north-northeast or north-northwest as well as due north. Moreover, the case-by-case method does not need to continue forever in the precise format of today. Mr. Landis has made some wise suggestions for the agency's own presentation of basic data;[12] and, at least in some types of proceedings, much might be said for the commission's starting the ball rolling with a tentative statement of agency or staff views.[13] I am not greatly impressed with the overall utility of one substitute the Board recommended, namely, the general investigation initiated by the agency;[14] this has its own problems, notably unwieldy size and un-

---

[11] I. & R. BOARD REPORT 82. See also LANDIS REPORT 18–19; REDFORD, NATIONAL REGULATORY COMMISSIONS: NEED FOR A NEW LOOK 15 (1959).

[12] LANDIS REPORT 41–42. Although the suggestions were made with specific reference to CAB route proceedings, they are applicable to other proceedings and agencies as well.

[13] It would seem that some such procedure could have been employed in the Seven States Area Investigation, 1A Av. L. REP. (Av. Cas.) ¶ 16113 (CAB 1958), which serves as Mr. Hector's horrible example. See *Problems of the CAB and the Independent Regulatory Commissions*, 69 YALE L.J. 931, 932–34, (1960). The CAB has followed such a procedure in "mail rate," *i.e.*, subsidy cases, as it has done very recently in Transatlantic Final Mail Rate Case, Order No. E–18018, Feb. 13, 1962; and the SEC employed it in some proceedings under the Public Utility Holding Company Act. The danger is that a "tentative" statement may be such in name only.

[14] I. & R. BOARD REPORT 83–85.

due delay. The case-by-case approach seems to have succeeded for the NLRB [15] and no reason is perceived why it could not have worked reasonably well with the FCC and the CAB; on the other hand, one can understand that for the ICC, the agency under particular study by the Board, sheer volume may create difficulty.

Although the case-by-case method should not be abandoned even if that were possible,[16] it should be supplemented by much greater use of two other devices — policy statements and rulemaking. It is partly because of their availability that I have no fear that the quest for better definition of standards must lead to what is opprobriously called the judicialization of the administrative process. The agencies, reluctance to employ such good tools has been rather curious — a result, perhaps, of undue emphasis on their "quasi-judicial" character. Yet the courts themselves have not hesitated to use such methods in their adjudicative task. Have the agencies not yet heard of the Rule in Shelley's Case?

The Board of Investigation and Research made a most helpful suggestion as to the issuance of policy statements, although, so far as I know, it has not been used. That is for the agency periodically to make a "systematic study of its own precedents on important questions" and to prepare, perhaps in its annual reports to Congress, an analysis of "past and present policies, where it could be carried through to some definite conclusions," a process having the further virtue that where the analysis could not be so carried through, "the attempt at statement might indicate, for the benefit of the Commission, inconsistencies which had not been fully appreciated." [17] The quotation itself suggests one of the values of the policy statement — the education of agency members in the

---

[15] See, however, note 22 *infra*. Of course, the agency must be free to draw on its general experience and should not be limited to the record of the particular "case." See Friendly, *A Look at the Federal Administrative Agencies*, 60 COLUM. L. REV. 429, 439 (1960).

[16] See Bernstein, *The Regulatory Process: A Framework for Analysis*, 26 LAW & CONTEMP. PROB. 329, 332 (1961).

[17] I. & R. BOARD REPORT 87, 88. Annual reports of the NLRB have contained chapters entitled "Principles Established."

agency's work. Such a statement of agency policy is likely to be the product of many meetings which the individual members will not have been able to avoid, and the issues will have been stripped of the trivia and personalities that may becloud decision in the individual case. Another merit of the policy statement is its utility in avoiding what may be a harsh retroactive application. Although a new rule declared in an agency decision could also be made prospective only, this technique seems to have encountered as much difficulty in gaining administrative as it has had in obtaining judicial adherence. Of course, there is no reason to limit the promulgation of policy statements to particular intervals; the agencies should be encouraged to put these forward whenever sufficient experience has accumulated for a proper formulation.[18] Yet a requirement of periodic review would have value; it would tend to overcome the inertia that usually prevents such "difficult and arduous undertakings."[19]

The next step beyond policy statements is the promulgation of rules with the effect of law, some examples of which we encountered in our study of the FCC.[20] This, too, is a most useful device for defining standards, although there may be a legal difficulty about it when rulemaking power has not been expressly granted; I fear that a norm promulgated as a rule would be more likely than one adumbrated in a decision, or even in a policy statement, to encounter outraged cries of "legislation" from the courts.[21] Even if the power to make rules is plain, the policy statement may still be preferable when the principle does not lend itself to, or is not ripe for, precise articulation, or when the agency desires

[18] See McFarland, *Landis' Report: The Voice of One Crying in the Wilderness*, 47 VA. L. REV. 373, 433–38 (1961). The article points out, at 433, that "agencies without such 'ad hoc' authority [to decide cases] do better in the way of formulating their policies in advance" than those with it, as witness the Wage-Hour Administrator.

[19] *Id.* at 436.

[20] Page 57 *supra*; see Baker, *Policy by Rule or Ad Hoc Approach — Which Should It Be?*, 22 LAW & CONTEMP. PROB. 658 (1957).

[21] We have seen that principles stated in decisions are not immune from this risk. See p. 49 *supra*.

to retain some freedom to modify its views without the steps prescribed by the Administrative Procedure Act for rules having the force of law.[22] In fact, there is no need to choose between the two devices; they can well be employed in tandem. When we add to all this the possibilities afforded by the declaratory order under section 5(d) of the Administrative Procedure Act, it becomes apparent that agencies do not suffer from lack of tools with which to get on with the job of defining standards. They have been given a variety of procedures sufficient to challenge the most skilled and imaginative administrators.[23]

The Role of the Executive

What role in the crystallization of standards of the agencies may properly be played by the executive? Professor Sharfman,

---

[22] Administrative Procedure Act § 4, 60 Stat. 238 (1946), 5 U.S.C. § 1003 (1958). Although § 2(c), 60 Stat. 237 (1946), 5 U.S.C. § 1001(c) (1958), defines "rule" as including "any agency statement of general or particular applicability and future effect designed to implement, interpret, or prescribe law or policy . . . ," § 4 exempts "general statements of policy" from rulemaking procedure "except where notice or hearing is required by statute." The Code of Federal Adminstrative Procedure of the American Bar Association, S. 1887, 87th Cong., 1st Sess. (1961), proposes to eliminate this exemption. See Benjamin, *A Lawyer's View of Administrative Procedure — The American Bar Association Program*, 26 LAW & CONTEMP. PROB. 203, 227–28 (1961). Cf. S. 3410, 87th Cong., 2d Sess., introduced by Senator Dirksen, June 13, 1962. One may wonder why, if an agency can include a policy statement in an opinion without rulemaking procedures, the latter must be employed if the statement is made separately. If it be said that in the former case the agency will have had the views of the parties, it can be answered that the statement may far outrun the issues litigated in the case, and that an agency that would make a policy statement without a background of experience is not going to be saved by prescribing procedures. As against this it has been claimed that the announcement of detailed policies in an opinion itself may violate § 4. See the recommendation of the Labor Law Section of the American Bar Association, 42 LAB. REL. REP. 513 (1958), and the response of the NLRB, 45 LAB. REL. REP. 407, 409 (1959); and Peck, *The Atrophied Rule-Making Powers of the National Labor Relations Board*, 70 YALE L.J. 724, 738–41 (1961). There is force in this when, as in the case of some of the NLRB's pronouncements, the "policy" is an inflexible rule. Surely much can be gained by obtaining a broad spectrum of views if this can be accomplished without impeding prompt and effective agency action.

[23] See Peck, *supra* note 22, at 755–56.

the historian of the Interstate Commerce Commission, answered, "None — no more than with the Supreme Court"; indeed, he deemed illegitimate any attempt to affect even the overall course of administrative determination by use of the appointing power [24] — a process perhaps not altogether unknown as to the Court itself. Professor Cushman, the historian of the agencies in general, reached an opposite conclusion: "there is no reason why he [the President] should not openly and frankly state his policies to the commissions and invite their agreement and co-operation," [25] a view recently taken also by Professor Redford.[26]

Surely the administrative purists went too far in seeking to raise a wall between the agencies and the President. There can scarcely be disagreement with President Kennedy's statements that it is the chief executive's obligation

> to staff the regulatory agencies . . . with men and women competent to handle the responsibilities vested in them and dedicated to the goals set forth in the legislation they are appointed to implement . . . [and also that] his duty to reward faithful public service by the reappointment of agency members . . . requires him to form opinions as to the capability of his or his predecessor's appointees to handle the affairs that the Congress has entrusted to them.[27]

---

[24] See 2 SHARFMAN 453–59 & n.209. Commissioner Eastman shared most of these views as to executive influence, although, significantly, not that as to the appointing power. See Eastman, *supra* note 7.

[25] CUSHMAN, THE INDEPENDENT REGULATORY COMMISSIONS 689 (1941). He adds, "When such a practice came to be sanctioned by tradition, it would lose its present superficial aspect of being a type of unauthorized interference on the part of the President with the commissions' activities."

[26] REDFORD, THE PRESIDENT AND THE REGULATORY COMMISSIONS 22–23 (1960) (Report submitted to the President's Advisory Committee on Government Organization).

[27] President's Message to Congress on the Regulatory Agencies, 107 CONG. REC. 5356, 5357 (daily ed. April 13, 1961), reprinted as H.R. Doc. No. 135, 87th Cong., 1st Sess. (1961). The President's message is as admirable for the claims it does not make on behalf of the chief executive as for the clear statement of those that it does. However, I would season the remark as to "capability" with a strong tradition of reappointment. See note 8 *supra*.

Neither can one reasonably quarrel with Mr. Landis' view that

> the congestion of the dockets of the agencies, the delays incident to the disposition of cases, the failure to evolve policies pursuant to basic statutory requirements are all a part of the President's constitutional concern to see that the laws are faithfully executed.[28]

Moreover, agency policies in certain areas might obstruct, whereas others might advance, the President's success in functions especially confided to him, such as the national defense or the conduct of foreign affairs; it is by no means plain that all he may properly do in such matters is to appear before the agency as a litigant.[29] Beyond all this the President has another very practical concern with the workings of the agencies — in all likelihood he will get the blame if things go too wrong.

Having said all this, I still find difficulty in the proposal that the President should not merely see to it that the agencies function but should tell them how. I do not have much trouble with

---

[28] LANDIS REPORT 33. I am far less convinced as to the desirability of the President's being allowed to forbid the agencies' submitting legislative proposals to Congress or making "other than casual comments . . . on bills pending before the Congress" without clearance from the Bureau of the Budget — a power which Mr. Landis says is "now generally acknowledged although at one time contested by Commissioner Eastman." *Id.* at 31. Perhaps "enforced" would be more accurate than "acknowledged."

[29] Recognition of this underlies the statutory provisions as to the relationship of the President and the Tariff Commission under the Tariff Act of 1930, 46 Stat. 590, see United States v. George S. Bush & Co., 310 U.S. 371, 379–80 (1940), and of the President and the Civil Aeronautics Board in the grant or denial of certificates to engage in foreign or "overseas" air transportation under § 801 of the Federal Aviation Act, 52 Stat. 1014 (1938) (now 49 U.S.C. § 1461 (1958)), see Chicago & So. Air Lines, Inc. v. Waterman S.S. Corp., 333 U.S. 103, 109 (1948). However, the President may have legitimate concerns of this nature even when he has not thus been made a part of the decisional process, *e.g.*, with policies of the transportation agencies that might affect the ability of carriers to respond to a national emergency, or of the FCC as to conflicting Government and private claims for frequency bands, especially in international communications and in connection with the problems of space satellites. See 48 Stat. 1083 (1934), 47 U.S.C. § 305 (1958).

the President's informing the agency of his policy when the policy is a very general one, for which he desires the cooperation not only of the particular agency but of all branches of Government, although I am skeptical that this would accomplish anything approaching what its advocates expect. I refer to such conventional virtues, universally praised but not always practiced, as curbing inflation or encouraging employment. I doubt that any agency would regard a presidential pronouncement on such subjects as infringing its independence; one reason is that the pronouncement would not really tell it much. For example, whereas opponents of a railroad or airline merger would argue that a policy of encouraging employment would require disapproval since the immediate effect would be the loss of jobs, the proponents would respond that the long-run consequence of disapproval would be the loss of more,[30] and the agency would end up having to decide, just about as if the policy had not been announced.

On the other hand, I would see a number of difficulties in the President's enunciating a more specific merger policy for the agencies to follow. As to one such, I have lots of company. Everyone, including the presidential activists, seems to agree that "the outcome of any particular adjudicatory matter is . . . as much beyond his [the President's] concern . . . as the outcome of any cause pending in the courts . . . ."[31] Yet this concession appears to contain the seeds of destruction of the whole proposal, at least when it is broadened as has properly been done:

> The President and all other executive officials should avoid any ex parte statement or communication with the intention of influencing any decision of a regulatory commission required by law to be made on a record . . . .[32]

---

[30] *Cf.* United-Capital Merger Case, 1A Av. L. Rep. (Av. Cas.) ¶ 21132 (CAB April 3, 1961), *aff'd sub nom.* Northwest Airlines, Inc. v. CAB, 2 Av. L. Rep. (Av. Cas.) ¶ 17809 (D.C. Cir. 1962).
[31] Landis Report 33. See also S. Rep. No. 168, 87th Cong., 1st Sess. 19 (1961).
[32] Redford, *op. cit. supra* note 26, at 20. See also *id.* at 2.

A statement in favor of or against mergers would, of course, have "the effect of influencing" decision in cases then pending even if no names were named; the only kind of statement that would not have that effect would be one so hedged that it had better not have been made. Even a very general statement has its dangers, as witness a proposal, sparked by the proposed American–Eastern Airlines and Pennsylvania–New York Central mergers, that before the agencies take action, "a national policy on transportation mergers must be developed by the Administration with the help of Congress." The suggested "policy" was to include certain principles which, although admirable, I should suppose the CAB and the ICC could be trusted to perceive without reminder, since they are either stated in or easily derivable from section 2 of the Federal Aviation Act, the *National Transportation Policy*, or other sections. Yet the very formulation of such a policy by the administration would be argued to have some implications for the agency; both the principle of noninterference and other considerations dictate abstention from nonlegislative policy declarations departing from the existing statutes, either consequentially or inconsequentially, while the contests are proceeding before the agencies in which the law vests responsibility for decision.[33] The sole escape from the dilemma would seem to be that presidential policy statements should be limited to issues of such little

---

[33] N.Y. Times, Jan. 25, 1962, p. 20, col. 3. The proposal under reference was later expanded into a bill that would forbid agency action until a new policy had been developed. This expansion removes any objection on the score of improper interference; if Congress wishes to change the rules, it is free to do so, see pp. 165–166 *infra*. The objections which remain are on the score of delay and of doubt how significantly any new policy adopted by Congress would differ from the present one, compare the history of the Transportation Act of 1958, pp. 131–136 *supra*. The "freeze" has been opposed by the ICC and also by the Departments of Justice and Commerce, the latter speaking through the Under Secretary for Transportation who is chairman of an interagency group appointed by the President; see p. 152 & note 34 *infra*. The two Departments indicated that Congress might well make the standards governing commission action on mergers more definite, but argued against delay while this was in process. N.Y. Herald Tribune, July 6, 1962, p. 21, cols. 3–4; *id.*, July 7, 1962, p. 17, cols. 1–3.

interest that no case presenting them is pending; that, if I may say so, scarcely accords with the realities of government.

A variation of this proposal is President Kennedy's recently announced formation of an interagency group which "after proper consultation with interested parties" is "to formulate general administration policies on mergers," these to include some rather generally accepted criteria and others which the group may develop, and "to assist the Department of Justice in developing a government position for presentation before the agencies." [34] The President properly recognizes that responsibility for decision is in the commission, before which, in form, the interagency group would simply be appearing as a litigant. However, one wonders whether, if a truly agreed administration position going beyond generalities were achieved, it would not be expecting too much to suppose that a commission would have the stamina to reject it. Also, although consultation among executive departments to see whether apparent differences of view are in fact as great as they initially seem is surely desirable, suppression of the views of one department in favor of another's is not. Where there is a true conflict, it is better that the departments present their views — as they do in the courts — and let the agency having responsibility decide.[35]

These illustrations will perhaps have shown why many advocates of presidential pronouncements on agency "policy" have been so chary of examples. Professor Redford is an honorable exception; let us take for further examination a proposal of his with respect to an area studied some time back — the FCC's award of broadcast licenses. Noting that "in no other field of domestic regulation has there been so much criticism of commission performance . . . for failure to establish standards of judgment

[34] H.R. Doc. No. 384, 87th Cong., 2d Sess. 8 (1962).

[35] Compare, for example, the differing views of the National Labor Relations Board and the Departments of State and Defense as to application of the National Labor Relations Act to the flag-of-convenience fleet; see Empresa Hondurena de Vapores, S.A. v. McLeod, 300 F.2d 223, 225–26 (2d Cir.), *cert. granted*, 8 L. Ed. 2d 497 (1962).

..." and that "this appears to be an area in which it would be particularly desirable to consider basic needs of public policy,"[36] he proposes to establish "a focal point" in an "executive center" to develop "policy guides" which the Commission is then to carry out through "day-to-day decisions."[37]

Quite simply, I find it hard to think of anything worse. Determination of "basic needs of public policy" within the general command of the statute is what Congress created the Commission to do. Either the Commission can perform the task or it cannot. If it cannot, it should be abolished and a new start made. What would be intolerable would be to leave it in existence but to shear it of its most important duty; that would defy the lesson that it is responsibility that breeds achievement. "Good men are primarily attracted by the challenge inherent in a job," Mr. Landis has reminded us;[38] "good men" would scarcely be attracted to the agencies by the prospect of making "day-to-day" decisions in line with the "policy guides" of White House assistants, whether or not the latter were characterized by a "passion for anonymity." Moreover, since even the "day-to-day decisions" would still involve a degree of policy making, the "focal point" on Pennsylvania Avenue would be only one of two foci; we would have exchanged a circle for an ellipse.

There is no reason to believe that such an "executive center" would be more sheltered from pressures than the agencies. Rather, it would be less so once the anonymity of the participants was shattered, since it would lack the "judicial" tradition of the commissions, and the chief executive himself is scarcely immune from considerations that are thought to affect votes, whether popular or congressional. Even if we could afford the extravagance of having two groups share a common responsibility, we would be worse off rather than better. For, in addition to the inevitable frictions of duplication, there is no reason to think the young

---

[36] REDFORD, *op. cit. supra* note 26, at 27.
[37] *Id.* at 25, 27–28.
[38] LANDIS REPORT 66.

bureaucrats in the "executive center" will have a wisdom denied to the "tribunal appointed by law and informed by experience," [39] composed of men, requiring confirmation by the Senate, who hold positions nearly of cabinet rank and, formerly at least, of great prestige.[40] I refer to young bureaucrats since it is indulging in fantasy to speak of "the President" as formulating policy pronouncements for the agencies himself. The spectacle of a chief executive, burdened to the limit of endurance with decisions on which the very existence of mankind may depend, personally taking on the added task of determining to what extent newspapers should be allowed to own television stations or whether railroads should be allowed to reduce rates only to or somewhat below the truck level, is pure mirage.[41] Yet a policy declaration with the honesty to avow that it has simply been prepared *for* the President, even by officials high in the executive branch, does not get much heed from the agencies — the Air Coordinating Committee's recommendation of May 1954, that "in the consideration of new route applications, particular care should be taken to avoid further duplication of service in the absence of proven substantial public need," [42] was followed, in the very next year and during

---

[39] Illinois Cent. R.R. v. ICC, 206 U.S. 441, 454 (1907).

[40] See Friendly, *A Look at the Federal Administrative Agencies*, 60 COLUM. L. REV. 429, 431 (1960).

[41] See GELLHORN & BYSE, ADMINISTRATIVE LAW, CASES AND COMMENTS 203–05 (4th ed. 1960), quoting, *inter alia*, Professor Corwin's statement, "to conceive of the President as a potential 'boss of the works' save in situations raising broad issues of policy would be both absurd and calamitous." THE PRESIDENT: OFFICE AND POWERS 98 (4th ed. 1957). All this has been clearly recognized in the Presidential Subdelegation Act, ch. 655, § 10, 65 Stat. 712 (1951), 3 U.S.C. § 301 (1958).

Mirages also are other statutes in which Congress has salved its conscience by placing "decision" in some high official, such as a cabinet officer, who cannot possibly find the time to take on the added assignment. See, *e.g.*, § 243(h) of the Immigration and Nationality Act of 1952, 66 Stat. 214, 8 U.S.C. § 1253(h) (1958), and Jay v. Boyd, 351 U.S. 345 (1956), sustaining the Attorney General's delegation to Regional Directors of responsibilities Congress placed in him.

[42] THE PRESIDENT'S AIR COORDINATING COMMITTEE, CIVIL AIR POLICY 13 (1954). President Eisenhower stated, at v, that the report could be "a milestone in the progress of American aviation" and that he would use it "as a guide

the same administration, by the wildest spree in the CAB's history.[43]

My negative reaction to Professor Redford's suggestion for executive oversight has been criticized as not taking into adequate account that his proposal does not extend to the whole gamut of policy making but only to great issues unsolved at the agency level. The marking of such a line between big and little issues would itself present a not inconsiderable problem in the definition of standards, with the executive group constantly trying to push the line farther down the field and the agency resisting; such pulling and hauling seems to me a new source of friction and a waste of governmental resources not to be suffered unless it must. Surely we do not want to create still a third group to umpire this game! Moreover, this redefinition of the proposal suggests other objections to it. If the reserved power of oversight is to be exercised only infrequently, we can hardly afford a special group in the White House devoted to each field, which, by hypothesis, would spend most of its time in thumb-twiddling; the proposal must thus be rather for a task force that can turn from one area to another as necessities demand. But where are the Nestors who one day can provide an assured answer with respect to port differential rail rates, next week determine how far our labor laws should apply to the flag-of-convenience fleet, then gaily pass on to the rate regulation of natural gas producers, and end up the month, or even the year, with a resolution of the ambiguities of the Robinson-Patman Act? Exceedingly bright young men on the staff of the executive there assuredly are. But they are not that bright — no one is. If they are truly interested in serving this cause, the President could make better use of their talents by appointing them to membership on the commissions, where

---

in the future consideration of questions related to the subject of civil aviation and in making appropriate recommendations to Congress." However, doubtless because of proper legal scruples, he did not *tell* the CAB to apply it and the act gave him no opportunity to "consider" the Board's actions in the domestic field.

[43] See pp. 94–96 *supra*.

their active brains and high ideals would have daily confrontation with refractory facts and obstinate human beings.

I am told also that my criticism ignores the apparent success of Presidents in overseeing executive departments; "good men" do not refuse cabinet or sub-cabinet appointments although they will be under some presidential control. Just how extensive presidential supervision of the great departments really is, I do not know. I would suspect that there is a rather wide variation between, say, State and Defense on the one hand, and Commerce and Interior on the other, and that the willingness of "good men" to accept a high degree of presidential control is thus in departments affording an interest and a challenge that a commission is unlikely to present. Yet, even assuming the intensity of presidential oversight of the departments to be greater than I would guess it generally to be, there are still a number of distinctions. Members of the cabinet and sub-cabinet are part of the President's "official family" and, almost always, of his political party, who have taken, and have been given, their posts because of their devotion to the President and their enthusiasm for his program. Members of the commissions are often not his appointees, at least not initially, and some are required by law to be of a different party. They took office not to carry out the President's policies but to exercise independent judgment in applying policies declared in general terms by Congress, in "the coldest neutrality." [44] The cabinet officer deploys federal employees and federal funds to attain the President's goals; the commissioner decides controversies between government and citizen or among citizens. The cabinet officer acts for himself without the frustrations more than occasionally afforded by commission colleagues; a combination of being first obliged to persuade a majority to a decision and then having to submit that, if on a truly important issue, to a White House group, does seem to me more than "good men" can or should normally be expected to bear, even if one were so naive as to believe the group on Pennsylvania Avenue would not attempt

[44] ICC v. Chicago, R.I. & Pac. Ry., 218 U.S. 88, 102 (1910).

to influence the decision before its transmittal. What the proffered analogy of the cabinet officer strongly suggests is that these sympathizers with Professor Redford's proposal really believe that the day of the independent commissions is over and that the functions of the agencies ought be transferred to the executive departments, but are not willing to recognize that this is where their thinking inevitably leads. That, of course, is an arguable position,[45] but it is not what we are discussing here.

There are still other troubles about executive determination of agency "policy." One President may have quite a different "policy" on such matters from his predecessors; yet an important value of the independent agency is to maintain a fair degree of continuity, a factor often quite as important as wisdom in a field where no policy can be assuredly wise. Moreover, might not such a bifurcation of the decisional process violate the principle of *Morgan v. United States*, that "the one who decides must hear"? [46] Although not expressly focusing on the danger of judicial invalidation, Professor Redford recognizes, as a problem in the way of White House policy directives, that commissioners "can still insist that law places the responsibility on them to determine the policy courses to be followed," [47] and that, in order to carry out his proposal, legislative authority for the President to direct the agencies might thus be required. It would have been well if he had tested out his idea by drafting a bill to that end; the degree of congressional abdication this would make evident would confirm one understatement, "Statutory provision for presidential guidance to all regulatory commissions is unlikely immediately." [48]

None of this denies that the President is properly concerned with whether an agency is proceeding in a way different from

---

[45] See pp. 3–4 & nn. 10–13 *supra*.

[46] 298 U.S. 468, 481 (1936).

[47] REDFORD, *op. cit. supra* note 26, at 27.

[48] *Id.* at 26. For an acute analysis of the place of the independent agencies in the constant power struggle between the President and the Congress, see I. & R. BOARD REPORT 22.

what he thinks Congress wanted or ought to want; if he believes that, Congress is the body for him to tell. Senator Dirksen has made a considered proposal to require the President to do exactly this on a regular and continuing basis. In an interesting passage he reasons that

> in connection with his daily execution of the affairs of the Government, the President may have a better opportunity than the Congress to observe the conduct of the administrative system and to note agency policies which may not represent the will of the people.
>
> . . . [Hence] the burden of the day-to-day review of agency policymaking [should] be placed upon the President. If the President determines that an agency policy is not consistent with the will of the people, it should be his responsibility to immediately inform the Congress as to the reasons for his determination. The Congress, by a majority of those voting, could then decide whether the agency policy should be changed. . . .
>
> By making his recommendations as to agency policies to the Congress, rather than directly to the agencies, the President would be acting through the Congress. . . .
>
> [T]here will be no reason for the President to communicate directly with the agencies . . . .[49]

Heartening though it be to see the Senate leader of one party thus proposing a new role for a chief executive of the other, one wonders whether the Senator may not, with the best of motives, have been unwittingly passing the President at least a bitter, if not a poisoned, chalice.

Under existing circumstances does the President really know better whether agency policies conform to the "will of the people" than does Congress? Surely not if "the President" means the President himself, *quaere* even if it means the White House — although of course the situation as to the latter might change if Senator Dirksen's proposal were adopted. Indeed, on most of

---

[49] S. REP. No. 168, 87th Cong., 1st Sess. 19–20 (1961).

these issues, do the people have any "will" that is identifiable until the contending forces have had their struggle on Capitol Hill? Yet, despite what I consider an overformalization, Senator Dirksen has rendered a distinct service in delivering this forceful reminder that the making of recommendations to Congress for the better definition of or change in the standards applied by the agencies is an important presidential responsibility that has not been sufficiently fulfilled in the past; and President Kennedy's message, of April 5, 1962, on transportation indicates his intention to discharge this.

A closely allied problem, requiring mention before we leave the relations of the agency and the executive, is that of "planning." If "substantive law has at first the look of being gradually secreted in the interstices of procedure," [50] it is equally true that not only "policy" but a good deal of "planning" evolves from, and should have a part in, the agencies' determination of particular controversies. Thus, the determination of an airline certificate case necessarily affects future planning, and planning ought to be the guide rather than the result, as has been forcefully pointed out.[51] Sometimes an agency has been expressly required to formulate a plan to guide itself, as, for example, the ICC with respect to railroad consolidation in paragraphs (4) and (5) of section 5 of the Interstate Commerce Act as amended in 1920,[52] in that instance with not very happy results; sometimes the agency has "planned" without such a direction; [53] sometimes, probably much

[50] MAINE, EARLY LAW AND CUSTOM 389 (new ed. 1891).

[51] Hector, *Problems of the CAB and the Independent Regulatory Commissions*, 69 YALE L.J. 931, 940–45 (1960).

[52] Transportation Act, 1920, § 407, 41 Stat. 481, as amended, 49 U.S.C. § 5 (1958). See also Merchant Marine Act of 1936, §§ 210–11, 49 Stat. 1989–90, as amended, 46 U.S.C. §§ 1120–21 (1958).

[53] Various instances are cited in LANDIS REPORT 18. Among them is the tentative plan of international air routes announced by the Civil Aeronautics Board in 1944 (Press Release, June 14, 1944), which has been the occasion for much self-congratulation in later years; I suspect the congratulation would be less if anyone were to look at the plan. Perhaps I will be pardoned for here expressing a long-held belief that the plan was geared to the preconceived view that competition

more often, it has "planned" too little, too late, or not at all.[54]

However, the kind of planning that is incident to the application of the general standards laid down by Congress does not exhaust the planning function with respect to the regulated industries, as an example will readily show. For an intelligent exercise of its powers with respect to railroad passenger rates under sections 1(5) and 13(4) of the Interstate Commerce Act or abandonments of lines under section 1(18) or discontinuances or changes in operation under section 13a, the Commission ought to have views as to how much railroad commuting service is necessary for our cities and what amount of passenger equipment in railroad service is required for the national defense. To the extent it applies such views to the decision of cases, it is using "planning" in administrative adjudication. Yet it may well be that neither such application, nor even any modification of the statutes within the general ambit of the existing regulatory

---

between American-flag carriers abroad should be on a "zonal" basis, avoiding competition at the same foreign point, later announced in Northeast Airlines, Inc., Atlantic Air Routes, 6 C.A.B. 319, 336-37 (1945), a view which, among other things, failed to take account of the realities of foreign-flag competition, rather than constituting an objective study of what international air routes were needed and could feasibly be operated in the national interest, regardless of who might be selected to fly them. Some of the routes would have been quite impossible to operate and others followed unnatural courses. The certificates actually issued, as a result of route proceedings in which the Board had the benefit of traffic and operating information from the carriers, were far more sensible. Thus the main virtue of the "plan" was the not inconsiderable one of making the hearings more meaningful. Its worst consequences lay in its omissions, dictated by the "zonal" philosophy; since United States negotiators for bilateral air agreements generally limited their requests to routes proposed in the plan, this country lost the opportunity to secure many needed routes, then rather readily obtainable, some of which had later to be acquired by important concessions and others of which have not yet been secured and may never be.

[54] See LANDIS REPORT 22-24. Commissioner Eastman recognized this long ago: "Our regulation in the past has operated too much on the cure basis, dealing with complaints after they arise but not forestalling them. National planning has been conspicuous by its absence." Address Before the American Life Convention, Oct. 10, 1934, quoted in BERNSTEIN, REGULATING BUSINESS BY INDEPENDENT COMMISSIONS 177 (1955). See also I. & R. BOARD REPORT 5, 65; 4 SHARFMAN 373-74.

scheme, would suffice to bring about the result needed in the national interest; some quite different type of plan may be required.[55] There is much feeling, well justified from what little I know, that today such planning outside the four corners of the statutes is nobody's business — not the business of the agencies because they are too preoccupied with specific tasks assigned them, not the business of the executive departments or of the congressional committees because they lack the expert staffs and information of the agencies and because they assume, ostrich-like, that the agencies are doing the job.

Identification of the problem is one thing; solution is quite another. There is a strong belief that the agencies are inherently incapable of this kind of planning. Commissioner Eastman's final report as Coordinator of Transportation, referring to "the absence of any sufficient provision for planning and prevention," said that "anyone who has served on the Commission knows that it is not well adapted to such work."[56] It is such a belief, among other things, that has led to the proposal that the agencies be shorn not only of planning *dehors* the statutes they administer but also of the planning which, as I see it, they must retain for the statutes' effective administration.[57] In contrast, Mr. Landis seems at one

---

[55] See DOYLE REPORT 273-328; N.Y. Times, Aug. 31, 1961, p. 18, col. 2 (excerpts from ICC interim report on the New York, N.H. & H.R.R.).

[56] See JAFFE & NATHANSON, CASES AND MATERIALS ON ADMINISTRATIVE LAW 176 (1961); 1935 FED. COORDINATOR OF TRANSP. ANN. REP. 41.

[57] Hector, *Problems of the CAB and the Independent Regulatory Commissions*, 69 YALE L.J. 931 (1960). See also the 1937 report of President Roosevelt's Committee on Administrative Management, quoted in JAFFE & NATHANSON, *op. cit. supra* note 56, at 174. See also *Hearings on Omnibus Transportation Bill Before the House Committee on Interstate and Foreign Commerce*, 76th Cong., 1st Sess. 1718 (1939), in which Commissioner Eastman proposed "a complete split between regulatory work and the issuing of orders, and this planning and promotional work," which he described as "continual and close study of the entire transportation system of the country from the standpoint of the general public interest, to determine where and how it is working badly, what can be done to improve it, what dangers are in sight, and how they can be averted"; CUSHMAN, THE INDEPENDENT REGULATORY COMMISSIONS 729-41 (1941), and the criticism of

point to lean toward placing in the commissioners the entire planning function for the industry under their care, and then making sure they "have the capacity and the time with which to discharge it," [58] with interagency coordination in the Executive Office of the President.[59] This echoes a suggestion, made many years ago by Professor Oppenheim, that " 'planning' is essentially just another label for research that is an indispensable adjunct to the effective discharge of the regulatory duties of the [Interstate Commerce] Commission," and that "the Commission has pursued a mistaken course in espousing the establishment of some other agency to explore the larger questions of over-all significance to the transportation system." [60] Such an answer may well be the best, Utopian as it may seem today; there scarcely is a perfect one. What I think vital is to recognize that an important part of the planning function must remain with the agencies as an essential part of their adjudicative task; to direct the agencies to apply "plans," made by others but not having the force of law, to the very issues whose decision is confided to them, would, as we have seen with respect to "policy," place them in a position of seeming responsibility for the activities they are directed to regulate, without the tools needed for its effective exercise.[61]

---

the latter by W. H. S. Stevens, Book Review, 34 AM. ECON. REV. 611, 615 (1944); and I. & R. BOARD REPORT 154-62.

[58] LANDIS REPORT 18.

[59] LANDIS REPORT 77-83. Mr. Landis has included in his agenda for the proposed executive office, along with some highly appropriate items not falling within any agency or crossing agency lines, others which, in my view, should remain with the agency. One example of the latter is "steps to establish cost of service, as the principal factor for determining the reasonableness of transportation rates." *Id.* at 79. To be sure, that problem can occur with other agencies, such as the CAB, especially in the cargo field, or the FPC, but today the great bulk of it is with the ICC, and methods of cost determination appropriate for one agency might not be useful for another.

[60] OPPENHEIM, THE NATIONAL TRANSPORTATION POLICY AND INTER-CARRIER COMPETITIVE RATES 123-24 (1945).

[61] *Cf.* I. &. R. BOARD REPORT 12. See also BERNSTEIN, *op. cit. supra* note 54, at 75-76.

The Role of Congress

Finally as to the legislature. Some years ago Professor Jaffe reminded us that "the legislature must be ready to intervene when administration runs into crucial issues for the settlement of which the existing standard is an inadequate guide."[62] We have seen examples of the legislature's doing this in the history of the fourth section and the National Labor Relations Act. Yet it will not have escaped notice that in the three areas later examined, where dissatisfaction with agency performance has been so great, Congress has not come to the rescue at all in two and not effectively in the third.

This is an alarming change. Commenting in 1931 on the legislative recommendations in the ICC's *Annual Reports,* Professor Sharfman could say: "While the Congressional response has often been tardy, it has seldom swerved, in essence, from the direction of the Commission's recommendations."[63] Former Commissioner Esch could write with satisfaction in 1937: "The foregoing incomplete review of the Commission's legislative activities indicates that to it was due in largest part some of the most constructive laws which it now administers."[64] No one would say anything like that today. Recommendations repeatedly made by the agencies have all too often remained dead letters, even — or perhaps particularly — when these are relatively uncontroversial.[65] Professor Bernstein has stated the unhappy

---

[62] Jaffe, *An Essay on Delegation of Legislative Power,* 47 COLUM. L. REV. 359, 366 (1947).

[63] 1 SHARFMAN 290.

[64] Esch, *The Interstate Commerce Commission and Congress — Its Influence on Legislation,* 5 GEO. WASH. L. REV. 462, 501 (1937). Commissioner Esch paid a well-deserved tribute to his predecessors: "The prescience of the original Commission as disclosed in its first annual report is remarkable, considering its lack of experience in transportation matters and the novel features of the Act which it began to administer." *Id.* at 467–68.

[65] So simple a change as a broadening of the civil penalty provision of the Civil Aeronautics Act, 72 Stat. 783, 49 U.S.C. § 1471 (1958), to include violations

truth, "While commissions frequently recommend legislative amendments to the appropriate Congressional committees, they have had little success in obtaining progressive revision of their statutes." [66]

Neither has the situation been different when what might have been a spark has come from an investigation launched by Congress or a report from the executive branch.[67] There have been countless "investigations" of the FCC; [68] yet the Communications Act, passed in 1934, has been significantly amended as to substance only once, in 1952, and, as has been shown, this made matters worse rather than better.[69] Investigations and reports as to the CAB's administration of the certificate provisions of the Civil Aeronautics Act have consumed literally thousands of pages; [70] yet in twenty-four years the economic regulatory pro-

---

of the economic regulatory provisions, recommended by the Board over many years, has never been enacted.

[66] BERNSTEIN, op. cit. supra note 54, at 292.

[67] "Congressional investigations tend toward the harsh side, with little clarification of basic regulatory policy." Id. at 151.

[68] See, e.g., COMMISSION ON ORGANIZATION OF THE EXECUTIVE BRANCH OF THE GOVERNMENT, COMMITTEE ON INDEPENDENT REGULATORY COMMISSIONS, STAFF REPORT ON THE FCC (1948); House Comm. on Interstate and Foreign Commerce, *Network Broadcasting*, H.R. REP. No. 1297, 85th Cong., 2d Sess. (1958) ["Barrow Report"]; McMAHON, REGULATION OF BROADCASTING: STUDY FOR THE COMMITTEE ON INTERSTATE AND FOREIGN COMMERCE, HOUSE OF REPRESENTATIVES, 85TH CONG., 2D SESS., ON H. RES. 99, 85TH CONG., 1ST SESS. (1958); Staff of a Subcommittee of the Senate Committee on Interstate and Foreign Commerce, 81st Cong., 1st Sess., Interim Report, 95 CONG. REC. 543-44 (1949); STAFF REPORT 56; *Hearings Before the House Select Committee To Investigate the Federal Communications Commission*, 78th Cong., 2d Sess. (1943-44).

[69] See Communications Act Amendments of 1952, ch. 879, 66 Stat. 711 (codified in scattered sections of 47 U.S.C.); p. 56 *supra*.

[70] The following is a partial list: STAFF OF SUBCOMMITTEE NO. 5, HOUSE COMMITTEE ON THE JUDICIARY, 85TH CONG., 1ST SESS., AIRLINES (Comm. Print 1957); S. REP. No. 949, 80th Cong., 2d Sess. 21-25, 49-54 (1948); H.R. REP. No. 2735, 79th Cong., 2d Sess. (1946); *Hearings on Monopoly Problems in Regulated Industries Before Subcommittee No. 5 of the House Committee on the Judiciary*, 84th Cong., 2d Sess., ser. 22, pt. 1 (1957); *Hearings on H.R. 4648, H.R. 4677, H.R. 8902, and H.R. 8903, Civil Air Policy, Before a Subcommittee of the House Committee on Interstate and Foreign Commerce*, 84th Cong., 1st Sess. (1955-56); *Hearings on S. 2674 To Provide for Regulation of Civil Aeronautics, Before the*

visions have not been altered in any material way, not even when the act was repealed and reenacted as the Federal Aviation Act in 1958.[71] The *Staff Report* of the House Legislative Oversight Committee contains an impressive list of recommendations for legislative change; the section entitled "Action by Congress" reports but a single enactment.[72]

Before I discuss the reasons for this seeming legislative paralysis and make a modest proposal as to what might be done about it, I must deal with the argument of the purists that further legislative definition of general administrative standards is not a really good idea. This is instanced by Professor Sharfman's criticism of the 1922 amendment of section 22 of the Interstate Commerce Act [73] requiring railroads to issue interchangeable mileage or scrip coupons at reasonable rates, and the Hoch-Smith resolution of 1925 directing the Commission to consider the conditions in various industries and to fix the lowest possible lawful rates on agricultural commodities.[74] He thought the former might "exert an unwholesome influence upon the independence of the Commission and upon the dominance of the method of administrative control," [75] and that the latter represented

---

Senate Committee on Interstate and Foreign Commerce, 83d Cong., 2d Sess. (1954); *Hearings on S. Res. 50, Airline Industry Investigation, Before the Senate Committee on Interstate and Foreign Commerce*, 81st Cong., 1st Sess., pt. 5 (1949–50); *Hearings on S. 1639, To Establish a National Air Policy Board, Before a Subcommittee of the Senate Committee on Interstate Commerce*, 79th Cong., 2d Sess. 131–33 (1946); Air Coordinating Committee, Civil Air Policy 6–25 (1954).

[71] 72 Stat. 754–60, 49 U.S.C. §§ 1371–86 (1958), as amended, 49 U.S.C. §§ 1373–78 (Supp. II 1961) (economic regulatory provisions). See, however, P.L. 87–528, July 11, 1962.

[72] See Staff Report 178–79, 181–83, 187–91. The one, Communications Act Amendments of 1960, 74 Stat. 889 (codified in scattered sections of 47 U.S.C.), consisted principally of procedural provisions, and did not include the amendment to § 310(b) to restrict transfer of licenses and to license networks introduced by Rep. Harris, H. 11340, 86th Cong., 2d Sess. (1960). See 106 Cong. Rec. 6413 (1960); p. 72 & note 58 *supra*.

[73] Act of Aug. 18, 1922, ch. 280, 42 Stat. 827.

[74] Act of Jan. 30, 1925, ch. 120, 43 Stat. 801.

[75] 1 Sharfman 227.

a type of Congressional interference, for the advancement of special interests, which may seriously threaten the independent performance of the Commission's tasks, and the unhampered adjustment of rate relationships on the basis of enduring principles, calculated to promote the general welfare.[76]

I cannot follow this conception of the agencies as satellites which, once having put them in orbit, Congress may not deflect. If Congress decided that commercial travelers or products of agriculture should receive special treatment from the railways, I see nothing wrong, as a matter of legislative-administrative relationship, in its saying so; that course is infinitely preferable to attempts by individual legislators or committees to bring about the same result by other means. My quarrel with these two measures, substance apart, is rather that they were so vaguely worded as to convey a mood rather than a message; in both instances the Supreme Court held the Commission had erred in following what had pretty plainly been the initial purpose of Congress but had become so hidden in qualifications that, as the Court saw it, nothing was left.[77] True, as the Board of Investigation and Research said, legislation of too high a degree of specificity "may . . . be unwise, destructive of the agency's usefulness, or so particular as to prevent necessary practical adjustments"; [78] but a clearer definition of an agency's mandate can scarcely impair either its independence or its impartiality.

Why is it that Congress seems to have lost the ability or the

[76] *Id.* at 230. See also 2 SHARFMAN 466. Professor Cushman also criticizes "this type of Congressional interference with the exercise by the commission of its quasi-judicial authority" as "highly undesirable from the point of view of commission efficiency and impartiality." THE INDEPENDENT REGULATORY COMMISSIONS 677 (1941).

[77] Ann Arbor R.R. v. United States, 281 U.S. 658 (1930); United States v. New York Cent. R.R., 263 U.S. 603 (1924). The former decision is criticized as failing to give effect to the declared congressional will, in Jaffe, *An Essay on Delegation of Legislative Power*, 47 COLUM. L. REV. 359, 367–68 (1947).

[78] I. & R. BOARD REPORT 14; see p. 14 & note 56 *supra*; N. Y. Times, Feb. 14, 1962, p. 71, col. 5, reporting a protest by the chairman of the FCC against legislation which had been proposed to reverse an agency decision.

will to legislate in the areas with which we are concerned, even when it is acutely dissatisfied with the performance of the agencies it has created to act for it? [79] Certainly not, as many would assume, because of laziness or incompetence. Few men put in as many hours of work each day as most members of the Senate and the House of Representatives, and the knowledgeability of those whose length of service has given them important positions on the great committees is astonishing. The legislative paralysis is much more likely to be due to Congressmen's having to work too much than to their working too little.

Lack of time, however, is only a partial explanation. For a deeper if somewhat cynical one, I go to a Gallic source; [80] no doubt American authors have spoken to the point, but what Dean Ripert has written of the Palais Bourbon could have been written of the Capitol just as well. I commend the entire discussion; here I can extract only a few plums: Every man with a privileged position tries to keep it; "When the legislator is asked to legislate, he knows the benefits he will be conferring on some will be matched by burdens on others; he will have his eye fixed on the relative number of his constituents on one side or the other." Moreover, he realizes that "the benefit accorded to some will bring less in gratitude than the loss suffered by others will in resentment"; [81] the optimum is thus to do nothing, since failure will be understood by those desiring the legislation whereas success will not be forgiven by those opposing it. If legislation there must be, the very necessity of a text arouses further opposition, hence the tendency to soften it in the sense of compromise or even of unintelligibility.[82] What better analysis than this of the

---

[79] See Cooper, *The Executive Department of Government and the Rule of Law*, 59 MICH. L. REV. 515, 527 (1961); Jaffe, *Administrative Procedure Reexamined: The Benjamin Report*, 56 HARV. L. REV. 704, 725 (1943); Bok, *The Tampa Electric Case*, 1961 SUPREME COURT REVIEW 267, 324.

[80] RIPERT, LES FORCES CRÉATRICES DU DROIT 88–129 (1955).

[81] *Id.* at 117.

[82] For an instance of deliberate legislative obscurity, see the analysis of § 8(c) of the Labor-Management Relations Act, 61 Stat. 142 (1947), 29 U.S.C.

failure of Congress to grapple with the concentration of control over media of mass communication, or of the emasculation of the rate provisions of the Transportation Act of 1958! [83] Doubtless pressure groups have long been with us; some, indeed, have said from the origins of the Constitution itself. But the increased pluralism of our society and modern techniques of organization and communication have sharpened their impact on the legislator.[84]

It is because of this unwillingness or inability of Congress to give better directives to its creatures that so much *Ersatz* has come into being. The shoddy character of some of this is apparent. Attempts by a congressman to influence the decision of a particular case, not by appearing before the agency as a witness [85] but by off-the-record pressure, have been generally condemned.

---

§ 158(c) (1958), in Cox, *Reflections Upon Labor Arbitration*, 72 HARV. L. REV. 1482, 1491 n.26 (1959).

[83] It is significant that the other provisions of the Transportation Act of 1958, dealing with financial aid and abandonments, which did not involve these sharp conflicts of private interests, are far less obscure.

[84] Princeton agrees with Paris on this: "The controversial character of regulatory policy cannot normally be resolved by Congress, which cannot risk the setting of a national policy that will antagonize important sources of political support." BERNSTEIN, *op. cit. supra* note 54, at 151. Although I do not disagree with this as an analysis, my belief is that legislators, like commissioners, are considerably overimpressed as to the power actually possessed by pressure groups in the areas here under review. See the statement by CAB Chairman Boyd at a meeting at Stanford University, N.Y. Times, July 1, 1962, § 1, p. 58, col. 6: "The sad fact is that we all want to be liked by everybody, and most of us tend to muddy up policy statements to harmless generalities so that we won't find ourselves read out of some segment of society as a traitor the following morning."

[85] See Mr. Landis' reference to testimony given before the CAB by Senator Hayden of Arizona in regard to feeder service in his own and a neighboring state, GELLHORN & BYSE, *op. cit. supra* note 41, at 181 n.41. Useful testimony of this sort, in favor of a service rather than of a particular applicant, is the exception. Compare the statement of the Aviation Committee of the Administrative Law Section of the American Bar Association that "congressional phone calls, particularly from legislators on the Commerce or Appropriations Committee, or from legislators with some influence on the appointment of Board members is [sic] far more effective." 9 AD. L. BULL. 204, 205 (1957). See also Friendly, *A Look at the Federal Administrative Agencies*, 60 COLUM. L. REV. 429, 439-40 (1960).

Others, such as questioning agency members in committee hearings as to their intentions in pending cases,[86] or pronunciamentos by individual legislators or self-constituted groups, whether on the floor of Congress or off of it, ought equally to be.[87] The debatable question is the degree to which the legislative duties that ought to be performed by Congress can be taken over by the appropriate standing committees, *faute de mieux*.

The Legislative Reorganization Act of 1946 recognized the duty of each such committee to "exercise continuous watchfulness of the execution by the administrative agencies concerned of any laws, the subject matter of which is within the jurisdiction of such committee."[88] The committee is something of a cross section of Congress; many of its members will have had a fair degree of experience in the subject; and it has at least the makings of a staff. Yet I take a rather dim view of committee pronouncements as to what agency policy should be, save when this is incident to proposals for amendatory legislation.[89] A more useful role would be for the committee to press the agency for policy statements, and not be satisfied with such weaselings as we have seen in the cases of the FCC and the CAB.[90]

My reasons for this negative view are various: one is that although the committee is something of a cross section, it is not a true one; there is still the danger of the committee's being "a

[86] One instance is recounted at 103 CONG. REC. 5001 (1957). See also Barrow Report, *Network Broadcasting, supra* note 68, at 36.

[87] Of course, this negative comment does not apply to open advocacy of a change in the law.

[88] 60 Stat. 832 (1946), 2 U.S.C. § 190(d) (1958).

[89] On this subject I find myself in general accord with the Report of the Committee on Administrative Law of the Association of the Bar of the City of New York, *Congressional Oversight of Administrative Agencies*, 5 RECORD OF N.Y.C.B.A. 11 (1950), which is criticized, to a somewhat indeterminate extent, in Newman & Keaton, *Congress and the Faithful Execution of Laws — Should Legislators Supervise Administrators?*, 41 CALIF. L. REV. 565 (1953). Admittedly congressional actions of the sort listed by Newman and Keaton do not "give rise to constitutional issues," *id.* at 570; however, the question is not simply constitutionality but wise policy.

[90] See, *e.g.*, pp. 65, 97–99 *supra*.

fraction which may be a faction."[91] A second is similar to what we identified in the proposal to have "policy" formulated by assistants in the White House; the committee would be taking over in an area for which Congress has given the commission responsibility.[92] A third is that the pressure of work is almost sure to mean that a report carrying the name of the committee will be at best that of a subcommittee and very likely that of a subcommittee chairman,[93] on some occasions dominating the committee staff and on others dominated by it. This latter institution requires a good deal more study before heavy responsibilities are assigned to it. Fears have been expressed, on the one hand, that the committee staff will be taken in by the staff of the agency and, on the other, that it will try to prove itself by endeavoring to outsmart its opposite numbers;[94] unhappily the fears are not mutually exclusive. Also there is a danger that the staffs of legislative committees, whose personal futures lie in other pastures, would prove easy game for special interests offering politically attractive solutions and financially attractive employment; the de-

---

[91] Macmahon, *Congressional Oversight of Administration — The Power of the Purse*, 58 POL. SCI. Q. 380, 414 (1943).

[92] What seems to me a practice of dubious utility is instanced by the Report of the Staff of the House Judiciary Committee, March 23, 1962, in regard to the proposed American-Eastern Airlines merger. The Report contains factual data and points up issues the Staff thinks the Board ought to consider. While the former would surely have been developed in the hearings, and the Board would hardly have been unaware of the latter, the Report in these respects does no harm, even though it may do relatively little good. However, although the Report is commendably moderate in tone, it drifts quite frequently into conclusory statements and leaves little doubt how the authors would answer the questions they propound; see, *e.g.*, pp. 1, 9, 13, 15–17. Despite disclaimers as to agreement by Committee members, it is hard to suppose the Report was not intended to have an effect greater than a similar study by a group of equally disinterested persons not occupying official status. Informal conferences between the staffs of the Committee and of the Board would have insured the latter's awareness of the Committee's altogether proper concern, without this potentially adverse effect.

[93] See BERNSTEIN, *op. cit. supra* note 54, at 152.

[94] GELLHORN & BYSE, *op. cit. supra* note 41, at 170, citing for the latter view, Perkins, *Congressional Self-Improvement*, 38 AM. POL. SCI. REV. 499, 508 (1944).

velopment of this work as a career would take years, if, under our system of government, it is possible at all. Most committee "investigations" of the agencies have been decidedly superficial — the usual process is to call up agency members who render laudatory accounts of their own performance ghostwritten by agency staffs, then to hear from the portions of the industry or the public that dislike what the agency has been doing, followed by those who support it, and to end up with a large amount of work for the public printer but little else. The thoughtful, well prepared report, such as the *Barrow Report* of 1958 on broadcasting or the *Doyle Report* of 1961 on transportation, is the rare exception. Little was done about the former, and only time will tell the latter's fate.

Is there then nothing that can be done? Ultimately the answer must lie with Congress. As Mr. Justice Jackson wisely said, "We may say that power to legislate . . . belongs in the hands of Congress, but only Congress itself can prevent power from slipping through its fingers." [95]

The need somehow to stimulate Congress to legislate is by no means limited to the areas of the administrative agencies. The leading text on admiralty comments that "the Limitation Act has been due for a general overhaul for the past seventy-five years; seventy-five years from now that statement will still be true, except that the overhaul will then be one hundred and fifty years overdue." [96] Although the authors understandably doubted that "any future body of law makers will ever surpass this extraordinary effort" in obscurity,[97] one may wonder whether they adequately weighed the claims of the framers of the Copyright Act of 1909,[98] an achievement scarcely rivaled in the truly superlative ambiguity of its few apparently simple provisions. Everyone agrees the Copyright Act should be amended, yet years pass

[95] Youngstown Sheet & Tube Co. v. Sawyer, 343 U.S. 579, 654 (1952) (concurring opinion).
[96] GILMORE & BLACK, ADMIRALTY 677 (1957). Perhaps the authors were too pessimistic, see S. REP. NOS. 1602, 1603, 87th Cong., 2d Sess. (1962).
[97] *Id.* at 676.
[98] 35 Stat. 1075, 17 U.S.C. § 1 (1958).

and nothing is done. Only the revenue act, for obvious practical reasons, seems to have escaped the general legislative inertia; but even that no longer lives up to Mr. Justice Holmes's rueful prediction of 1928, "We all know that we shall get a tax bill every year."[99]

Could not Congress be persuaded to amend the Legislative Reorganization Act so that each standing committee would be charged not only with the vague mandate to "exercise continuous watchfulness" but with the obligation to render a comprehensive report each ten or fifteen years on each major piece of legislation subject to its jurisdiction, either with specific proposals for amendment or with a considered statement that none is required? It would be provided or at least understood that any such report would be preceded by a true investigation — not the superficial sort I have depicted, but a thorough and searching inquiry, preferably conducted with the aid of private research organizations, and with publicity withheld at least until tentative conclusions have been formulated.

There are ample precedents; the most famous goes back thousands of years: "Ye shall hallow the fiftieth year, and proclaim liberty throughout the land unto all the inhabitants thereof . . . and ye shall return every man unto his family."[100] Jefferson thought constitutions should be revised every generation.[101] The United Nations Charter, perhaps not the happiest of examples, provides that if a conference looking toward amendment has not been called before the tenth annual session of the General As-

---

[99] Untermyer v. Anderson, 276 U.S. 440, 446 (1928) (dissenting opinion).

[100] *Leviticus* 25:10.

[101] He defined this as nineteen years, the period after which, under "the European tables of mortality, of the adults living at any one moment of time, a majority will be dead . . . ." Letter to Samuel Kercheval, July 12, 1816, in 12 THE WORKS OF THOMAS JEFFERSON 11–13 (Ford ed. 1905). Professor Julian Boyd has kindly pointed out to me that this thought, that "the earth belongs in usufruct to the living," goes back to Jefferson's Letter of September 6, 1789, to Madison, discussed in 15 THE PAPERS OF THOMAS JEFFERSON 384–91 (Boyd ed. 1958); and see Madison's Reply, 16 *id.* at 146–54.

sembly, a proposal for its call should be placed upon the next agenda.[102]

No one could be sure that such an amendment, if adopted, could force committees to make meaningful recommendations, much less that it could compel Congress to pass them. Still, the requirement of periodic review and report, with its implicit corollaries that in these years the committee would be relatively freed from other major tasks and that no similar opportunity for an attempt at general revision would recur for a long interval thereafter, may afford some promise. At least we would have nothing to lose by trying that and the other means for attaining the sharper definition of standards governing the agencies that have been here reviewed. If there be still better mousetraps, no time should be lost in finding them.

One such, of no small importance, may lie rather near at hand — in the critical work of law teachers and law students. Cardozo remarked nearly forty years ago how "judges have at last awakened . . . to the treasures buried in the law reviews."[103] If our machine age has invented any counters for detecting the fallacious and the equivocal as sensitive as the professors and students of the great law schools, I have not seen them. Yet, with a few distinguished exceptions, the law teachers and the law reviews have not yet begun to do for the administrative agencies what, for many years, they have been doing for the courts. Perhaps I am quite wrong about this, but I have the impression that the study of administrative law in most law schools, at least until very recently, has been concentrating unduly on procedure at the expense of substance, as the criticism of the agencies in the profession surely has. Another way of stating this would be that instruction has been too much concerned with what the courts do with the agencies rather than with what the agencies do

---

[102] Art. 109, ¶ 3. The Pennsylvania Committee on Constitutional Revision of 1959 advocated an amendment calling for study and review every fifteen years.
[103] THE GROWTH OF THE LAW 14 (1924).

with themselves.[104] Yet the procedural battle has been largely won in the type of agency with which we have been here concerned — indeed, attempts to wage it further in some respects may do more harm than good; it is in the substance of administrative adjudication that improvement is sorely needed.

Of the scores of administrative adjudications we have considered, I do not recall one that has raised an issue as to denial of a hearing, the right to compulsory process, lack of proper post-hearing procedures, the right to judicial review, or any of the other important adjective rights that are the staples of the usual administrative law course. All the formalities have been faithfully pursued — the book has been duly kissed; the trouble has been with the product. Should not the law schools recognize the full implications of what Mr. Justice Jackson said in the opinion with which we began,[105] that administrative agencies are creating, or ought to be creating, a body of substantive law, requiring constant critical analysis, almost as important as that produced by the courts? Although the law schools are the source

[104] This statement requires qualification as to two fields now rather largely governed by commissions — labor law and securities regulation. It requires qualification in another respect — Professor Frankfurter's famous course, misnamed "Public Utilities," actually a study of the Interstate Commerce Act, was the very sort I had in mind. I should make clear also that I do not suggest that instruction in the important "adjective" side of administrative law ought be abandoned; I urge rather that it be supplemented by "substantive" instruction in the administrative regulation of transportation, communications, energy, and other forms of business, and that somewhere along the line, an insight should be afforded as to how administrative agencies work. AUERBACH & NATHANSON, FEDERAL REGULATION OF TRANSPORTATION (1953), illustrates what I have in mind for such a course. Whether this "substantive" instruction had better be given in an added elective course or courses, separate from the basic and often compulsory course, is a pedagogical problem beyond my competence. My appeal is that proper emphasis should be given to the "substance" of administrative adjudication; I am not concerned with where and when.

I find that some of these views have been anticipated in Miller, *Prolegomenon to a Modernized Study of Administrative Law*, 12 J. LEGAL ED. 33 (1959); and Schwartz, *Oversight and Oversights in Administrative Law Teaching*, 11 J. LEGAL ED. 358, 362 (1959).

[105] 343 U.S. 470, 487 (1952), see p. 2 *supra*.

most readily available, still more might be accomplished by drawing also on other disciplines, notably political science and economics. Continuing critical study by scholarly groups uniting all these talents would be of great value both to the agencies and to the congressional oversight committees; such groups would also be in a position to undertake for the committees the more comprehensive periodic surveys I have suggested.[106] Coordination and cross-pollinization could be achieved through the Admintrative Conference. The day when commissioners become concerned how their work in defining the general standards laid down by the legislature will be dissected by professors and students, as judges' decisions applying statutes regularly are, will be a good day for administrative adjudication.

The administrative agencies have become a vital part of the structure of American government. Nothing is accomplished by merely negative criticism or by petulant proposals to abolish them. All of us, legislators, judges, lawyers, professors, students, citizens, have a responsibility to help them in their difficult assignment of developing wise and intelligible standards and applying these consistently and fairly. The first step is to understand how essential it is that this be done.

[106] The need for facilitating such regular and disinterested study of the functioning of the administrative agencies on a multidiscipline basis has been noted of late by observers in several fields. Correspondence with Professor David F. Cavers of the Harvard Law School; see Herring, *Research on Government, Politics & Administration*, in RESEARCH FOR PUBLIC POLICY, BROOKINGS DEDICATION LECTURES 6–7 (1961), and comment by Waldo at 22; Miller, *supra* note 104, at 34, 37–38; STEIN, PUBLIC ADMINISTRATION AND POLICY DEVELOPMENT xix (1952). For a similar suggestion in the antitrust area, see Bok, *supra* note 79, at 329–32. See also Davis, *Ombudsmen in America: Officers To Criticize Administrative Action*, 109 U. PA. L. REV. 1057 (1961).

Index

Administrative adjudication: compared to judicial adjudication, 14f; definition of, 5–8, 14–16; desirability of certainty and stability in, 16, 19f, 157; impracticability for Congress, 10f; legislative or judicial, 8f. *See also* Overruling of prior decision; Standards

Administrative agency, *see* Agency

Administrative Conference, 4, 90n, 175

Administrative law, study of, 173f

Administrative Procedure Act, 3, 43n, 147

Agency, administrative: antidemocratic implications of, 21; appointments to, 142f, 148, 155f; discontent with, 2f, 5; discretion, evils of excessive, 19f; importance of, 2, 175; independence of, 22, 148, 157, 165f, 168–71; lawmaking function of, 6f, 14–18, 174f; methods of defining standards, 143–47; partnership with legislature, 32–35, 36f, 163f; permanence of, 4, 175; planning function, 159–62; policy statements, 145–47; pressures on, 22f, 54, 71, 168f; proposals for improvement of, 142f; prospective action, 50f, 146; relations with Congress, *see* Congress, Congressional committees; relations with President, *see* President; reorganization of, 4; role of examiners, 24, 70f; role of staffs, 24; rulemaking, 43n, 50n, 70n, 145, 146f. *See also* Certainty; Overruling of prior decision; Stability; Standards

Antitrust laws, 17f

Certainty, as goal, 16f, 20

Civil Aeronautics Board: competition by more than two carriers, 84, 85, 86f, 94–96, 104; criticisms of, 74n, 91, 101–5; disingenuous opinion writing, 85, 86–91, 92–94; failure to anticipate technological changes, 81, 101f; failure to explicate standard as to competition, 78, 81–83, 97–99, 103–5, 142; failure to make economic studies, 78, 84, 87f, 99–101, 104f; favorable initial auspices, 74f; growth of industry, 75; legislative history and meaning of Civil Aeronautics Act, 75–78; plan of international air routes, 159n; selection of carrier by, 55f, 79f, 96n; unwillingness to admit error, 88, 103; use of data not introduced at hearing, 90n; use of unrepresentative data, 89f

Clark, Mr. Justice Thomas C., 49

Commission, *see* Agency

Congress: committees of, *see* Congressional committees; criticisms of, for too detailed legislation, 165f; delegation to agencies by, 7, 10f, 21f; disapproval of interpretations by NLRB, 45; enactment of ICC interpretations of long-and-short-haul clause, 33f; enactment of ratemaking standards for ICC, 110f, 113f, 132–36; enactment or endorsement of interpretations by NLRB, 38, 42–45; failure to amend Civil Aeronautics Act, 164f; failure to evolve more definite standards, 163–73; failure to furnish FCC with intelligible standard, 54–57, 65f, 164f; investigations of agencies, 164f, 171; pressures by Congressmen on agencies, 168f; pressures by interests on Congress, 167; proposals for stimulating revision of standards by, 158, 172f; reasons for legislative paralysis, 166–68; Transportation Act of 1958, 131–136; unfitness for administrative adjudication, 10f; vagueness of standards initially prescribed, 6, 11f, 13f, 21f, 54f

Congressional committees: duty of oversight, 169; investigations, 164f, 171;

INDEX

policy guidance by, 168–71; proposal for periodic reports by, 172f, 175
Cooley, Chairman Thomas, 28–32, 142
Courts: role in promoting development of standards, 14, 18n, 141; similarities of judicial and administrative adjudication, 14–16

Delegation, *see* Legislation, delegated
Dirksen, Senator Everett McK., 5n, 143nn, 158f
Douglas, Mr. Justice William O., 19, 49

Eastman, Commissioner Joseph B., 111–113, 126, 140, 148n, 149n, 161
Eisenhower, President Dwight D., 154n
Examiners, *see* Agency, role of examiners
Executive, *see* President

Federal Aviation Act, *see* Civil Aeronautics Board
Federal Communications Commission: "criteria" of, 57f; criticisms of, 53f, 152f; disingenuous opinion writing, 59–64, 66f; frustrating task of, 54–57; local interest criterion, 58–63; Multiple Ownership Rules, 57, 69f; problem of choice among equally qualified applicants, 70–73; problem of concentration of control over mass media, 63–70; relations with Congress, 54–57, 65f; review of program proposals, 71–73; suggestions for standards in diversification cases, 68–70; suggestions on handling of cases in general, 70–73; transferability of broadcasting licenses, 56n, 59, 72f
Federal Maritime Board, 13n, 14n, 28
Federal Power Commission, 4f, 106n
Federal Reserve Board, 7
Federal Trade Commission, 4, 13n, 15; failure to define unfair competition, 106n
Frankfurter, Professor (later Mr. Justice) Felix, 1, 27, 42, 50n, 174n

Interstate Commerce Commission: legislative recommendations by, 163; momentum given by early commissioners, 142, 163; motor carrier certificate cases, 55, 75f; powers granted by Transportation Act, 1920, 13; prohibition of excessive rates and discrimination, 13n; ratemaking standards, 110f, 113f, 131–36

Long-and-short-haul clause, 27–35; initial interpretations, 29–32; Mann-Elkins amendment, 1910, 32f; amendments in Transportation Act, 1920, 33f; amendment in Transportation Act of 1940, 34; amendment of 1957, 34f

Minimum-rate power, 106–40; apportionment of traffic, 119f, 129–31; attempts at definition of standard, 109f, 112f, 115–17, 119f, 126–31, 136–40; criticisms of use of, 107; differing definitions of costs, 114f; effect of intermodal competition, 111–14; initial grant, 108–10; need for cost data, 107, 112; *New Automobiles* case, 127–29; "not lower than necessary" principle, 126–30; proscription of rates covering fully distributed costs, 116f, 126–31, 136–39, covering out-of-pocket costs but not fully distributed costs, 116f, not covering out-of-pocket costs, 115f; *Sea-Land* case, 122, 138f; *Seatrain* case, 126f; Transportation Act of 1940, 113f, 120–22; Transportation Act of 1958, 131–36; "value of service" principle, 111, 126f, 130f

Jackson, Mr. Justice Robert H., 2, 5n, 124n, 174
Judiciary, *see* Courts

Kennedy, President John F., 4, 140, 148, 152, 159

Labor Law, *see* National Labor Relations Board
Landrum-Griffin Act, *see* National Labor Relations Board
Law schools, role of, 173–175
Legislation, delegated, 7, 10, 21f

INDEX

Legislative Oversight, Subcommittee on, 3, 165
Legislative Reorganization Act, 169, 172
Legislature, *see* Congress; Agency, partnership with legislature

Motor Carrier Act, 55, 75f, 111

National Labor Relations Board, 36–52; *Bonwit Teller* rule, 38–41; "contract-bar" rule, 43f; criticism for failure to follow rulemaking procedures, 43n, 50n, 147n; discharge of employee for union activity, 15; duration of employer's duty to bargain with certified union, 42; employers' acts manifesting refusal to bargain, 44f, 52; employees' acts manifesting refusal to bargain, 45f; exclusive union hiring halls, 46–51; injunctions against unfair labor practices, 24n; Landrum-Griffin Act, 36; overrulings by, 41; picketing premises of secondary employer, 51n; statement of principles in annual reports, 145n; Taft-Hartley Act, 9, 36, 42, 43, 45; union solicitation on company property, 36–41
National Transportation Policy, 113f, 121–23, 134f, 151

Overruling of prior decision: by CAB, 85f, 87f, 91, 92, 94; by FCC, 62–64; by ICC, 20n, 131–33; by NLRB, 41; need for candor where prior decision not followed, 20f, 41, 63; when proper, 20f
Oversight, *see* President; Congressional committees

Per se doctrine, 17
Planning, 159–162
President: concern with workings of the agencies, 149; directions to agencies, 147–57; forbidding agencies to submit or comment on legislative proposals without consent of Bureau of Budget, 149n; impracticability of personal oversight of agencies, 153f; responsibility as to agency appointments, 148; responsibility to recommend legislation, 157–59; responsibility to see that work of agencies gets done, 149; role with respect to agencies, 147–58
Public convenience and necessity, 54f, 75–78, 97f

Rulemaking, *see* Agency, administrative

Securities and Exchange Commission, 4; *Chenery* decision, 50f; Public Utility Holding Company Act, 13, 106n; short sale rules, 7, 10
Sherman Act, per se violations of, 17
Shipping Act, *see* Federal Maritime Board
Shipping Board, *see* Federal Maritime Board
Stability, need for, 20f, 157
Staffs, *see* Agency, role of staffs
Standards: definition or failure of definition of, by Congress, 6, 12–14, 131–36, 163–72, by courts, 14f, by FCC, 53–73, by FPC, FTC, and SEC, 106n, by ICC, 27–35, 106–40, by NLRB, 36–52, in administrative adjudication, 5f; feasibility of, in administrative adjudication, 11f, 16f; need for, 14, 19–25; problems of defining, in licensing, 107
Stare decisis, *see* Agency; Overruling of prior decision
Stone, Mr. Justice Harlan F., 118n
Supreme Court: approval of NLRB actions, 38, 42f, 52, of SEC standard, 106n; attitude toward definition of standards by agency, 51f, 146; distinction between "quasi-legislative" and "quasi-judicial" action, 9; invalidation of ICC interpretation, 31f, of NLRB holdings, 45f, 46–51; on meaning of "unfair methods of competition" in Federal Trade Commission Act, 15; on per se violations of Sherman Act, 17; principle that "the one who decides must hear," 157
Decisions thought relevant to mini-

mum-rate power of ICC: Texas & Pacific Ry. v. United States, 118; Scandrett v. United States, 119–22; Eastern Central Motor Carriers Assn. v. United States, 122f; ICC v. Mechling, 124f

Taft-Hartley Act, *see* National Labor Relations Board

United States Shipping Board, *see* Federal Maritime Board

FEB 21 1970
MAR 32 1972
MAY 15 1972
MAY 31 1972

PRINTED IN U.S.A.

23 236